AN ACT OF
KINDNESS

AN ACT OF
KINDNESS

CHUCK HUSTMYRE

BERKLEY BOOKS, NEW YORK

THE BERKLEY PUBLISHING GROUP
Published by the Penguin Group
Penguin Group (USA) Inc.
375 Hudson Street, New York, New York 10014, USA
Penguin Group (Canada), 90 Eglinton Avenue East, Suite 700, Toronto, Ontario M4P 2Y3, Canada
(a division of Pearson Penguin Canada Inc.)
Penguin Books Ltd., 80 Strand, London WC2R 0RL, England
Penguin Group Ireland, 25 St. Stephen's Green, Dublin 2, Ireland (a division of Penguin Books Ltd.)
Penguin Group (Australia), 250 Camberwell Road, Camberwell, Victoria 3124, Australia
(a division of Pearson Australia Group Pty. Ltd.)
Penguin Books India Pvt. Ltd., 11 Community Centre, Panchsheel Park, New Delhi—110 017, India
Penguin Group (NZ), 67 Apollo Drive, Mairangi Bay, Auckland 1311, New Zealand (a division of
Pearson New Zealand Ltd.)
Penguin Books (South Africa) (Pty.) Ltd., 24 Sturdee Avenue, Rosebank, Johannesburg 2196, South
Africa

Penguin Books Ltd., Registered Offices: 80 Strand, London WC2R 0RL, England

AN ACT OF KINDNESS

A Berkley Book / published by arrangement with the author

PRINTING HISTORY
Berkley mass-market edition / March 2007

ISBN: 978-0-425-21342-1

BERKLEY®
Berkley Books are published by the Berkley Publishing Group,
a division of Penguin Group (USA) Inc.,
375 Hudson Street, New York, New York 10014.
BERKLEY is a registered trademark of Penguin Group (USA) Inc.
The "B" design is a trademark belonging to Penguin Group (USA) Inc.

PRINTED IN THE UNITED STATES OF AMERICA

10 9 8 7 6 5 4 3 2 1

AUTHOR'S NOTE

There were parts of this book that I found very difficult to write; there were records, including gruesome photographs of the crime scene that were hard to review, but I felt it was an important story that needed to be told. The brutal murder of Genore Guillory was as horrendous as it was senseless. As a single act of violence it was as bad as murder can get. However, Genore Guillory's murder wasn't just a simple act of violence. It was something more. It was a demonstrative act from one of the many subcultures in this country that have no regard for human life and think that violence, particularly cross-racial and cross-ethnic violence, is perfectly acceptable. The Bubba subculture of southeastern Louisiana described in this book is certainly not unique in its hatred of other races and ethnic groups, or in its propensity for bloodshed. Unfortunately, it's just one small part of this country's subculture of violence.

I would like to thank the many people who helped me with this book. Although my name is on the cover, I could not have written it without the help of a host of people. Among that host, I would like to particularly thank East Feliciana Parish Sheriff Talmadge Bunch, Detective Don McKey, District Attorney Sam D'Aquilla, former Detective Joel Odom, Louisiana State Police Sergeant Dennis Stewart, Caddo Parish Assistant District Attorney Hugo Holland, reporter James Minter, and the many others who helped me.

I would also like to thank my literary agent, Scott Miller, of Trident Media Group in New York City and my editor, Tom Colgan, of the Penguin Group/Berkley Books, for their invaluable assistance.

ONE

*The smell got stronger as East Feliciana Parish Sher-*iff's Deputy Ronald Johnson pushed deeper into the house. It washed over him and turned his stomach. It choked him. Johnson knew what it was. He had smelled it once before, on a suicide call. It was a smell you never forgot. It was the smell of decaying human flesh. It was the smell of death.

He willed himself to breathe more shallowly. With his pistol in one hand and his flashlight in the other, Deputy Johnson crept across the kitchen.

He called out. "Hello. Sheriff's Department. Is anyone home?"

A sudden noise came from upstairs. Fast thumping, like someone running. Johnson squeezed the grip of his service pistol and scanned the open stairwell. The sound got closer. Something moved at the top of the stairs. Johnson aimed his flashlight and his gun. A big black-and-white dog, a Dalmatian, rushed down the stairs. Johnson tensed, his finger on the trigger. Outside, a vicious chow had lunged at Johnson on his way into the house. He'd only gotten past it because the chow had been tied up. Now this dog was charging right at him.

But instead of attacking, the Dalmatian brushed past him with barely a glance. It, too, was scared.

Johnson was shaken. He sucked in the foul air to steady his nerves. Something was definitely wrong in this house. He could feel it.

The portable police radio on Johnson's gun belt crackled to life. The tinny voice of the Sheriff's Department dispatcher called to him. "Dispatch to E-F 38, can you read me?"

Johnson tugged the radio from his belt. He keyed the microphone and tried to respond, but the signal wasn't strong enough. The dispatcher couldn't hear him.

"E-F 38?" she called again. "Can you hear me? Is everything all right?"

From Johnson's perspective, things were definitely not all right. He replaced his radio on his gun belt. Just past the kitchen was a short hallway and an open door that led to another part of the house. Johnson inched into the hall.

In the tomblike silence of the house, the chatter on the police radio was a welcomed distraction. A couple of other patrol deputies told the dispatcher they would head toward the house on Oakwood Lane and check on Deputy Johnson.

In the hallway, Johnson peeked around the edge of the open door. He saw a bedroom. A four-poster, queen-sized bed stood against the far wall, the bedcovers piled together on top of the mattress. A small table had been knocked over and sat upended in the middle of the floor. From inside the room the smell came at Johnson hard. He felt sick, like he was going to throw up. He fought past it and stepped through the door.

Inside the bedroom, the walls were splashed with blood. A window that looked out on to the yard had a bullet hole through it. Another bullet had punched through the wall above the bed, and a third had pierced the headboard. The body of a woman lay on the floor beside the bed. She was mostly naked, bloated, disfigured. Blood was everywhere.

Johnson refused to believe what he was seeing. The body looked like a mannequin. It's not real, Johnson thought. He took another step closer. The woman lay on her back near the far corner of the room, her swollen body covered only by a green nightshirt that had been pushed up to her breasts. Her head was tilted to the left, and her tangle of black hair only partially masked a face that had been beaten nearly flat.

She wasn't a mannequin. She was real. And she was as dead as dead can get.

Deputy Johnson bolted from the house.

Outside, the sun was shinning. It was a beautiful early summer morning.

In the driveway, Johnson braced a hand against the fender of his Jeep Cherokee. He bent over and retched. From the police radio mounted inside the Jeep, Johnson heard the nearly frantic voice of the dispatcher calling for him. "E-F 38, E-F 38, I need you to respond."

Johnson opened the driver-side door and grabbed the microphone, but he was so overcome with emotion that he couldn't speak.

Several minutes passed before Johnson pulled himself together enough to find his voice.

When he did, he keyed the microphone and called for the dispatcher. Still short of breath, Johnson gasped out, "I have a signal twenty-nine [dead body] out here. I need you to notify the detectives and E-F one."

TWO

East Feliciana Parish Sheriff's detectives Don McKey and Drew Thompson arrived at the house on Oakwood Lane at 10:50 a.m.

The home where Deputy Ronald Johnson had discovered the mutilated body was a two-story Acadian style, with dark siding and a big front porch. It sat at the end of a long driveway on several acres of semiwooded property. Beside the house stood an attached carport stacked with fifty-pound sacks of dog food and baled hay. Twenty yards behind the house was a cement slab surrounded by a chain-link fence. It was a kennel for twenty-five, maybe thirty dogs, all of them barking. Other than the sheriff's cars, two Toyotas were parked near the house. One was a small pickup truck, the other a Camry.

The address was 11856 Oakwood Lane. It was about five miles northeast of the town of Clinton and less than ten miles south of the Mississippi state line. Oakwood Lane is a dead-end gravel road no more than a mile long. It runs off of Rist Road, a dirt road to nowhere that cuts between two backwoods state highways. Only a few residences dot the landscape along either side of Oakwood Lane. The dark side of the moon is more out of the way, but just barely.

The dispatcher told McKey that a State Police forensic team and the deputy coroner were on the way. The two detectives started their initial crime scene survey. They moved from outside to inside, from farther out to closer in.

The purpose of the survey was to get an overview of the crime scene, to look at the big picture prior to getting into the detailed, inch-by-inch examination and before beginning the process of collecting evidence.

After nearly a dozen years with the Sheriff's Department, the last three as a detective, McKey knew that processing a crime scene, particularly a murder scene, was a time-consuming and resource-draining operation; and for a small department like East Feliciana's, with only eight patrol deputies and two detectives, it could be a ball buster.

Even with State Police help, the job of securing and processing the crime scene and of taking witness statements was going to take all day and probably all night. If something else broke loose in another part of the parish, if calls for service started backing up and drawing the patrol deputies away, if the State Police got called to another scene, it would stretch McKey's resources too thin and affect the quality of the work he wanted done on Oakwood Lane.

McKey had heard about what was waiting for him inside the house, and from what he'd been told it sounded like this killer didn't just need to be caught, he needed to be stopped.

The extreme violence suggested that whoever had done it wasn't squeamish. That could mean one of two things: either the killer was enraged or else he got off on the violence. Maybe both. An enraged killer was one thing. Someone or something could push a person to the edge of sanity, could drive him to commit a heinous act of murder, but typically after that it was over. The killer retreated back into the real world. Thinking about what he'd done, he probably felt some remorse. That was someone who needed to be caught.

But a killer who got off on the act of killing, who had acquired a taste for blood, a taste for terror, who maybe even got some sexual satisfaction out of it and felt no remorse about what he'd done, that was someone you had to really worry about. That was someone likely to kill again. That was someone who needed to be stopped.

The initial crime scene survey would help McKey focus on what was most important and decide what needed to be done first. The killer's actions would dictate what had to be done. They weren't going to dig up the yard or dismantle the house unless they had to. McKey needed to find out where the killer had been and what the killer had touched.

He and Thompson also needed to pry open the victim's life and find out who she was and what she had been like. They needed to know who might have been mad at her and who might have profited from her death. Anger and greed are two of the most common motives for murder.

The survey of the outside of the house went quickly. Nothing appeared to have been disturbed. There were no obvious blood trails, tire impressions, or footprints. From all appearances it looked to McKey as though the crime scene was contained within the confines of the house. That was good. Houses maintained evidence a lot better than the outdoors. It didn't rain inside houses, the wind didn't blow, wild creatures didn't munch on corpses.

As McKey and his partner stepped toward the side door that connected the carport and the house, a tan chow, a vicious bundle of hair and teeth, lunged at them from under the short set of wooden steps that led up to the house. The detectives jumped back. Instinctively, McKey reached for his pistol. A rope looped around the dog's neck and tied to the near step railing jerked the chow to a sudden stop. McKey asked a uniformed deputy to pull the rope tight while he and Thompson skirted around the dog and slipped into the house.

Inside, the two sheriff's detectives found a comfortable den filled with bookshelves and reproduction antique furniture and a hardwood floor covered with rugs. A glass-enclosed, six-foot display case stood just inside and to the right of the door. Arranged on its shelves were a dozen collectible dolls in elaborate dresses. Figurines of horses and more dolls adorned the rest of the den. The room was neat. Everything seemed to be in its place. It had a homey, lived-in feel.

Except for the dried blood.

McKey found the first traces of it on the threshold. There was more on the door. A faint blood trail ran along the left side of the den, past the front door, and toward the kitchen. The two detectives followed it. On the inside of the front door they found more blood. The door handle, an old-fashioned brass lever, was splattered with it. A set of keys hanging from the dead bolt had also been smeared with blood.

Neither door showed signs of forced entry. The killer had likely gained access to the house through an unlocked door or window or been let in.

In the kitchen, an antique-style wooden box phone hung on the wall beside the refrigerator. The handset dangled by its cord almost to the floor. Below the kitchen counter, a drawer had been left open. The utensil tray inside was smeared with blood. A couple of the dinner knives were out of place, their ceramic handles spotted with more blood. On the countertop was a reddish-brown smudge.

McKey nearly gagged on the fetid odor that washed over him in the kitchen. He knew the smell. There was no mistaking it. He also knew what was waiting for him in the next room.

The bedroom was a wreck. Blood-splattered walls, an upended table, overturned houseplants, bullet-riddled surfaces, a mangled lamp on the floor, its shattered base lying beside the body—they told the story of what had happened in that room. There had been a fight, a hell of a fight, and the lady lying naked on the floor had lost. But she had fought hard.

The body was that of a middle-aged black woman. She lay on her back, her torso angled toward the back right corner of the room, her bare feet aimed at the door. Her green nightshirt had been pushed up to her chest. She was naked from her breasts down. Her legs were splayed apart, revealing a wide patch of dark pubic hair and the outer labia of her vagina. Dark smears covered the insides of her thighs and milky fluid drained from her crotch. Her head lay twisted over her left shoulder at an unnatural angle, and her face, partly obscured by a mop of black hair, had been crushed. Bloody rips in her skin, which McKey recognized as stab wounds and bullet holes, dotted the woman's body.

The detectives threaded their way around the room. Other than the broken lamp base next to the victim's head, there were no obvious murder weapons—no guns, no knives, no blunt objects.

Based on the bloating and the smell, McKey guessed it had been at least a couple of days since she'd been killed.

The deputy coroner arrived at 12:15 p.m. The crime lab techs pulled up at 12:55. McKey and Thompson started working the crime scene.

Everything indicated that the woman lying dead on the floor of the master bedroom was the owner of the house, Jane Nora Guillory. Positive ID would come when a family member identified the body, but there was certainly enough information lying around—mail addressed to her, bills in her name, one of the cars outside registered to her—for McKey to make an educated guess as to the identity of the victim.

If it was her, Jane Nora Guillory had been forty-two years old. She had lived at 11856 Oakwood Lane for several years. The first few with her boyfriend, Eddie Dixon. In October 1998, Eddie had died in a car crash on his way home from the overnight shift at the Georgia-Pacific paper mill in St. Francisville in neighboring West Feliciana Parish. Since then Jane Nora had lived alone. She was an animal lover, especially dogs. That was obvious from the twenty-five or so dogs kenneled in the backyard. She also liked horses. She had four of them stabled on her property and figurines of horses scattered throughout the house.

McKey talked to Deputy Ronald Johnson. He'd responded to the house on Oakwood to do a welfare check. Jane Nora Guillory's coworkers, they called her Genore, had phoned the Sheriff's Department at ten o'clock. Genore hadn't shown up for work, and they couldn't get through to her by telephone. The line had been busy, according to what one of the coworkers, Ann Fendick, told the dispatcher. Fendick said she checked with the telephone company, and the operator told her that there was no activity on the line. It was either out of service or off the hook.

The dispatcher sent Deputy Johnson to the house to check on Ms. Guillory. Johnson told McKey that he had first pulled up to the mobile home across the street, thinking that was the right address. Few of the mailboxes had numbers on them. The guy who lived there pointed out Ms. Guillory's house. Johnson drove across the street and pulled into the driveway of 11856. He'd blown his horn but got no answer. Then he tooted his siren, but still no one came out. The side door had been open, so he walked into the house. When he found the body in the bedroom, he got out of the house as quickly as he could and notified the dispatcher.

That's all he knew.

McKey found no bullet casings in the bedroom or

anywhere else in the house. From the looks of the victim, she'd been shot at least three times, maybe more. There were four additional bullet holes in the room: one in the headboard, one in the wall, one in a baseboard, and one through the window. All small-caliber. At least seven shots fired but no shells. That suggested to McKey that a revolver had been used, but most revolvers held only five or six shots.

Did the killer reload? If so, what happened to the empty shells? Did he pick up his brass? In the old days, when cops carried revolvers, they'd been trained to dump the empty brass in their hands and shove it into their pockets.

In addition to the gunshots, Ms. Guillory—if it was indeed her lying on the floor—had suffered several stab wounds. They dotted the left side of her chest and abdomen. She also had what appeared to be defensive scraping and bruising on her arms and legs.

McKey tried to make sense of the bedroom, to bring some semblance of order to the chaos. Blood was everywhere. The bed was unmade. The rest of the house was neat. Ms. Guillory had probably been the type of person who made her bed every day. She had been wearing a nightshirt. The attack had probably come late at night or early in the morning.

The cord from the shattered lamp was stretched taut and still plugged into a wall outlet behind the nightstand. McKey guessed the killer had jerked the lamp off the nightstand and smashed it down on top of the victim. The damage to her face and head, however, looked too severe to have been done with just the lamp. Another blunt object must have been used.

Shot, stabbed, and beaten. McKey was looking for at least three weapons.

A digital clock lay on the floor, its red numbers flashing. Sometime after the murder, the power had gone out.

While McKey and Thompson tried to read tea leaves in

the bedroom, Adam Becnel, a forensic scientist with the Louisiana State Police Crime Lab in Baton Rouge was scouring the crime scene picking up trace evidence. He swabbed blood from the front and side doors. He bagged the contents of the utensil drawer and the telephone handset. He cut out blood-splattered pieces of carpet and upholstery. He stuffed household documents into evidence envelopes and bagged a hat to preserve any strands of hair that might be inside it. He unscrewed the plate from the bedroom light switch, took a pantyhose package with a bloody fingerprint on it, collected the victim's jewelry box because it showed traces of blood on the lid, and picked up every knife he could find. He also dusted nearly every flat surface in the house for fingerprints.

In the bedroom, McKey eyed a pillow lying on the ground. Like nearly everything else in the room, it was stained with blood. But there was something else about it that attracted his attention. He saw a pattern. Like one of those pictures you have to stare at for a while before you see the hidden images. The pillow had a tread pattern. A tread pattern from a shoe. It was right there on the pillowcase. Sometime during the fight the pillow was knocked to the floor, the floor was covered in blood, the killer got blood on the bottom of his shoes, the killer stepped on the pillow, and left behind an evidentiary gold mine—a bloody shoeprint.

McKey called Adam Becnel over. Wearing surgical gloves, the forensic scientist slipped the pillowcase off the pillow and cut out the shoeprint. Then he bagged the cut-out tread mark and the rest of the blood-spattered pillowcase as separate pieces of evidence.

Upstairs was clean, just a bedroom and a bathroom. No blood, no sign of a struggle, no sign anyone had been there.

THREE

By early afternoon, one of Genore's coworkers showed up. Carl Chenevert had made the one-hour drive from his office as soon as he learned from the East Feliciana Sheriff's Department that something was wrong at Genore's house.

Chenevert had worked with Genore at the BlueCross BlueShield insurance company in Baton Rouge for eleven years. For the first several years their desks had been three feet apart. When the company moved into another building a few years back, Genore and Chenevert had been assigned offices on different floors; he went to the third floor, she went to the second, but they still saw each other every day.

A big man with a hairline that had retreated all the way back to the crown of his head, Chenevert considered himself a close friend of Genore's. At work she confided in him about personal problems, particularly relationship issues, most of which, at least recently, concerned a man who had been hounding Genore for a date for the last several months.

By the time Chenevert arrived, Detective McKey had already posted Deputy Ronald Johnson at the end of the driveway. He was to keep everyone off the property. Although McKey was fairly certain that the crime scene and any useful evidence were contained inside the house, he didn't want to take the chance that a curious neighbor or coworker, or even an overzealous law enforcement officer, would trample something important.

Chenevert tried to pry information out of the deputy about what had happened, but Johnson kept quiet. Finding the body inside the house had shaken him badly, and he had no clear idea who was and who was not a suspect. Like most good cops, Deputy Johnson considered almost everyone a suspect until proven otherwise.

After thirty minutes of standing at the end of the driveway, Chenevert saw a couple of Genore's neighbors walk over. Phillip and Amy Skipper. Chenevert had been to Genore's house a few times and had met the Skippers before. They lived with their son—a toddler, still in diapers—and a teenage stepson, named John, in a trailer across the street. Chenevert noticed that Amy was pregnant.

At work, Genore had often talked about her neighbors. Both Phillip and Amy did odd jobs for Genore around her house, more so since Eddie had died. Genore helped the young couple out a lot with money and gifts for their son. She had even paid for a party at a pizza joint in the nearby town of Denham Springs, just south of Clinton in neighboring Livingston Parish. When the Skippers first moved in across the street, Phillip and Amy had been living in a dilapidated trailer. After she got to know them better, Genore lent the couple the money to buy a much newer mobile home. The two women talked on the telephone at least once a day while Genore was at work, sometimes two or three times a day.

Amy looked devastated at the news she heard when she and Phillip walked over from their trailer: Barring some miracle of mistaken identity, Genore Guillory was dead.

A half hour later, a thin nervous woman walked to Genore's house from the Skippers' trailer. She joined Phillip and Amy, who'd been standing with Chenevert at the end of the driveway. She introduced herself as Phillip's mother, Isabella Skipper. The four of them stood together, talking in muted tones about what had likely happened to Genore.

Isabella Skipper said she'd spent Sunday night with her son and daughter-in-law. She mentioned having heard Genore's dogs barking a lot the previous night. They'd woken her up sometime around two o'clock in the morning. Other than that she hadn't heard or seen anything suspicious.

Amy Skipper said she'd been home all weekend, and, like her mother-in-law, she hadn't heard or seen anything out of the ordinary.

Phillip said he had been out of town most of the day Saturday, helping a friend move, but had gotten back home Saturday night. He had not noticed anything unusual. Phillip said he'd been helping Miss G a lot, especially since Eddie Dixon had died, feeding the dogs and horses and mowing the grass. He'd never known Miss G to have an enemy or to say a bad word about anyone. Only once had there ever been anything even close to trouble at her house. When some male friend of hers wouldn't leave, Miss G—that's how Phillip referred to Genore—called Phillip for help and he came over and escorted the man off of her property.

Carl Chenevert had never known Genore to have a problem with anyone. "She never met a stranger," he later said. "Anybody she would meet, she treated them just like they were a family member."

Later that afternoon, Genore's family arrived at her house. It started to rain. Don McKey pulled Deputy Johnson in from his post at the end of the driveway and let

Genore's family, friends, and neighbors huddle under the carport. Having them all close at hand would make it easier for McKey and his partner to interview everyone.

McKey pulled Phillip Skipper aside. Did Ms. Guillory have any regular visitors? Did she have a boyfriend? What was his and his wife's relationship to Ms. Guillory? His home was the closest to Ms. Guillory's. Had he seen or heard anything unusual over the weekend?

Skipper was very cooperative and repeated what he'd told Carl Chenevert. Then he added something. He told McKey that his wife had gotten into an argument with Ms. Guillory about a month ago. The Skippers had owned a goat. One day a dog got loose from the kennel behind Genore's house and wandered over to the Skippers' trailer. After spotting the goat, the dog attacked and killed it. Amy got upset. She and Genore exchanged harsh words. They didn't speak for a few weeks, but eventually the two women worked everything out.

Genore had few visitors, Phillip said. She mainly kept to herself. She was gone at least ten hours a day during the week at her job in Baton Rouge and spent her weekends tending to her animals and working on her property. She had a few admirers. A guy named Donald Johnson came by every couple of months and delivered hay for Genore's horses. They'd known each other for a long time, something like ten or fifteen years. He would always stay and chat for a while.

A guy named Tommy Alexander came by sometimes. He had horses, too. Alexander and Genore were friendly, they may have even had something going on, but Phillip had never seen him spend the night.

The guy Phillip had run off of Miss G's property was named George. Phillip couldn't remember if that was his first name or his last name. He knew that George lived somewhere in East Feliciana Parish. Phillip said he couldn't give McKey directions to George's house, he didn't know it well enough, but if the detective wanted him to, he could probably find it for him.

Phillip said his wife used to have a key to Genore's house, but Genore had asked for it back after the two women got into the argument about the goat. Genore also kept a spare key under a seashell in the carport. Later, when McKey picked up the seashell, the key was gone.

While they talked, McKey noticed scratches on Phillip Skipper's arms. The detective pointed at them. "Where'd you get those?"

Skipper rubbed the palm of one hand across his arm. "Horsing around with my stepson. We was wrestling in the yard and trading punches."

"What's his name?"

"John Baillio. We call him Little John. He's scratched up, too."

"How old is he?" McKey asked.

"Fifteen."

"Is there anything else you can tell me about Ms. Guillory's personal life?" McKey asked. "Besides George, was there anyone else she ever had a problem with?"

"Just one person," Skipper said.

"Who?"

Genore had told Skipper about a guy she was having trouble with, a guy from Baton Rouge who'd been bothering her for a while. Recently, the problem seemed to be getting worse. His name was Steve Williams. He was a Baton Rouge policeman.

Carl Chenevert knew a good bit about Steve Williams. Williams was in his mid-forties and lived in Baton Rouge. He was a retired corrections officer and had recently been hired by the Baton Rouge Police Department. Chenevert told McKey that for the last few months Williams had been calling Genore at least twice a day at her office. The calls were like clockwork, the first one at noon, the second one around four p.m.

Genore and Williams sometimes got into loud arguments on the telephone. Genore often asked her coworkers to tell Williams that she wasn't in or that she was busy on another line and couldn't talk. Williams left messages for her all the time.

From what Genore had told Chenevert, Steve Williams's actions and phone calls had reached the point of harassment. Although Genore had known Williams for many years, she was fed up with him. She told Chenevert that she wished Williams would just leave her alone.

According to Chenevert, things with Williams had recently gotten worse. In early May, Genore had invited Williams to stop by her house after he mentioned to her that he was going to be in the area that weekend visiting his mother in St. Francisville, a small town twenty miles west of Clinton on Louisiana Highway 10. Shortly after Williams arrived, however, he and Genore got into an argument about her dogs. Williams said she had too many of them. He thought it was cruel to keep them penned up in a kennel. Genore later told friends at work that inviting Williams to her house had been a mistake.

A couple of weeks later, Williams talked Genore into going out to lunch with him. When Genore got back to the office, she told a friend: "I will never go out to lunch with him again. Steve is crazy. He had his hands all over me."

After their lunch date, Williams showed up unannounced at a barn on U.S. Highway 61 where Genore stabled a couple of her horses. He was wearing military-style pants. Genore later told Chenevert that she had not seen Williams until he was practically on top of her and that his sudden appearance startled her.

After Genore stopped taking Williams's phone calls at work, she told her coworkers that she'd seen him a couple of times waiting for her in the parking lot when she got off from work. Chenevert said Genore starting staying late at the office to avoid running into Williams.

"The situation with Steve was pretty tense at the time," one of Genore's coworkers later said.

On Friday, June 23, three days before sheriff's deputies discovered her body, Genore got into a heated argument on the telephone with Williams. She later told Chenevert that Williams said he was going to St. Francisville the next day to do some work around his mother's place and that he planned to stop by Genore's house sometime Saturday.

Around noon Friday, Genore told friends at work that she was taking a half day of vacation time. She was going home to do some work on a fence. Before she left, Genore told Chenevert that she hoped Steve Williams wouldn't show up that weekend.

It was the last time Chenevert ever spoke to Genore.

FOUR

At 6:00 p.m., McKey and Thompson sent the dead woman's body to Lane Memorial Hospital in Zachary, twenty miles south in East Baton Rouge Parish, for an autopsy. Drew Thompson arrived at the hospital at 7:20. Don McKey got there at 8:45.

Louisiana law requires that an autopsy be performed in the case of any death not attended by a physician. What that means is that anyone who dies outside of a hospital or who is not under the direct care of a doctor has to be cut open.

The autopsy, or postmortem examination as it's also known, is crucial to a homicide investigation. The word "homicide" means the killing of a human being. A homicide can be legal or illegal, depending on the circumstances. People kill one another all the time. Sometimes by accident. Sometimes on purpose. Sometimes it's legally excusable. Sometimes it's not.

If a drunk decides to take a nap under your car and you roll over him and crush his head, it's a tragic accident. If someone breaks into your house and tries to rape your eleven-year-old daughter and you fire a string of .40-caliber bullets into his chest, it's a justifiable homicide.

The line that separates homicide from murder is occasionally a little hazy, but in most cases it's pretty clear. If you meant to do something, then by definition it wasn't an accident. So if you meant to kill someone and you lacked a legally justifiable reason, then it was murder.

However, in Louisiana, as in every state, not all murders are created equal. There are varying degrees of murder.

In the Louisiana hierarchy of criminal homicide, aka murder, the act of manslaughter occupies the lowest rung. (In a case in which death is caused by accident but happens as a result of sheer stupidity or recklessness on the part of the killer, the perpetrator is usually charged with negligent homicide, known as involuntary manslaughter in some states.) The crime of manslaughter is loosely defined as murder for a reason. Someone does something that would enrage an average person to the point that he or she loses control and takes a human life.

The key phrase in the manslaughter statute is "an average person." Whatever it is that the troublemaker did that led to his or her death must be of sufficient seriousness that it would make *an average person* so mad and so unable to control himself that he could take a human life. There is also a time element. The killing must be close enough in time to the event that *an average person* would not have had time to regain control of his emotions or to cool off.

If you kill your best friend when you catch him in bed with your wife or if you kill your neighbor immediately after finding out he beat your son senseless and put him in the hospital, it's manslaughter. If you wait a week, or a month, or a year, it's not manslaughter anymore, it's murder.

Nor is it manslaughter if the provocation wasn't sufficient. If *an average person* wouldn't have become so enraged that he could lose control of his senses and be driven to kill—you stab your boss to death with a letter opener because he asked you to work late—it's not manslaughter, it's murder.

Manslaughter also covers the unintentional killing of a person during the commission of certain nonviolent crimes—both felony and misdemeanor. You grab a handful of cash from the open register of a store and run off with the store manager in hot pursuit, but during the chase he dies after falling and cracking his head on the pavement. You didn't mean to kill him, but he died as a result of your crime. It's manslaughter.

In Louisiana, manslaughter is punishable by up to forty years in prison.

Second-degree murder is your average, run-of-the-mill killing. Somebody pisses you off and you kill him. There was no reasonable provocation as in a case of manslaughter. You're shooting dice with a friend, sharing a bottle of Mad Dog. He drains the last quarter of the bottle in a single gulp. You pull out your Lorcin .380 and punch a couple of holes in his chest. Second-degree murder carries a mandatory life sentence without the possibility of parole.

Then there's the top rung of the hierarchy of criminal homicide, first-degree murder. In Louisiana, the charge of first-degree murder is reserved for that special brand of killer who, through stupidity, bad luck, or just a gut full of evil, kills a policeman, kills more than one person, kills a child, is a contract killer, or kills someone in what would normally be considered second-degree murder but does so while committing a violent felony such as armed robbery, burglary, rape, or kidnapping. The punishment for first-degree murder is left up to a jury, but includes only two options: death by lethal injection or life in prison without parole.

The key to any successful murder prosecution is the establishment of proof beyond a reasonable doubt that a specific person or persons caused the death of the victim. To do that, a prosecutor needs to know the answers to two questions: How did the victim die? And who killed the victim?

Law enforcement answers the second question. Science answers the first.

Enter the autopsy. The prosecution can't prove murder unless they can prove how the victim died. Expressed another way, to prove murder means to eliminate the possibility that death came as a result of natural or accidental causes.

The postmortem examination has a single purpose: to determine the cause of death.

The term "autopsy" comes from the Greek word autopsia *and means "to see for oneself."* Italian physician Giovanni Battista Morgagni first catalogued autopsy procedures in 1769 in his classic book *The Seats and Causes of Diseases Investigated by Anatomy.*

Sometimes cause of death is easy to determine. A shotgun blast to the head of a person who is otherwise healthy and uninjured doesn't leave a lot of room for doubt as to the reason the victim is lying naked on a stainless steel table in a morgue. But a charred body with a crushed skull found in the collapsed remains of a house fire is a different story. Did the victim die in the fire and then get crushed in the collapse, or did someone bash the victim's head in and then set fire to the house to make the death look accidental? In that case, the presence, or lack thereof, of scorching along the trachea or soot in the lungs means the difference between an accident and a murder.

Because they are always gruesome and often quite bloody, autopsies are usually performed in out-of-the-way corners of hospitals, far from public view. The basement is a popular place for a morgue. The symbolism is hard to miss.

To get a body to a hospital morgue requires subtlety and

a bit of discretion. Dead bodies aren't rushed to the hospital in ambulances with lights flashing and sirens wailing. Once the death scene investigation—whether criminal or unexplained—is completed and the detectives release the body, the body snatchers, usually a couple of coroner's men, sometimes assistant medical examiners or funeral home attendants, zip the remains into a clean, black rubber body bag and load it into a vehicle. Most of the time the body travels in an unmarked van, sometimes in a hearse. The trip to the hospital is made with no fanfare. Once there, the body is usually wheeled on a collapsible gurney through a discreet back entrance.

The reason for the discretion is one of faith, not the religious kind, but rather the institutional kind. The dead must be kept hidden so that the public's faith in the institution of medicine is maintained.

No one wants to see the dead hauled from the rear of an ambulance and rolled through the brightly lit entrance of the emergency room. No one wants to see the dead carted out of hospitals. Once the paramedics reach someone, that person is supposed to survive. Once the sick or injured make it to a hospital, they're supposed to get well or be healed. They're not supposed to die.

Death is taboo. Real death—as opposed to the sanitized fictional version portrayed on television and in the movies—is messy and unpleasant. It's also scary. You may escape your taxes, but you won't escape your death.

Because death is messy, because death is unpleasant, because death is scary, people don't want to hear about it, they don't want to talk about it, and they sure as hell don't want to see it. Left in their natural state, one of advancing decomposition and putrefaction, and without the preservative arts of the mortician, the dead are just . . . gross.

The reason people spend so much time, effort, and money on preserving and clothing the dearly departed is so they don't look so . . . dead. People want to be deceived.

They want the last time they see a deceased friend or loved one to be pleasant. They want the dead to look more . . . alive.

Because death is taboo, the public demands it be kept hidden. To look death in the face, to actually see the dead in all their horror, is to say, at least on some level, *that could be me* or, even worse, *that will be me.*

Autopsies begin with an exterior examination. The body lies on a stainless steel table. The surface of the table is rimmed and slightly concave and looks something like a one-inch-deep bathtub. The examination table comes equipped with a flexible hose with an attached spray nozzle and a drain to wash away the blood and other bodily fluids.

The corpse is stripped of all clothing and jewelry. Naked, it's weighed and measured and, in the case of a homicide investigation, photographed. The pathologist examines the surface of the deceased inch by inch, noting each mark, scar, and blemish. Exterior injuries and wounds are probed and their exact measurements catalogued. Wounds are photographed. Bullet holes are tracked and their angles calculated. In the case of a homicide, hair and nail clippings are collected for later comparison to suspects. In suspected rape cases, the mouth, genitals, and rectum of female victims—sometimes male victims also— are examined for abrasions, tears, lacerations, or the presence of semen or foreign objects.

Then comes the interior examination. To begin the examination, the autopsist uses a scalpel to make the initial opening, called a "Y" cut, along the torso. The incision is really shaped more like a letter "T" than it is a "Y," but for some reason that's what it's called. It's a two-part incision, with the first cut a lateral slice across the top of the chest, just below the collarbone. The blade carves through the muscle until it hits bone. The second cut is linear and runs from the top of the sternum, down the belly, past the navel to the pubic bone. Once the flesh is peeled back from the ribs and abdomen, the pathologist uses an electric, high-speed circular saw to split the breastbone. The rib cage is pulled apart, and the interior of the thorax and abdomen are exposed.

In the case of a homicide victim who's been shot or stabbed in the upper body and whose insides have been ripped apart or punctured, the opened torso can resemble a pool of blood. The circular saw the autopsist uses to cut through the rib cage can sling blood across the examination room.

The internal organs, which sit in the freshly opened corpse like a bowl of Jell-O, are given a detailed examination. Their general condition and any indications of the presence of disease are noted. They are removed and weighed. The contents of the stomach and intestines are extracted and inspected. Tissue and fluid samples are collected from each of the organs for later analysis, and vials of blood are drawn for toxicology testing. The completed autopsy report will list the presence and amount by volume of any drugs—legal or illegal—or alcohol.

In many cases, particularly those in which there has been head trauma, the dead person's brain needs to be examined. To get to the brain, the autopsist has to open the skull. To the uninitiated, it's a messy and gruesome process.

It begins with a scalpel slice across the scalp. The cut starts at the bony notch behind one ear and runs laterally across the top of the head to the notch behind the opposite ear. The pathologist then jams his gloved fingers into the front edge of the incision and yanks the face and ears down to the chin.

It's surprising how easily someone's face—without a doubt a human being's most recognizable feature, and the one that serves as a window into their personality, into their mood, into their very soul—can be torn off. Similarly, the back of the scalp is pulled down and away from the bone, leaving nothing but a bloody, sticky, gooey mess, and what appears to be an almost grinning skull.

Again the high-speed saw. The pathologist makes a circular cut around the circumference of the skull an inch or so above where the top of the ears once reached. A stainless steel pry bar—called a skull chisel—is wedged into the cut and used as a lever to force open the top of the calvarium, the vaultlike part of the skull that houses the brain. A quick scalpel incision at the base of the skull severs the brain stem and allows the entire brain to be pulled out.

If the head trauma wasn't too severe, the brain comes out intact, wet and pink and looking like a three-pound ball of compressed hamburger meat. If the trauma was severe, say from a high-velocity bullet that carried with it a pressure wave many times larger than the bullet itself, the brain slides out in a gelatinous ooze that looks remarkably like cranberry dressing. Either way, the pathologist deposits the brain into a steel pan so that it can be measured, weighed, and later dissected.

FIVE

McKey and Thompson met Dr. Emil Laga in the morgue at Lane Memorial Hospital for the autopsy. Laga had been a forensic pathologist since 1968 and had performed more than five thousand autopsies.

The first step in the process was to try to get a positive identification before the body was cut up. At 8:00 p.m., Genore Guillory's brother-in-law, Elbert Guillory, an attorney from Opelousas who'd married Genore's sister twenty years before and who, coincidentally, had the same last name, stepped into the morgue at Lane Memorial. Detective Drew Thompson stood beside him. Elbert Guillory looked at the mutilated face lying before him. The woman's head had been beaten almost beyond recognition. After a few moments, Elbert Guillory nodded. There was no doubt about her identity. As everyone had suspected all day, the body was indeed that of his sister-in-law, Jane Nora Guillory.

Dr. Emil Laga began his postmortem examination immediately after Elbert Guillory made the identification.

Detectives Don McKey and Drew Thompson, along with State Police forensic scientist Adam Becnel, were there as witnesses and to collect the evidence.

Dr. Laga started with Genore's green nightshirt. Manufactured by Simply Basic, the nightshirt was one-size-fits-all. It bore no logos or cleaning labels. Along the front left side of the nightshirt Dr. Laga found five thin holes. The fabric around the holes was covered with dried blood. Embedded in the blood were hard splinters, possibly of bone, and strands of hair. He identified the holes as having been made by a knife or other sharp object.

High on the back right-hand side of the nightshirt, up near the shoulder, was a single small-caliber bullet hole. There were no powder burns around it. To Dr. Laga, that suggested a shot fired from at least a foot away. Shots fired from closer than a foot usually leave traces of burned gunpowder around the edge of the hole.

Dr. Laga removed the nightshirt and handed it to Adam Becnel; then he began his exterior examination of Genore Guillory. Along her front left side, corresponding to the holes in the nightshirt, the pathologist found five stab wounds. They were lined up vertically, each about one to two inches from the next. The stab wounds measured approximately three-quarters of an inch long. When he probed the wounds, Laga found they measured from five to seven inches in depth. The uppermost wound pierced the bottom of the left lung; the three in the middle penetrated the stomach; and the bottom wound sliced through one of the ligaments that connect the liver to the stomach. In Dr. Laga's opinion, none of the stab wounds had been fatal.

Next, he examined the gunshot wounds. One corresponded to the hole in the back of Genore's nightshirt. The bullet had struck the upper right portion of her back and blown apart the joint between her shoulder and upper arm. Another had hit her in the left buttock. One bullet struck her left forearm, and another buried itself in her left wrist. A fifth shot tore completely through the ring finger of Genore's left hand.

Laga recovered four of the five bullets from Genore's body. All of the bullets appeared to McKey and Thompson to be .22-caliber. In the pathologist's opinion, although all five bullet wounds were inflicted while Genore was alive, none of them were the cause of her death.

The most severely damaged part of Genore's body was clearly her head. Laga identified five separate blunt impact injuries to her skull. Later in his report, Dr. Laga described the condition of Genore's head and face as "markedly disfigured, swollen, blood splattered . . . with blood plastering together curly hair strands and embedded batches of dried grass."

Genore's eye orbits were smashed, her nasal bones shattered, her upper and lower jaws fractured, her front teeth knocked out. Crusty reddish brown streaks showed where she'd bled from her ears, nose, and mouth. The back of her skull had been crushed.

The killing blow had come from behind. It came at high speed, traveling upward at a thirty-degree angle and from left to right. It struck Genore just behind her left ear and severed her spinal cord. Paralysis was instantaneous. Death was not.

According to Laga's examination, the impact ruptured Genore's brain stem, the mechanism responsible for most of the body's autonomic functions, life-sustaining functions such as respiration and blood pressure. The blow cracked Genore's skull and ripped open the arteries that carried blood to her brain. The hemorrhage inside Genore's head was severe. It was as if a tap had been opened inside her skull.

"There was a massive loss of blood," Dr. Laga later said.

In Genore's stomach and lungs, the pathologist found at least seventy milliliters of blood. Its presence meant that after having her head nearly crushed, Genore was still gasping for air as she tried to swallow the blood that was pouring into her mouth through her shattered sinus cavities. Laga estimated that Genore may have lived for as long as five minutes after being struck in the back of the head.

The blow that landed across the bridge of Genore's nose, one that McKey and Thompson thought had likely come from the lamp base they found broken beside her head, was potentially fatal and might have killed her had she not suffered the one to the base of her skull. But Laga was sure it had been that one, the high-velocity strike to the back of her head, that was the cause of death. "The one behind her left ear killed her," he explained later.

There were indications of rape, but nothing definitive. Although there was no tearing or abrasion of the vaginal walls or inside the rectum, Laga noted in his report what he described as a "white . . . fluid running out of the vagina."

Genore's fingernails were trimmed off and bagged. Later, technicians at the State Police Crime Lab would put them in a chemical wash to leech away any skin scrapings that might have been trapped under them. A comparison sample of hair was pulled from her scalp. Oral, vaginal, and rectal swabs were taken. And a combing from her pubic hair as well as pulled hair follicles were collected. Genore's blood was collected in test tubes for toxicology screening and alcohol testing.

Dr. Laga finished his postmortem examination of the remains of Genore Guillory at 1:30 Tuesday morning. East Feliciana Detectives Don McKey and Drew Thompson went back to Clinton. Adam Becnel took the evidence and photographs to the State Police Crime Lab. Dr. Laga went home. Genore Guillory traveled by hearse to the Owens-Thomas Funeral Parlor in her hometown of Eunice, Louisiana, in St. Landry Parish, halfway between Baton

Rouge and the Texas state line. Two days later, she was laid to rest in St. Mathilda Cemetery in Eunice.

Later, in his report, Dr. Laga would estimate the time of Genore's death to have been between noon, Saturday, June 24, and noon, Sunday, June 25. The manner of her death he listed as homicide. The cause of that death, the doctor explained in his report, using the necessarily cold and stilted language of the autopsist, was "multiple trauma, including lethal blunt trauma to head (5 blows), fracturing skull, directly injuring brainstem and causing intracranial subdural hemorrhage (50 ml), in addition to five nonlethal gunshot wounds to left upper/lower extremity and right shoulder, five nonbleeding trunk-penetrating stabwounds . . ."

The report went on to say that Genore's blood alcohol concentration had been 0.03 grams percent. Enough to indicate she'd had a glass of wine with the partially digested dinner Dr. Laga had found inside her stomach.

Tuesday morning, the day after Genore Guillory's body was discovered, Steve Williams, the Baton Rouge police officer who, according to Genore's coworkers had been harassing her, called Genore's office. Linda Cueno answered the call.

Linda had worked next to Genore for eleven years. The two women were close friends. Linda had attended Eddie Dixon's funeral a year and a half before. She had also screened many of Steve Williams's telephone calls for her friend. A week before her death, Genore asked Linda to tell Williams not to call her anymore. When Linda told Williams what Genore had said, that she didn't want to speak to him ever again, he launched into a monologue about what a wonderful woman Genore was and how someday the two of them were going to be married. Linda listened politely then hung up. Later, the two women laughed about it. "That Steve is crazy," Genore said.

On Tuesday, Williams told Linda that he'd heard about Genore's murder on the television news the previous night. He seemed genuinely upset, but Linda didn't feel like talking about it with him. She asked for his telephone number and said she would call him later. Williams refused to give her his number. He said he would call back. Then he hung up.

The next day, Williams called again. This time he asked Linda Cueno for the telephone number for Genore's parents. Linda said she didn't have it nearby. She would have to go to another office to get it. She told Williams that she would call him back with the number. Williams again refused to give her his telephone number. He said he would call her later, and he hung up.

SIX

Wednesday morning, two days after Genore Guil-lory's body had been discovered, McKey and Thompson were in their cinder block–walled office in the jail complex. They'd gotten in early and were going over the list of evidence they'd collected and reviewing witness statements. The case was a stone-cold whodunit, and on top of that it was a *real* murder.

In the world of homicide investigation there are misdemeanor murders and there are real murders. There are so-what victims and there are true victims.

A misdemeanor murder always involves a so-what victim. So-what victims are nearly always of the male persuasion. When a so-what victim winds up dead, the cops often classify it, although certainly not officially, as a misdemeanor murder because the victim deserved what he got. He brought death upon himself; he invited it, so the cops reason, because of the poor choices he made in life and because of the lifestyle he engaged in. In the often cynical world of homicide investigation, most dope killings are misdemeanor murders, and a doper who gets whacked is always a so-what victim.

However, just because a case is a misdemeanor murder, at least in the eyes of the investigators, doesn't mean that it isn't going to get worked. After all, cops like to put bad guys in jail, so they'll usually work a misdemeanor murder as hard as they can, but if the physical evidence doesn't pan out and witnesses don't come forth, very few detectives are going to lose much sleep over a dead dope dealer.

But if the victim is a child or a woman, or a man who lived a relatively clean life, then the crime gets bumped up a notch on the priority list. A true victim turns a run-of-the-mill killing into a real murder.

In the mind of nearly every detective, child killers deserve a special place in hell. The murder of a child can transform a cynical, coldhearted detective into the right hand of God and launch him on a crusade to strike down the wicked.

Most detectives feel the same way, if to a slightly lesser degree, about the murder of a woman. The reason is simple. Law enforcement is a profession dominated by men, mostly conservative men. They look conservative—short hair, maybe a neatly trimmed mustache. They act conservatively—most vote Republican. And they think conservatively. What that means is, despite the best efforts of modern feminism to stamp out the last traces of that old misogynistic code once known as chivalry, most cops still have a touch of it in them. And that code says that you're not supposed to kill women. So the murder of a woman—even if her old man is a drug dealer or she's been in and out of jail since she was thirteen years old or she's a prostitute or she's a dope fiend—is likely to strike a homicide detective as just plain wrong.

The killing on Oakwood Lane was a real murder, and Genore Guillory was a true victim. From what McKey had pieced together from talking to Ms. Guillory's family and friends, she hadn't done anything to deserve what happened to her. She had a low-key, low-risk lifestyle. She worked hard. She wasn't involved in anything illegal. And she spent most of her spare time taking care of her animals. McKey had to find her killer. He had to put this case down.

About ten o'clock Tuesday morning, McKey called Deputy Ronald Johnson and told him to go back to Oakwood Lane and find Genore's closest neighbor, Phillip Skipper. McKey wanted to talk to him.

When Johnson turned into the Skippers' driveway and pulled his Jeep to a stop in front of their trailer, it had been almost exactly twenty-four hours since he'd pulled into the same driveway the day before. Then he'd been on a welfare call. Now he was helping with a murder investigation. Phillip's wife, Amy, who stood about four feet, ten inches tall and had long, dark hair, told Johnson that her husband was across the street at Miss G's house.

Why was the Sheriff's Department looking for her husband? Amy Skipper asked. Johnson didn't say. He really didn't know, so he just thanked her and climbed back inside his police cruiser.

Across the street, several cars were parked at Genore's house. Johnson eased down the long driveway and stopped near the house. He got out of his Jeep and walked up to a couple of Genore's relatives. He asked if Phillip Skipper was around.

Genore's brother briefly questioned Johnson about why he wanted to see Phillip. There was a challenge in his voice. Skipper hadn't done anything wrong, the brother said. In fact, he'd been extremely helpful to the family. Johnson explained that it was just routine. The detectives had to question everybody.

A moment later, Skipper came out of the house through the side door. He said he'd been helping clean the house.

"I need you to come with me," Deputy Johnson told him.

Skipper looked wary. "Why?"

"The detectives want to talk to you."

"Am I under arrest?"

"No," Johnson said. "The detectives just want to ask you some questions."

Skipper wasn't convinced. "Why do they want to talk to me?"

"I don't know. They just want you to come in for questioning."

Skipper shrugged and walked with Johnson toward his Jeep Cherokee. It must have come as a relief to Skipper that Johnson opened the front passenger door for him and didn't pull out a set of handcuffs.

On the ride to the detectives' office, Skipper told Johnson about how generous Miss G had been to him and his wife and son. She had lent them the money for their new trailer, Skipper said, and he hoped the Sheriff's Department found whoever killed her.

At the detectives' office, Phillip Skipper reiterated what he'd told McKey the day before. He and his wife had lived across from Miss G for a few years. They'd gotten friendly with her and her boyfriend Eddie. When Eddie died in a car crash, Phillip and his wife had been there to help Genore tend to her animals and to maintain the house and yard.

"What about the argument over the goat?" McKey asked.

That had been nothing more than a neighborly spat, Skipper said. They'd worked it all out.

McKey inquired again about the man Ms. Guillory had asked him to run off of her property, the man named George. Skipper said he didn't know George's full name but remembered enough about where he lived to find his house. McKey asked Skipper to point out George's house to Deputy Johnson on the ride back to his trailer.

As Skipper was about to leave the detectives' office, McKey tossed out a question. "Would you be willing to take a polygraph, a lie detector test, about the things we've talked about?"

"Sure," Skipper said.

McKey also talked that morning to John Baillio, Skipper's fifteen-year-old stepson. John, too, had scratches on his arms. He confirmed that he and Phillip had been wrestling around in the yard. Baillio said he'd been close to Miss G. She'd been like a grandmother to him. He had no idea who'd killed her. She had no enemies. Everyone loved her.

Like his stepfather, John Baillio agreed to take a polygraph test.

On Friday, June 30, 2006, Don McKey and Drew Thompson drove Phillip Skipper to Baton Rouge police headquarters, to the office of Vicki King, the police department's polygraph examiner.

McKey knew that just because Skipper had agreed to take the polygraph test a couple of days before didn't mean he was actually going to do it. Now it was time to find out just how sincere he'd really been about taking the test and how truthful he'd been when he said he didn't know anything about Genore Guillory's murder.

East Feliciana didn't have a polygraph machine, so McKey had made arrangements with the Baton Rouge Police Department to use theirs.

Although criminal courts in the United States generally do not accept the results of polygraph examinations, investigators frequently ask witnesses and suspects to take them anyway. Part of it is a bluff. Most people believe in the machine's ability to detect deception.

Just a person's reaction to the offer of a polygraph test is often enough to tell an investigator whether he's on the right track. Generally, innocent people are not afraid of the test. They accept the offer. They're not worried about being caught lying because they're not lying. On the other hand, a refusal to submit to a polygraph examination usually means the person has something to hide. Not necessarily guilt, but something they don't want exposed.

Most career criminals, however, are smart enough to realize that a flat refusal looks suspicious, so the clever ones cooperate—at first. They accept the initial offer for the test. *Of course I'll take a lie detector test. I've got nothing to hide. I'm innocent.*

But the devil is in the details. Any veteran investigator knows that a yes is not always a yes. What often happens is that as soon as a detective starts setting up the specifics, such as the time and place for the test to be administered, the test subject comes up with an excuse not to take it. There are a lot of excuses, but one of the most common is a recommendation from a doctor. The subject has a nervous condition or is on heart medication. Another is advice from an attorney. Sometimes the subject says he knows people who've failed polygraph tests even though they were telling the truth. Some subjects say they are afraid the cops will rig the test to make them look guilty, an argument that doesn't make a lot of sense given that the test results aren't admissible in court. Sometimes they just don't show up. *My car wouldn't start. I missed the bus. My kid got sick.*

But if a refusal to take the test or a last-minute equivocation is an indicator of deception, then actually sitting down and getting hooked up to the box has to be considered an indication of truthfulness.

Phillip Skipper didn't come up with a last-minute excuse. During the ride to Baton Rouge he seemed relaxed. At police headquarters on Mayflower Street, he dropped into the chair next to the polygraph machine without complaint. Officer King hooked him up.

A polygraph machine doesn't actually detect lies. It measures physiological responses to questions based on the theory that the responses will be greater when a person lies. The theory is founded on the idea that lying is stressful and that stress can be detected and measured.

The thing that makes lying so stressful is the fear of being caught. If a person was absolutely certain that his lies would not be detected, then there wouldn't be any stress, other than perhaps from a guilty conscience. If, on the other hand, a person was sure that even the slightest deception would be exposed, then there would be a tremendous amount of stress associated with lying. Therefore, the key to a successful polygraph examination is that the subject believes in the machine's ability to detect deception.

William Marston invented the first polygraph in about 1917. The machine measured only one physiological variable—systolic blood pressure. Since then, lie detection machines have undergone dozens of major modifications. Modern machines use electrodes attached to the tips of two fingers, a pair of pneumographic tubes that encircle the chest and stomach, and a pressure cuff wrapped around the bicep to measure four variables: blood pressure, heart rate, respiration, and galvanic skin response, also known as perspiration.

Old-style polygraph boxes were the size of a small suitcase. During the test, electric rollers fed a spool of graph paper across the top of the machine. L-shaped stylus pens jerked from side to side, leaving a jumble of squiggly lines.

In the last decade or so, most of the old clunkers have given way to laptop computers. The physiological monitors feed information directly into a slim electronic device about the size of a computer's external hard drive. The data is then routed into the computer via a cable connection. As the graphs and wavy lines slide across the monitor, electronic algorithms make thousands of microsecond calculations in an attempt to determine whether the subject is lying.

But a polygraph test isn't really a test at all. It's a rigidly structured and recorded interrogation. The "test" consists of two, sometimes three interviews. The pre-test interview is a meet and greet between the subject and the polygraphist. It's rapport building, a chance to get to know a little bit about each other and to establish some common ground. In any structured interview, rapport building is an important first step. People usually tell secrets to their friends, not their enemies.

It might go something like this:

> POLYGRAPH EXAMINER: What'd you do last night?
> TEST SUBJECT: I went to a baseball game.
> POLYGRAPH EXAMINER: Really? You like baseball?
> TEST SUBJECT: Uh-huh.
> POLYGRAPH EXAMINER: Me, too. It's a great game. My son—he's nine—he plays ball at the park out near our house. I've been helping out this season, acting as sort of an assistant coach.

The examiner might or might not have a nine-year-old son, who might or might not play baseball at the park near his house. Whether the story is true or not isn't important. It's better if it is, but if it isn't, it doesn't really matter. What does matter is that the interviewer and the interviewee now have a connection—baseball. They've established common ground. They're friends.

During the pre-test interview, the subject isn't hooked up to the machine, but he can see it. Belief in the machine is the key to the test. Once the examiner establishes rapport with the subject, the two of them go over the questions that will be asked during the real test.

There are three types of questions: irrelevant questions, control questions—also known as "probable-lie questions"—and relevant questions. Irrelevant questions are throwaways. *Is your name John? Are you thirty years old? Are you married?* They seem like control questions but they're not. The examiner knows the answers and doesn't expect the subject to lie about them.

The real control questions are designed to encourage the subject to lie. *Have you ever lied to an authority figure? Have you ever stolen anything from work? Have you ever operated a car while under the influence of alcohol?* Once the examiner gets the subject to give an answer that is almost certainly a lie, a physiological baseline for deception is established.

Then come the relevant questions. In the case of a criminal investigation, they're the questions about the crime. *Did you burn down your business to collect the insurance money? Did you have sex with so-and-so? Did you kill what's-his-name?*

If the physiological reaction to the relevant questions is stronger—an increase in blood pressure, more sweating, a higher heart rate, more rapid breathing—than to the control questions, then boom, the subject fails. But since it's not really a test, there actually is no pass or fail. Results are rated in one of three ways—truthfulness, deception, inconclusive.

Belief in the box, fear of the box, is crucial.

When Vicki King hooked Phillip Skipper up to the polygraph machine in her office at Baton Rouge police headquarters on the morning of June 30, 2000, Skipper knew he was there because he was at least a potential suspect in a homicide investigation.

To even be considered a possible culprit in a brutal murder is enough to make almost anybody nervous, yet Skipper appeared calm as he waited for the test to begin. He didn't know a thing about sophisticated interview techniques or lie detector tests. He was a country boy, not a detective. The twenty-three-year-old Skipper had trouble holding a job because of a childhood accident that left him with only one lung. He hadn't finished high school and could barely read and write. On the signature line of the consent form King read to him before he took the test, Skipper scrawled his name in fourth-grade print. In all likelihood he had never even seen a polygraph machine before.

Vicki King saved the hard stuff for last. Near the end of the forty-five-minute interrogation, King asked Skipper a series of questions about the murder. Her voice was measured, her tone even.

"Do you know for sure who killed Ms. Guillory?"

"No," Skipper said.

"Did you kill Ms. Guillory?"

"No."

"Did John make those scratches on your arm?"

"Yes," Skipper responded.

"Did you shoot or stab Ms. Guillory?"

"No."

In the report Officer King typed up later that day, she wrote, "In the polygraph recordings there were definite indications of truthfulness when Mr. Skipper answered the test questions. It is the opinion of the polygraphist, based upon the polygraph examination of Phillip Skipper, that he told the truth to the listed questions."

Skipper had "passed" his polygraph test with flying colors.

SEVEN

On Saturday, July 1, 2000, exactly one week after Dr.
Emil Laga's estimated time of death for Genore Guillory,
Talmadge Bunch officially took office as East Feliciana
Parish's new sheriff. The fifty-one-year-old Democrat had
been sworn in the previous Sunday, one day after Genore's
murder and the day before her body was discovered.

Before being elected sheriff, Bunch spent five years
with the Sheriff's Department, where he had risen to the
rank of sergeant. Before he hired on with the Sheriff's Department, Bunch spent a year as a guard at the state prison
on Highway 10 near the East Feliciana town of Jackson.
He'd also worked for ten years at a local lumber company.
He had played on the baseball team at Southeastern
Louisiana University in the nearby city of Hammond.

Bunch was a law enforcement legacy. His father, George
Bunch, had been an East Feliciana sheriff's deputy for
forty years. When Talmadge Bunch announced his candidacy in 1999, he vowed to get tough on dope dealers and
violent crime. He promised voters that he would be "a

sheriff who will never rest until the scourge of drugs and drug dealers is gone from our parish."

In May 1999, a month after Bunch announced he was running for sheriff, a drive-by shooting wounded six people outside a juke joint north of Clinton. The place was called the Lo' Key Lounge and had a history of dope dealing and violence.

A year later, in May 2000, just a month before Bunch was sworn in, one man died from a bullet wound to the head and three more were shot after a 2:00 a.m. brawl at the Lo' Key. Sheriff's deputies recovered spent shotgun shells and casings from 9mm handgun cartridges and 7.62mm rifle ammunition. A car in the parking lot had four bullet holes in the passenger door and two windows shot out.

"There were a lot of rounds fired . . . and numerous vehicles were shot up," Chief Deputy James Norsworthy said the morning after the shooting.

Trouble was nothing new to that part of East Feliciana Parish, but it nearly always involved people who were looking for it—drunks, dopers, and miscreants who hung out all night at backwoods bars. "There's no closing time on bars in the parish, and it seems the fights always start about one-thirty or two o'clock in the morning," Chief Deputy Norsworthy said. "There's a lot of gunfire in that area on Friday and Saturday nights."

The day after Talmadge Bunch took the oath of office as East Feliciana Parish's new sheriff, he found out that trouble had reached out and touched someone who wasn't looking for it. Someone innocent. Someone named Genore Guillory.

On July 2, Detective Don McKey interviewed Donald Johnson, who turned out to be related to Ronald Johnson, the deputy sheriff who discovered Genore's body, although at the time of the murder, the two men didn't know they were related.

Johnson said he'd met Genore fifteen years earlier when she'd been working at a dentist's office in Baton Rouge. The two of them became friends and kept in touch after she began working for BlueCross. Johnson said he hauled hay out to Genore's property every two or three months. The last time he'd spoken to Genore had been sometime around the middle of June.

According to Johnson, Genore had recently been dating a guy named Tommy Alexander. Genore had said she and Tommy Alexander often got into arguments because Alexander had another girlfriend.

Genore had also told Johnson about a man named Steve Williams. She said that on a recent lunch date, Williams had been very physical, that he'd touched her too much.

Johnson said he was afraid of Genore's dogs, especially the tan chow named Cleo. He said Genore relied on Cleo for protection. She never tied the dog up. No one could get near Genore if Cleo was around. Even her boyfriend, Eddie, when he was alive, had to be careful around Cleo.

That same day, McKey talked to Tommy Alexander. The forty-seven-year-old Alexander said Genore had been one of three women he was seeing. One of the other two lived with him most of the time in Zachary, and the third one lived in Lafayette, forty miles west of Baton Rouge.

Alexander said he met Genore at a feed store in Zachary about a year, maybe a year and a half, before her death. They both owned horses. He had been to Genore's house a few times, but he had never spent the night. He was afraid of her dogs, he told McKey. Especially Cleo. "I was scared of that chow," he said. A couple of times Cleo latched on to Alexander's pants.

When Alexander came over, Genore would put Cleo outside. Still, Alexander wasn't comfortable there. "I didn't want to be around him," he explained to McKey. "He would bite."

Alexander said he talked to Genore two or three times a week. They often took walks together. He said he hadn't been to her house since December, but he had seen Genore either the Tuesday or Wednesday before her death. She had come to his house in Zachary so he could help her fill out paperwork to transfer ownership of a couple of horses that she'd purchased.

Recently, Genore had complained to Alexander that she had discovered some of her clothes were missing from her closet. A few other items from around the house were also missing.

Alexander said he'd first learned about Genore's death from a friend. Then he'd seen it on the television news.

McKey asked Tommy Alexander where he'd been the weekend of June 24 and 25.

With his girlfriend, Alexander said, the one he lived with in Zachary.

On July 6, 2000, one week after Genore Guillory's funeral, Steve Williams called Genore's friend and coworker Linda Cueno again at her office. Williams blurted out that the police suspected him of Genore's murder. He told Cueno that he had nothing to do with Genore's death. He loved Genore and would never have hurt her. Cueno signaled to a coworker to ring her phone. Within seconds it emitted an electronic bleat that could be heard over the line on which she was talking to Williams.

"Steve, my phones are ringing off the hook," she said. "Can I call you back?"

Ever since their conversations the previous week, Cueno had become increasingly suspicious of Williams and wanted to get the number he was calling from.

Williams mumbled something Cueno couldn't quite

make out and then hung up. She never heard from him again.

On Friday, July 7, eleven days after Genore's body was discovered, Don McKey drove Phillip Skipper's fifteen-year-old stepson, John Baillio, to Baton Rouge police headquarters. His stepmother, Amy Skipper, rode with them. Polygraphist Vicki King was there to meet them.

After Baillio and Amy Skipper signed a consent-to-question form, and after the pre-test interview, King hooked Baillio up to the box. Again, as she had with Phillip Skipper, King saved her most important questions for last:

"Do you know for sure who killed Ms. Guillory?"

"No," Baillio answered.

"Did you kill Ms. Guillory?"

"No."

"Right now, can you take me to the gun used to shoot Ms. Guillory?"

"No."

"Did you shoot or stab Ms. Guillory?"

"No."

In the report King typed up later that afternoon, she cited what she referred to as "definite indications of truthfulness" in Baillio's answers to critical questions. King concluded her report, "It is the opinion of the polygraphist, based upon the polygraph examination of John Baillio, that he told the truth."

Baillio, too, had passed his polygraph test with flying colors.

Steve Williams was fast becoming Don McKey's primary suspect in the murder of Genore Guillory. Williams had the means. At five feet, eleven inches and 210 pounds, he was certainly strong enough to have done it. His twenty-four years as a corrections officer and recently completed stint at the Baton Rouge Police Academy had given Williams extensive training and experience in physical control techniques. It was also certainly no stretch to suspect that Williams might have access to a .22 pistol or rifle.

Williams also had the opportunity. He knew where Genore lived. He had even been to her house at least once. On the Friday before she was killed, Genore told her friend Carl Chenevert that Williams had said he was planning on doing some work at his mother's in St. Francisville and was going to stop by Genore's house on his way there, on Saturday, May 24—the day Dr. Laga identified as the most probable day of Genore's death.

Motive in a murder case is almost always speculation, unless the murderer confesses his reason, and even then a detective may never know the whole truth about why one person decided to take the life of another. But in the case of Genore Guillory, McKey had at least a credible theory as to why Steve Williams might have killed her—unrequited love.

Williams was enamored with Genore. He had told her friends that he loved her and wanted to marry her. The problem was, she just didn't feel the same way about him. According to her friends at work, Genore didn't want to have anything more to do with him.

After their one lunch date—about which Genore complained that Williams wouldn't stop touching her—she had refused to go out with him again. She quit taking his calls and asked her coworkers to tell him that she was out of the office or too busy to talk. When he couldn't reach her by telephone, Williams began hanging out in the parking lot at Genore's office. He had gone so far as to sneak up on her at the pasture where she stabled some of her horses.

Genore's caller ID box showed eleven calls from Williams since May 27. The last call was on Saturday, June 24.

Did Williams visit Genore on Saturday like he said he was going to do? Did they fight, as they had on the telephone on Friday, June 23? Did Williams snap? Did he kill Genore because she rejected his romantic advances?

Don McKey had a lot of questions for Steve Williams.

*McKey met Williams at Baton Rouge police head-*quarters on July 7, the same day John Baillio took his polygraph exam. To McKey, Williams, who stood fidgeting in civilian clothes, looked nervous.

Williams said he and Genore had been just friends. They'd known each other since the early 1980s. Like Donald Johnson, Williams met Genore while she was working for a dentist in Baton Rouge. They'd kept in close contact for a while, although they never dated, Williams explained. They drifted apart after he got married and she became involved with Eddie Dixon.

Several years later, they ran into each other at a Sears store in a mall in Baton Rouge and exchanged telephone numbers. They'd talked on and off since then. Williams claimed their relationship was more like that of a brother and sister rather than a romantic one.

Williams admitted that he had been calling Genore at work at least twice a day for some time, but he resented that Genore's coworkers were characterizing him as a stalker. He denied the accusation some had made that he had left notes on Genore's car and sometimes followed her home. Yes, Williams said, he had gone to that pasture off U.S. 61 to see Genore, but he didn't scare her, at least not that he could recall. He had tossed a rock into some bushes to get Genore's attention. Perhaps that was what she had been talking about. He may have been wearing military-style fatigue pants, but he wasn't sure.

Williams said he went to his mother's house the weekend of Genore's death. He worked in her garden while his son attended a Boy Scout event at Camp Avondale, located just a few miles from Genore's house. Williams said he spoke to Genore briefly on the telephone Saturday, but she told him she had company and couldn't talk. Sunday, Williams called her again but couldn't get through because the telephone was busy. He had not been to her house that weekend, he said.

"Did you ever argue with her?" McKey asked.

Williams recalled that the one time he went to her house—sometime in late April or early May—they had a disagreement over her dogs. Williams said he didn't think it was right to keep so many dogs cooped up in pens.

He also didn't like that Genore had so many male friends.

"I didn't feel comfortable that she had all these friendships because she was like a sister to me," Williams said.

Williams, who was married, said he kept his interest in Genore secret from his wife—his second. "She's young and wouldn't have understood the friendship," he explained.

Williams said he had never owned a .22-caliber firearm.

After the interview, McKey wasn't satisfied with Williams's answers. Not by a long shot. In fact, they had only fueled the detective's suspicions about the rookie Baton Rouge police officer.

McKey decided to dig into Williams's background a little more deeply to see what he could unearth.

EIGHT

Steve Williams retired from the Louisiana Depart-ment of Corrections in 1999 after twenty-four years of service. According to the department's records, Williams had a distinguished career at Hunt Correctional Center, a state prison just south of Baton Rouge. He had risen to the rank of colonel and had a clean employment record with no history of discipline problems.

Within months of his retirement from the Department of Corrections, Williams joined the Baton Rouge Police Department. Because he was forty-five years old, a generation older than his academy classmates, he had sought and been granted a special waiver of the maximum age limit of thirty-five.

One of Williams's police academy classmates was Tabatha McCants.

Shortly after the Baton Rouge Police Department's Academy Class Number Sixty-three began training in December 1999, twenty-nine-year-old police cadet McCants noticed that she was getting extra attention from fellow cadet Steve Williams. During a class banquet at the police union hall, Williams told McCants that she reminded him of a friend with the last name of Guillory who lived in Clinton. Williams asked if she was related to any Guillorys in the Clinton area. She told him she wasn't.

Sometime after the banquet, Williams pressured McCants into accepting an invitation to lunch. Later at the restaurant, McCants found herself becoming a little nervous about Williams's behavior. Something about him troubled her. She later described it as "the stare and weirdness." Williams picked up on her discomfort as they ate, and he asked her why she was scared of him. Then he made a strange comment. He reassured her that he wasn't going to hurt her, McCants later said.

McCants declined Williams's next offer to go to lunch. She declined the one after that, too. But Williams kept asking. According to McCants, Williams started calling her at home on the pretext of asking questions about her class notes.

McCants, who was married, finally confronted Williams and demanded that he stop calling her house.

When Don McKey talked to McCants in July, she recalled that while her academy class had been training at the firing range, Williams had talked about shooting a .22-caliber pistol at his mother's house near Clinton. She also recalled that Williams spent a lot of time during class breaks talking on one of the two student pay phones at the academy. McCants said she often overheard Williams asking the person he was talking to questions like: *Why are you doing this? What's wrong with you?*

McCants told McKey she was sure Williams had been speaking to a woman.

McKey subpoenaed the telephone company records for the two pay phones at the Baton Rouge Police Academy. The telephone company's records showed that during the four months Williams spent at the academy, he made at least thirty-five calls to Genore's office.

McKey also found out that Genore Guillory wasn't the only woman whom the very married Steve Williams had the hots for. There was also a woman named Dora. Williams knew practically nothing about her, not even her last name, but he knew where she lived and what car she drove.

In early 2000, Williams began leaving love notes and romantic cards for Dora. Williams's printed handwriting was elaborate, each letter "Y" had a curlicued top and a hooked bottom. In the notes, Williams never identified who he was and referred to himself only as Dora's secret admirer. The prose was semiliterate slush, more like the musings of a lovesick teenager than the feelings of a forty-five-year-old married man.

Williams wrote things like "You are a classic lady that sit [sic] among the extraordinary people of yesterday, today and tomorrow." And "My heart burns to take our very first walk in the park. Me holding the lovely petite body close to mines [sic]." In another profession of feeling, perhaps love, perhaps just lust, Williams wrote, "If I had you I would be the best lover that you ever had." In another, he wrote, "Smile baby, I love you."

Williams told Dora through his notes that he wished he had her telephone number or knew her last name. He offered to leave her his pager number. Since he was married—something he never mentioned in his notes— Williams probably didn't feel comfortable giving Dora his home telephone number and taking the chance that his wife might answer her call. One of his notes included instructions on where Dora could leave her telephone number so he could find it.

It's clear from Williams's writings that he had been watching Dora. At the end of one note he warned her, "P.S. Don't park the car on the sidewalk (may cause injuries)." In another, he said, "I don't want you to feel like I am stalking you . . . but I have noticed one of you [sic] tail lights is out for you [sic] breaks."

McKey asked Williams if he would be willing to take a polygraph examination. Williams agreed. They scheduled the exam for July 14. Because Williams was a Baton Rouge police officer, Police Chief Greg Phares asked that the East Baton Rouge Sheriff's Office conduct the exam.

At 9:45 on the night before the polygraph exam, Steve Williams called Genore's parents' house in Eunice, Louisiana. Genore's mother, Evelda Guillory, answered the telephone. "Hello," she said.

"Is this the Guillory residence?" Williams asked. "Is this where Genore's dad lives?"

"Yeah."

"I'd like to speak to him very much."

"He's not home."

"Do you know where I can reach him?" Williams asked.

"No, where he is doesn't have a phone."

"I'm Steve Williams. Who am I speaking to? Is this her mother?"

"Yeah."

"I sure would like to speak to Mr. Guillory and I am sorry about what happened to Genore. I met Genore and she told me where she lived and her phone number and where she worked. Oh, I went to her house one time. I told her something about her dogs."

"And she told you not to go back, huh?" Mrs. Guillory said.

"Yes," Williams admitted, then added, "We went out one time."

"Why you kept calling her? You should not have kept calling her like that."

"But I just wanted to talk to her."

"When you went out with her, you kept mashing her foot," Mrs. Guillory said.

"Yeah, but I liked her," Williams said. "Oh, my mother raised me better than that. I would have never done nothing like that. After it happened, I talked to Manuel (Sanders, another friend of Genore's) and Tommy (Alexander). I went for a test, but I have to go back tomorrow morning," Williams said, referring to his pending polygraph exam. "You don't know really when I can reach Mr. Guillory? I really want to talk to him. I want to talk to her dad. I am working for the police force."

"I know, she told me," Mrs. Guillory said. "I don't know why you kept calling her."

"Because I like her and she didn't want to talk to me."

Genore's mom wanted to cut the chitchat. She wanted to get to the point of Williams's call and find out why he wanted to speak to her husband. "What do you want to ask him?" she said.

"I want to ask him where to go to put some flowers on her grave," Williams said.

"Ask the people at her work."

"I wouldn't know where to go."

"Where did you get this phone number?" Mrs. Guillory asked.

Williams dodged the question. "Well, I'll keep calling to talk to Mr. Guillory," he said, then hung up.

At seven-thirty the next morning, Williams called again.

When Mrs. Guillory answered the telephone, Williams said, "I'd like to speak to Mr. Guillory, please."

"He's not here."

"Where is he?" Williams asked.

"I don't know."

"Okay, then," Williams said before ending the call.

Just a couple of hours after Steve Williams's second call to Genore's mother, Sergeant David Use hooked Williams up to the polygraph machine inside the Sheriff's Office headquarters building at Third Street and North Boulevard in downtown Baton Rouge. After the irrelevant questions and after the control—"probable-lie"—questions, Sergeant Use got to the heart of the matter.

"Did you kill Genore Guillory?" the sergeant asked his nervous test subject.

"No," Williams said.

"Did you stab Genore Guillory?"

"No."

"Did you shoot Genore Guillory?"

"No."

"Do you know for sure who killed Genore Guillory?" Sergeant Use pressed.

"No," Williams insisted.

As Use studied the graph of Williams's physiological responses, he was sure Williams was lying. His reactions to the relevant questions were all over the place.

"In the polygraph recordings, there were present significant emotional disturbances, which are usually indicative of deception, when Mr. Williams answered the relevant questions," Sergeant Use later wrote in his report. He concluded his report by offering his professional evaluation of the test results: "It is the opinion of the polygraphist, based upon Steve Williams's polygraph examination, that there was DECEPTION INDICATED." (Emphasis included in original.)

As soon as the polygraph exam was over, McKey asked Officer Williams if he would be willing to answer a few more questions. Williams refused to cooperate any further. He said he wanted a lawyer.

Once a suspect requests an attorney, the police can't ask any more questions. If they do, courts consider whatever information they get from the suspect to be tainted and therefore inadmissible. Under the *fruit of the poisonous tree doctrine*, even evidence the police might derive independently, but that was uncovered based on the tainted statements of a suspect, is inadmissible.

The only exceptions to the doctrine that would allow the police to continue questioning a suspect, or to use information obtained from him after he invoked his right to an attorney, are if the suspect initiated a subsequent interview without any prompting from the police, or if, in a fit of absolute stupidity, the suspect blurted out something that incriminated him.

Courts haven't yet managed to rule as inadmissible excited utterances such as "I buried her in the backyard next to my barbecue pit!"

But with Steve Williams asking for a lawyer, the prospect of him granting McKey another interview or of him making some kind of spontaneous admission jumped from not very likely to no way.

Criminal cases are built on three things: witness statements, circumstantial evidence, and physical evidence. Often, the best witness to a crime is the person who committed it.

When a suspect waives his Fifth Amendment right against self-incrimination and decides to do incredible damage to his prospects of staying out of jail by making incriminating statements to the police and thereby becoming a witness against himself, the case is hard to beat, provided the prosecution wins the inevitable challenges to the confession. One of the first things a criminal defense lawyer asks a client is "Did you make any statements to the police?" If the answer is anything but a resounding "NO," then the lawyer's job just got harder by a factor of about ten. If criminal defense lawyers had their way, there would be two iron-clad rules clients had to follow. To make sure the rules weren't forgotten, most lawyers would probably like to tattoo them on to the backs of their clients' eyelids.

Rule No. 1—Don't ever say anything to the police.

Rule No. 2—No matter what, don't ever say anything to the police.

McKey didn't have a confession from Williams, but he did have witness statements. Genore's coworkers could testify about Williams's strange behavior, his harassment—what some would even perhaps call his stalking—of Genore. Williams's academy classmate, Tabatha McCants, could testify that he'd done much the same thing to her. Dora, if McKey could find her, might tell a similar tale.

McKey also had circumstantial evidence. Williams and Genore had argued on the telephone the Friday before she was murdered. Williams had told Genore he was going to stop by her house Saturday, the likely day of her murder. Williams admitted to having been in the area of Genore's home around the time she was murdered. Williams had been spotted lurking around the parking lot at Genore's office, and he had admitted to sneaking up on her at the pasture where she kept some of her horses.

There were other pieces in McKey's circumstantial puzzle. There had been no sign of forced entry at Genore's house. The lack of evidence of a break-in suggested that Genore had known her killer. Then there was the ferocity of the attack. Jealous boyfriends, spurned boyfriends, wannabe boyfriends—all had a reputation for overzealousness when it came to murdering the objects of their affections. Williams had admitted he wasn't happy about Genore having so many male friends. He also told classmates at the police academy that he used to shoot a .22-caliber pistol at his mother's house in St. Francisville, which was not too far from where someone shot Genore with a .22-caliber firearm, most likely a pistol.

Then there was Williams's failure on the polygraph test and his refusal to cooperate with investigators. Although the former was clearly inadmissible in court and the latter was certainly Williams's right under the Fifth Amendment of the United States Constitution, they were plenty enough to make an already suspicious detective even more so.

What McKey lacked was physical evidence. Although a trial could be won on circumstantial evidence alone, it was certainly more difficult. McKey wanted something physical, a piece of evidence that directly linked Steve Williams to the murder of Genore Guillory.

To get it, he needed to search Williams's house. He also wanted to search the policeman's vehicles.

McKey dragged his feet after the polygraph exam to keep Williams busy at the Sheriff's Office while an East Baton Rouge Parish sheriff's detective wrote an application for a pair of search warrants. The first warrant was for Williams's single-story brick house on Landis Drive. The description of the property to be searched included any of Williams's personal vehicles parked at his house. Williams owned a green 1998 Toyota pickup truck and a 1990 red and gold Toyota Corolla.

The second warrant was for an additional vehicle Williams kept at his home, a 1996 white Ford Crown Victoria that was registered to the Baton Rouge Police Department.

In the application for the search warrants, East Baton Rouge Sheriff's Detective Dale Hodges explained in clipped police-ese that Williams knew Genore Guillory, that he continued to make frequent calls to her at work after she asked him to stop, that he had failed a polygraph examination that very morning, and that he had refused to answer questions about the murder. Hodges completed his affidavit by writing, "Detectives further learned that the suspect, Mr. Williams, had a long history of making unwanted advances towards the deceased."

The warrant application specifically sought permission for investigators to search for .22-caliber firearms and ammunition; edged weapons; footwear with a particular tread pattern (one that matched the bloody footprint on Genore's pillowcase); clothing that might contain blood, hair, fabric fibers, or traces of bodily fluids; and documents such as telephone bills, letters, or other records showing contact between Steve Williams and Genore Guillory.

State District Judge Don Johnson signed both warrants at 6:35 p.m., July 14, 2000.

NINE

McKey, Thompson, and East Baton Rouge Detective Dale Hodges hit Williams's house at eight o'clock that night. No one was home. Williams was still cooling his heels downtown at the Sheriff's Office. Before he left for Williams's house, McKey made a cursory search of Williams's 1998 Toyota pickup truck, which Williams had driven to the Sheriff's Office and had parked in a downtown lot. McKey made arrangements for the truck to be towed to the Louisiana State Police Crime Lab for further examination.

While Williams sat at the Sheriff's Office, McKey and the other detectives combed through his Baton Rouge home. It turned out, Williams didn't have much to worry about. Inside the house, McKey found very little of anything that had potential evidentiary value. He seized a videotape and several photographs but nothing else.

Outside, a sheriff's crime scene tech searched Williams's police car. The tech lifted several fingerprints and collected a white hand towel and a hairbrush. To McKey's naked eye there didn't appear to be any blood on either the towel or the brush, but he knew it would take only one droplet of Genore's blood to link Williams to her murder.

McKey ordered the Toyota Corolla and the Police Department's Crown Vic towed to the State Police Crime Lab. There, the state's forensic scientists could treat the interior surfaces of the vehicles with luminol and examine them for hidden traces of blood. If applied in a dark environment, chemical compounds in luminol have an oxidation reaction with the iron in blood hemoglobin. The result is temporary phosphorescence. The blood literally glows in the dark. While not foolproof—luminol can also react to things other than hemoglobin—it is a strong indicator of the presence of blood. In most cases, trace amounts of blood on a carpet fiber or swatch of cloth are enough for a DNA comparison.

While the presence of Genore's blood inside any of Williams's vehicles or on his clothes would have been a slam-dunk piece of evidence that he had been involved in her murder, hair strands and fingerprints were another matter. Steve Williams and Genore Guillory had known each other. They'd been out on a lunch date. He'd been to her house at least once. He'd met her at her horse pasture.

In a stranger murder, a strand of the victim's hair found on or near a suspect can lead to a conviction. Likewise the fingerprint of someone the suspect claims to have never met, discovered inside the suspect's home or vehicle, is damning evidence. In a case in which the victim and the suspect knew each other, and when there has been physical contact, regardless of how slight, even a freshman defense attorney can convince a jury that a fingerprint or a misplaced hair means nothing.

DNA from hair, skin tissue, even semen doesn't prove guilt, only contact. All evidence has to be evaluated in context, but particularly DNA evidence. In a stranger murder, the presence of DNA is usually a cinch; but in a murder involving two people who have some type of relationship, even a casual acquaintanceship, the presence of DNA means a lot less. People swap DNA all the time. A handshake, a scratch, a backrub, sex—all cause the transfer of varying amounts of DNA material.

But even in an acquaintance murder, blood is hard to explain. Murder weapons are even tougher. Either at Williams's house or inside his cars, McKey had hoped to find traces of Genore's blood, or a .22-caliber gun to compare to the bullets recovered from Genore's body, or a knife that matched the wounds, or a shoe that matched the bloody footprint on the pillowcase.

He got none of that. He got nothing.

Baton Rouge Police Chief Greg Phares placed Officer Steve Williams on administrative leave late Friday after he learned that East Feliciana and East Baton Rouge sheriff's detectives had served search warrants on Williams's home and vehicles in connection with a murder investigation. Despite the failure of the search warrants to turn up anything significant, Williams was still the prime suspect.

"Right now, given what I know about the case, I am not at all comfortable having him act as a police officer," Chief Phares said shortly after suspending Williams. "I don't want him on the streets of Baton Rouge."

Steve Williams wasn't the only one of the twenty graduates of the most recent police academy training class to find himself in hot water within just a few months of being on the street. Officer Calvin Brown, who graduated from the academy with Williams in March, wrecked his police cruiser under what Chief Phares called "questionable circumstances." Department policy required any officer involved in the wreck of a police vehicle to give a urine sample, but Brown tried to get his brother to give him a sample to use instead of his own. Brown resigned before being fired.

Officer John Sauls, another of Williams's academy classmates, was arrested after investigators from the department's Internal Affairs unit discovered the rookie cop had had sex with a prostitute in his police car on July 4 and then wrote her a check for forty dollars.

On July 20, the Baton Rouge newspaper *The Advocate* ran a story about Steve Williams headlined "Police officer suspected in slaying."

In August 2000, Steve Williams resigned from the Baton Rouge Police Department and continued to refuse to cooperate with the Guillory investigation.

Don McKey ran out of leads but didn't have enough to charge Williams with Genore's murder. "The case went cold," McKey says.

Meanwhile, things started to get hot in East Feliciana. Shootings, murders, and the bizarre disappearance of a two-year-old boy stretched the sheriff's tiny detective office pretty thin.

In August 2000, Don McKey and Drew Thompson arrested three bouncers from the Lo' Key Lounge for the wild parking lot shoot-out in May that left one man dead from a high-velocity rifle shot to the head and three others wounded.

Less than a month later, someone burned the Lo' Key to the ground. McKey suspected arson but couldn't prove it.

In November, a late-night telephone call from the Sheriff's Department dispatcher jerked McKey out of a sound sleep. There had been a shooting at Jesse's Speed Shop, a roadhouse bar in the unincorporated community of McManus, halfway between Clinton and Jackson. Like the Lo' Key, the Speed Shop was a late-night juke joint and a hangout for dope dealers and thugs.

Nine people had been shot.

After a couple of hours, McKey and his partner pieced

together enough of the story to understand what had happened. Somewhere around one-thirty in the morning, one guy shoved another. Words were exchanged. The guy who got shoved wasn't man enough to shove back. Instead, he pulled a gun and started shooting. More guns were pulled, more shots went off.

It was a hip-hop gangsta movie played out in real life.

As bedlam broke out inside the bar, dozens of drunk patrons bolted for the exits. Others dove for cover. The gunfight spilled out into the parking lot. More guns, more gunshots. Bullets smacked flesh. Most of those hit were probably not even the intended targets. Drunken barroom shoot-outs are not normally demonstrations of precision shooting, and the gunfight at Jesse's Speed Shop was no exception. Most of those involved in the melee used the spray-and-pray method of target acquisition and engagement. They ducked for cover while spraying bullets around the parking lot, and prayed they hit something.

Someone pulled out an AK-47. A woman in the parking lot went down hard.

By dawn, McKey and company had recovered .25-caliber, 9mm, and 7.62mm shell casings, the latter from the AK-47. They also arrested the man they suspected of being the original shooter, twenty-one-year-old Satterius Cobb, and charged him with two counts of attempted second-degree murder.

Sherrell Beauchamp, thirty, the woman hit in the parking lot, clung to life for six weeks before she died. Cobb, who wasn't charged with Beauchamp's murder, later pled guilty to three counts of aggravated battery. He was sentenced to a nickel in state prison.

In December, less than a month after the Wild West shoot-out at Jesse's Speed Shop, McKey was back at the same bar, this time examining a car that had been shot up in the parking lot.

An hour or so earlier, Joe Reese, a thirty-year-old East

Feliciana dope dealer who went by the nickname Mooney, had been parked in front of the Speed Shop. He had a crack whore with him. A van pulled up next to Reese's car, and someone inside the van started shooting. Several bullets punched through Reese's windshield. At least three of them hit Reese. The crack whore was lucky. The bullets missed her.

Reese was dead but didn't know it. As the van peeled away, he crawled out of his car and staggered across the parking lot. He managed to flag down a passing car and convinced the driver to take him to Lane Memorial Hospital in Zachary. Somewhere along the way, Joe Reese bled out. Doctors at Lane pronounced him dead on arrival. The crack whore claimed she hadn't seen a thing.

As 2000 slipped into 2001, a few more bodies were added to the pile in East Feliciana, and a few more case files found their way on to Don McKey's desk.

On January 21, 2001, Roosevelt "Buddy" Mack, an eightysomething-year-old black man in feeble health, disappeared. Mack lived with his brother and sister on Lane Road near the East Feliciana community of Ethel. Lane Road sits tucked away in a maze of unmarked gravel roads that crisscross the parish's piney woods and pastures. No one wanders onto Lane Road. You have to work hard just to find it.

Mack's sister said she helped him get up about three a.m. to use the bathroom and saw him go back to bed. The next morning she got up and cooked his breakfast, but when she called for him to come eat, Mack didn't answer. She went to check on him and found he was gone. At first she wasn't alarmed, because her brother—despite having to walk with a cane and suffering from poor eyesight—often took early morning walks. But when he didn't come back, she went looking for him. When she didn't find him, she called the sheriff.

Sheriff Talmadge Bunch organized a search party but

wasn't able to find the old man. One troubling sign the search did uncover was a single shoe. Sheriff's deputies found one of Mack's shoes on top of a thicket of briars about twenty feet from the road, not on the ground under the thicket but on top of it. Chief Deputy Paul Perkins told newspaper reporter James Minton that he thought the shoe had been thrown into the thicket from the road. He suspected it had been planted there to mislead the search effort. "It's looking more and more suspicious," Perkins said.

According to family and friends, Mack often carried what they referred to as large sums of money on him, probably his cashed Social Security checks. Chief Deputy Perkins learned that Mack had been robbed more than once while on his walks by people Mack had described as young men.

A weeklong search turned up nothing other than the one shoe and a baseball-style cap that may have belonged to the missing man.

Roosevelt Mack was never found.

On Tuesday, May 15, 2001, nineteen-year-old Ruby Renee Havard called the East Feliciana Parish Sheriff's Department and reported that her two-year-old son, Wesley Dale Morgan, had disappeared. Havard claimed she had last seen her toddler son playing in the front yard of their rental house in the community of Bluff Creek about nine-forty-five that morning. Havard said she'd gone inside to make him something to eat. When she came out, Wesley was gone. He'd been wearing blue shorts, a gray Mickey Mouse T-shirt, and sandals.

East Feliciana is the second poorest of Louisiana's sixty-four parishes. With a predominately rural population of just under twenty thousand, it ranks ahead of only East Carroll Parish in wealth.

East Feliciana was once part of the short-lived Republic of West Florida, a nation cobbled together from what are now known as the Florida Parishes: East and West Feliciana, East Baton Rouge, St. Helena, Washington, Livingston, Tangipahoa, and St. Tammany. The region declared its independence from both the United States and Spain in 1812 after a bloodless revolution, but was folded into the Louisiana Territory just seventy-four days later. Then, after officially becoming part of the newly created state of Louisiana in 1812, East Feliciana, supported by its affluent plantation society, grew into a regional center for commerce, banking, and culture. Traveling theatrical troupes regularly made stops in Clinton, and the town boasted its own Shakespearean society.

The genteel Southern aristocracy of the western Florida Parishes differed markedly from their neighbors to the east. The eastern Florida Parishes—St. Helena, Washington, Livingston, and St. Tammany—were made of hard-packed earth and pine.

Few roads penetrated the piney woods of the eastern Florida Parishes. Navigable waterways and the commerce they brought were scarce. Residents fought hard to eke out a living as subsistence farmers. There were no plantations, few slaves, and fewer jobs. Those who lived in the piney woods lacked the cultural sophistication and social structure of their neighbors to the west, and their isolation from the rest of the state and the country bred a stubborn resistance to authority that would explode more than a century later during the civil rights battles of the 1960s.

The roots of that sense of rebelliousness trace back to the end of the American Revolution. Tories—those who supported the British in America's bid for freedom and independence—fled the East Coast after the war to escape retribution from the victorious Americans. They ran west to wild, untamed places where no one would find them. And they ran south to places where no one would want to find them, to the piney woods and low-slung hills of what would one day become known as the eastern Florida Parishes.

In his 1996 book *Pistols and Politics: The Dilemma of Democracy in Louisiana's Florida Parishes, 1810–1899*, Samuel C. Hyde Jr. wrote, "Prior to its incorporation with the rest of the state in 1812, the region served as a haven for Tories, army deserters, and desperados."

Then came the Civil War and its aftermath—Reconstruction. With the destruction of the plantation society, what little social controls piney woods residents had, mostly those imposed by their rich plantation and slave-owning neighbors in East and West Feliciana and East Baton Rouge parishes, disappeared.

According to Hyde, after the Civil War, "The piney woods of the Florida Parishes began a rapid descent into anarchy."

In the eastern Florida Parishes, rebellion turned to resentment; then over the course of the next hundred years, that resentment boiled over into racial hatred.

TEN

Despite his cash-strapped financial situation and lack of resources, Sheriff Talmadge Bunch committed his entire department to the search for little Wesley Dale Morgan. The sheriff called in favors from friends and allies. He asked other agencies for help. He begged and borrowed until he managed to organize a search effort unparalleled in parish history.

For two days, sheriff's deputies on horseback and on four-wheelers, along with firemen, prison guards, bloodhounds, cadaver dogs, National Guard troops with helicopters and thermal imaging equipment, state troopers, nearly a dozen FBI agents, and an army of volunteers combed the countryside in ever-widening circles around Bluff Creek, a tiny community ten miles southeast of Clinton. They drained a sewage oxidation pond near the boy's house and probed the bottom of a nearby creek. They searched a neighbor's house. They even consulted a psychic.

Back in April, Sheriff Bunch had organized a search that

found a missing three-year-old after he'd wandered away from his home.

But in the case of Wesley Dale Morgan, the searchers found nothing. Even the bloodhounds couldn't pick up a trace of the missing toddler.

After two days of fruitless searching, Sheriff Bunch and his small staff of detectives turned their attention toward the baby's nineteen-year-old mother and her thirty-seven-year-old live-in boyfriend, Burnell Hilton. McKey brought the mother in first. He questioned her for four hours. Then the FBI polygraphed her. The results showed deception, but Ruby Havard stuck to her story that her son had disappeared while playing in the front yard.

About five p.m., after Havard had left the Sheriff's Department sobbing, McKey brought in Burnell Hilton. They questioned him on and off for twelve hours. Hilton occasionally napped on an old sofa in the cinder-block detective office. They also polygraphed him.

According to Sheriff Bunch, Hilton's test also indicated deception. "Both of them failed their polygraphs," Bunch said. "They know something about this. His was off the charts."

During the twelve hours Hilton was being questioned at the Sheriff's Department, something unexpected happened. Detectives got a call from Hilton's former girlfriend, Winnie Mae Edwards. Edwards had spent twenty years with Hilton before he ditched her for a woman half his age.

Hell hath no fury . . .

Edwards told the cops that Hilton had shot a man in Zachary a few years before and had never been caught. She explained that on October 31, 1998, she and Hilton had been watching the television program *America's Most Wanted.* That night, the show featured an episode about the unsolved murders of two women in Zachary and a bloody machete attack on two kids parking in a Zachary cemetery.

In 1992, forty-one-year-old Connie Warner disappeared from her Zachary home. Eleven days later her body was found dumped in a ditch in downtown Baton Rouge.

On a rainy night in April 1993, two young lovers were doing what young lovers do in a car parked late at night in a cemetery. As their attention was thus occupied, a figure slipped from the shadows and approached the car. It was a man. In his hand he clutched a three-foot cane knife. He jerked the door open and started hacking. Fortunately for the two in the car, a Zachary police officer pulled his cruiser into the cemetery at that moment. The attacker dropped the cane knife and ran.

Then in April 1998, Randi Mebruer, a twenty-eight-year-old beauty with thick brown hair that fell past her shoulders, was dragged bleeding from her house while her three-year-old son slept in the next room. Her body was never found.

Zachary cops thought the three cases were connected. The young woman who'd been attacked in the cemetery described her assailant as a black man, probably in his twenties, with close-cropped hair. After *America's Most Wanted* profiled the case on Halloween night 1998, Burnell Hilton hopped in his new Dodge Dakota pickup and drove to Zachary.

About eleven o'clock that night, Hilton spotted a black man walking down Flonacher Road just west of Zachary. Burnell Hilton was a Bubba from the "They All Look Alike" school of race relations. He pulled up next to the man, whose name was John Lavallais, stuck his pistol through the open window of his truck and shot the man in the face.

Lavallais survived, but for two and a half years he had no idea who shot him or why. Not surprisingly, it turned out Hilton was wrong. Lavallais had nothing to do with the murder of Connie Warner, the disappearance of Randi Mebruer, or the bloody attack on the kids who were getting it on in the cemetery. All three crimes were later linked to serial killer Derrick Todd Lee. Lee was arrested in 2003 for a string of brutal abductions and murders in and around Baton Rouge. He was convicted and sentenced to death.

After confirming the story of Lavallais's shooting with the cops in Zachary, Sheriff Bunch ordered Hilton arrested for attempted second-degree murder.

While McKey was questioning Havard and Hilton, the FBI sent an evidence collection team to search the couple's home. The team scanned the house and Hilton's pickup truck with an ultraviolet light, looking for traces of blood. Police also set up a command post in a converted travel trailer they parked across the street from the missing boy's house. Deputies established around-the-clock surveillance of the boy's mother.

One of the deputies assigned to watch her was Tim Brasseaux. A few days into the surveillance, Brasseaux followed Havard to a mobile home where she was staying temporarily with another woman and the woman's boyfriend, who was also an East Feliciana Parish sheriff's deputy. Havard later claimed she and Brasseaux had sex inside the trailer. Brasseaux denied it. He admitted following Havard inside the trailer but claimed he didn't have sex with her. "I know what her background is," Brasseaux said. "And I would be stupid to have anything to do with her."

Regardless of whether Brasseaux did or did not have sex with Havard, the accusation cost Brasseaux not just one job, but two. At the time he followed Havard into that trailer—Brasseaux said he did it because he knew that another deputy lived there—the East Feliciana deputy had already accepted a job with the East Baton Rouge Parish Sheriff's Office and turned in his resignation to Sheriff Bunch. But when Havard came forward with her allegation, not only did Talmadge Bunch fire Brasseaux, but the East Baton Rouge Sheriff's Office also withdrew its job offer.

For weeks, Bunch and McKey continued to focus their investigation on Havard and her boyfriend but were never able to develop enough information to charge either of them.

"That baby never left that house walking," Sheriff Bunch later said. "He was carried out of there."

Wesley Dale Morgan is still missing.

Television detectives work one case at a time. They can solve even the most complicated murder in an hour, forty-four minutes if you subtract for commercials. Real police work doesn't work that way. New cases come in, old cases pile up. Even in a small town, and sometimes especially in a small town, particularly one with a two-man detective office, time marches on and so does crime. In East Feliciana Parish, neither stopped just because Don McKey couldn't solve the Genore Guillory case.

On May 19, 2001, at two-fifty in the afternoon, thirty-four-year-old William Rushing was bushogging his boss's property just outside Jackson, Louisiana, a few miles down Louisiana Highway 10 from Clinton. Rushing's boss, Martin Macdiarmid, used the wooded property behind his house on Millwood Drive for deer hunting. Rushing was pushing a tractor down a deer trail, getting the property ready for the start of hunting season in the fall, when he came upon a white pickup truck parked at the end of the trail.

Rushing couldn't see anyone in the truck. Still, it was a little early in the day for kids to be screwing. He climbed off of his tractor and approached the truck. One of the first things he noticed was that the hinged door covering the gas cap was open. A white T-shirt, partially singed, hung from the end of the gas tank filler tube. Some of the white paint near the hinged door had been seared black. It looked like someone had tried to set the truck on fire.

A couple of steps closer and Rushing noticed the smell. Later, he described it as a "rank odor," but that was probably only because he couldn't come up with a more accurate descriptive phrase. The smell was bad, maggot-gagging bad.

Rushing choked back the bile that welled up in his throat and pushed forward. He peeked through the driver's side window, but a greasy film covered the glass and prevented him from seeing clearly into the cab. From what he could see, though, there didn't look to be anyone inside the truck.

There was no reason to open the truck and certainly no reason to hang around it, not with that nasty smell threatening to overwhelm him and make him toss his lunch, so Rushing climbed back onto his tractor and went to get his boss.

A few minutes later, Rushing walked back to the truck with his boss and his boss's wife. Macdiarmid, fifty-eight, and his wife looked at the truck and saw the same thing Rushing had seen: a white Dodge pickup jammed in among scrub pine trees. The truck had a rusted back bumper and a partially burned T-shirt sticking out of the gas tank. The truck looked like it had been there awhile. They nearly choked on that awful, sickly sweet smell.

The three of them beat feet back to the Macdiarmids' house and called the cops.

The East Feliciana Sheriff's Department dispatcher sent Jackson Police Officer Cary Quiet to investigate. He arrived at Mr. Macdiarmid's house at about three-twenty. Macdiarmid, his wife, and Will Rushing were waiting for him.

A five-minute walk through the woods took Officer Quiet to within smelling distance of the pickup truck. After Quiet worked his way through his initial gag reflex, he borrowed a work glove from Macdiarmid and threaded his way through the pine brush to the passenger door. He peeked inside, but just like Rushing, the officer couldn't really see anything because of the greasy film covering the windows. With his gloved hand, Officer Quiet grabbed the door handle and yanked the passenger door open.

He turned his face away and held his breath as a putrid wave of rancid air crashed against him and threatened to overwhelm his respiration and cause him to regurgitate the contents of his stomach. When the initial shock passed, Quiet turned back toward the truck.

There was a body inside it. Badly decomposed, it was stretched across the floorboard. The head, not much more than a skull with dark pieces of meat and some hair clinging to it, lay on the passenger side, wedged between the bottom right edge of the seat and the door frame. The legs were sprawled across the drivetrain hump that ran down the centerline of the truck, and the feet, encased in black tennis shoes, rested on the floor beneath the steering wheel.

The body appeared to be that of a man, but there was no way to be sure, and certainly no way to identify the race. The guess as to its sex was based mainly on the clothing. He—if it was a he—wore a sweatshirt and dark long pants, possibly green.

Quiet backed away and caught his breath. The truck was a potential crime scene and was now his responsibility to protect. He couldn't go back to his patrol car, so he used his cell phone to call the Sheriff's Department. He asked the dispatcher to send his supervisor, sheriff's detectives, State Police crime techs, and someone from the coroner's office.

Detective Don McKey arrived at the secluded scene at 3:50 p.m., just an hour after William Rushing first spotted the white pickup. As usual, McKey started his initial survey from the outside and circled his way toward the center of the crime scene, although at that point it was really just a potential crime scene.

McKey took his time. The stiff inside the truck wasn't going anywhere, and there was the very real danger that if McKey rushed, valuable evidence could be blown away by the wind, crushed under the foot of a curious policeman, or deputy sheriff, or just overlooked in the soon-to-be-fading daylight. The good thing about the unholy smell oozing from the cab of the truck was that it kept everyone away.

The truck was a 1987 Dodge Ram, Louisiana license plate number V945109. It was registered to Dionne Chaney, who lived on Hollywood Street in Baton Rouge, thirty miles from where the truck now sat in the woods of East Feliciana Parish.

When McKey got close to the truck, he saw the plastic gas cap and a cigarette lighter lying on the ground below the filler tube, the one with the partially burned T-shirt sticking out of it and the nearby scorch marks.

While it was theoretically possible that the dead guy in the truck had brought some young lady out to this secluded spot on a starry night to make a little whoopee, or maybe gone out there on his own to engage in some amateur astronomy, or maybe just parked his truck back in the pines to whack his weenie, and then had the unfortunate luck to drop dead of a heart attack or some other natural cause, that didn't explain the presence of the T-shirt stuffed down the gas pipe, the burn marks, or the cigarette lighter.

Someone had tried and failed to destroy the body inside the truck, or at the very least, had tried to significantly alter the scene, and that almost always meant a homicide.

The body inside the truck was so badly decomposed, and exuded such a horrible stench, that after McKey finished his outside scene examination and the lab techs had photographed the truck from nearly every conceivable exterior angle, McKey ordered the truck hauled to the State Police Crime Lab in Baton Rouge with the body still inside. Maybe the ride to Baton Rouge would vent out some of the stink.

Meanwhile, a routine check with the Baton Rouge Police Department turned up a surprising bit of information. Dionne Chaney, the registered owner of the pickup, had recently reported her boyfriend missing.

ELEVEN

Dionne Chaney last saw her boyfriend, Emile Anthony Jackson, the night of May 3. He'd gotten a telephone call about 11:45 p.m. and had left their home moments later. Late night calls and mysterious trips weren't unusual for Jackson, and Chaney had gotten used to them. What was new was him not coming home.

That night and the next morning, Chaney called Emile's cell phone repeatedly but got no answer. She confronted his mom. Did he have another girlfriend? No, the mom said, Emile didn't have any other girlfriends. Chaney really started to get worried.

Neither Chaney nor Jackson were strangers to trouble. Chaney had pleaded guilty in February 2001 to money laundering, possession of stolen property, and conspiracy. Thirty-one-year-old Emile Jackson had a string of arrests dating back to 1985, when, as a fifteen-year-old, the cops caught him with a stolen car. In 1988, he got popped trying to sneak marijuana into a correctional facility, and later that same year he was arrested for possession of cocaine.

He got five years for the cocaine charge but got out early. After a few more cocaine arrests, the cops grabbed Jackson for possession of a firearm with an obliterated serial number, later for distribution of cocaine, and finally for murder. He did a little more time for manslaughter; then after he got out of prison he tried to run over a cop while fleeing and got caught with more cocaine.

On May 6, three days after Jackson vanished, Chaney walked into the Baton Rouge Police Department's First District station on Plank Road and told Officer Carnel Bell that her boyfriend was missing. She was honest with Officer Bell, brutally honest. "Emile is a drug dealer," Chaney said, "and I'm scared something happened to him. He's never stayed away from home this long."

He still hadn't called and he was not answering his cell phone.

Bell typed up a report and faxed it downtown to the Criminal Investigation Bureau. There, it landed on the desk of Detective Todd Quebedeaux.

Not satisfied with waiting for the police to find her boyfriend, Chaney started her own investigation. She put together a flyer and passed out copies. The flyer showed a photo of a serious-looking Emile Jackson in the top right-hand corner. Below that and to the left was a picture of the white Dodge truck he drove. Printed across the top of the flyer was the word "MISSING."

Chaney called local television stations and pleaded with them to air a segment about Jackson's disappearance.

She also obtained a copy of Jackson's cell phone bill. The last call Jackson received, the one that sent him on his mysterious middle-of-the-night errand on May 3, had come from a phone registered to Pat Collins at 2326 Riley Street in Baton Rouge.

On May 8, two days after Chaney reported her boyfriend missing, two carloads of young men, eight total, showed up at Collins's house on Riley Street. There, according to a police report, they demanded to know where Jackson was and accused two people they found at the house, twenty-six-year-old Shiquoya Blunt and nineteen-year-old Joseph Flowers Jr., of withholding information about Jackson's whereabouts. As soon as the cars left, Blunt called the police to report the incident.

Mary Manhein met Detective Don McKey and the white pickup truck at the State Police Crime Lab. Manhein was the director of the Louisiana State University FACES program, also known as the Forensic Anthropology and Computer Enhancement Services Lab. As a forensic anthropologist, Manhein had worked on hundreds of cases involving the identification of bodies in nearly every imaginable state of decomposition. Cops dubbed her "the bone lady."

A native of the hill country of southwest Arkansas, Mary Manhein was born in 1943 and spent her first seven years living in three rooms of a semi-abandoned hotel that sat beside a railroad switching yard on the outskirts of the small town of Lewisville. She spent those years poking around the dusty nooks and crannies of the hotel and helping her mother care for the sick men housed on the hotel's second floor, which had been converted into a convalescence ward at the end of World War II.

As a child Mary was fascinated by puzzles. She loved figuring out where each piece fit and would often fight with her five brothers and sisters for the honor of putting the last piece of the puzzle in place. To Mary's young mind, a puzzle was a mystery, a mystery whose solution lay in tiny pieces scattered on the floor. To examine those pieces, to organize them, and to place them back in their original position was the secret to unlocking the mystery of any puzzle.

"I admit it," Manhein wrote in her 1999 book, *The Bone*

Lady: Life as a Forensic Anthropologist. "I am fascinated with death or, more precisely, with the rest of the story that continues after death."

In her book, Manhein traces her fascination with death back to the early 1950s and the death of her younger brother, Kevin Paul, whose birth and funeral she attended less than a year apart. Kevin Paul died on an operating table while surgeons tried to repair a faulty heart valve. When Mary next saw her baby brother's body at a funeral home, he had copper pennies pressed onto his eyelids. Her mother said the pennies were there to keep the baby's eyelids from popping open.

Many years later, Manhein wandered through Louisiana State University as what she described as a mature—she was in her mid-thirties with a husband and two sons—undergraduate student, majoring in English. In her senior year, she happened upon an anthropology class. After just one course, Manhein said she was hooked. "I had found a field . . . that was filled with puzzles and mysteries," she wrote in *The Bone Lady*. The next semester she entered LSU's master's program in anthropology.

Manhein had spent the years since then working in the field of applied anthropology, a combination of the anthropological subdisciplines of archaeology and physical anthropology, and had examined human remains from all over the United States. One of only a few dozen to earn the distinction of being named a "fellow" in the field of physical anthropology by the American Academy of Forensic Sciences, Manhein once described her job as a forensic anthropologist as "a scientist who works with human bones in a medico-legal context and who sometimes digs them up."

In law enforcement circles, old-school homicide investigators constitute an elite, almost exclusively male fraternity whose members take great pride in their cast iron stomachs. So when veteran homicide detectives encountered a wisp of a woman whose intestinal fortitude exceeded their own and whose corresponding puke factor rested higher than even the hardiest homicide man, they paid homage to her by bestowing upon her the nom de guerre "the bone lady."

As soon as McKey stepped inside the garage at the State Police Crime Lab, he realized that the drive from Jackson to Baton Rouge had done nothing to dissipate the smell pouring out of the truck's cab. In fact, if anything, inside the confines of the garage at the State Police laboratory, the stench from the victim's rotting flesh had actually gotten worse. When they cracked open the truck's doors, McKey's stomach sounded retreat and the veteran detective puked all over the garage floor.

Heat does terrible things to a decomposing body. Hunks of hair can begin to separate from the scalp in just two days. Teeth, particularly the upper and lower front teeth, can also fall out within a couple of days. After two weeks, it's likely that all that will be left of a once vibrant human being is a pile of bones with a few attached tendons.

But sick or not, McKey had work to do, so he held his breath and poked his head inside the truck. He was careful not to disturb anything. The protocol McKey used for the close-up examination was based on the same principle he had used at the crime scene—outside to inside. One of the first things he noticed was that the passenger-side window was smeared with blood. So was the inside door panel. There was also a good bit of blood on the blue vinyl bench seat.

On the driver's floor, between the victim's legs, lay a Nokia cell phone. With any luck it wasn't broken. Once the techs bagged and printed it, the data the phone held— names and numbers of contacts, text messages, and missed calls, things not available through phone company records— might reveal important clues about the last few hours of the victim's life. One of the most important first steps in any homicide investigation is to establish a timeline for the victim. If an investigator can establish where the victim went, what the victim did, and whom the victim saw, he's taken a major step toward solving the crime.

Although vitally important to the case, victim timelines are a bit unusual in the sense that they're written in reverse order. They begin at the end, with the discovery of the body. There are almost always gaps, usually a lot of gaps at the beginning of a homicide investigation. How far back the timeline reaches depends on the circumstances of the case, but without question, the most difficult, and the most important, gap to fill in is the one right before the discovery of the body. It's the moment at which the victim went from relatively healthy to stone dead. It's the moment when the victim was killed. Filling that gap means identifying the last person to see the victim alive, and as a rule, that person is usually the killer.

So the cell phone McKey spotted lying in the puddle of maggot-infested human soup on the floor of the Dodge pickup truck could very well help fill in several gaps in this victim's timeline, and maybe, if McKey got lucky, it could help him fill in that all-important gap—the one that identified the killer.

But the cell phone wasn't the only thing slopping around in the puddle of goo on the floor of the truck. A foot or so closer to the driver's door, staring up from between the victim's black Reeboks, was an eyeball. The glass kind.

A quick check of the skull-like remains of the victim's head and McKey was able to determine that he—they were unofficially calling the victim a he—was missing his right eye. It wasn't something you saw every day, and it would make identifying the victim a bit easier.

The reason the glass eye was on the floorboard was simple physics. As a body deteriorates, gases released from the decomposing tissues expand and get trapped beneath the skin. The body starts to swell. The hotter the air temperature, the more it swells. A body closed up inside the cab of a pickup truck and left in the woods in south Louisiana during the summer is going to swell a lot. Eventually, a decomposing body will reach its bursting point and pop like an overinflated balloon. The weakest parts explode first. When the victim in the truck reached his bursting point, the built-up gasses shot his glass eye across the cab of the truck like a champagne cork.

As the body continued to bake in south Louisiana's subtropical climate, the heat further broke down the victim's soft tissue, until his body began to collapse on itself. Essentially, it dissolved and began to liquefy. "He was actually melted into the floor of the truck," McKey recalls.

The lower part of the victim's legs angled down from the knees, which rested on top of the drivetrain hump, toward the driver's side floorboard. Encased in a pair of soggy dark pants, the legs were so thin they looked like sticks. The reason they were so thin was that by the time the body was discovered, most of the flesh had fallen off of them and oozed down the pant legs onto the floorboard. There, the flesh had continued to decompose until it eventually formed a dark puddle of liquid human remains. Flies had worked their way inside the truck and dropped off their larvae. The result was maggot stew. The same thing had happened on the passenger side, where the victim's ruptured abdomen had leaked guts all over the floor.

Once McKey and the other investigators finished photographing the interior of the truck, it was time to remove the body. The problem was, the victim was in such a bad state of decomposition that he was stuck to the floorboard. Eventually, somebody—McKey can't remember who—came up with the idea of using shovels, so they scooped the victim off the floor of the pickup truck and dumped him into a cadaver bag.

McKey knew an autopsy was pointless. That's why he had called the bone lady. At 11:30 p.m., Mary Manhein formally took possession of the body, minus the victim's hands, which McKey had ordered cut off and kept for identification purposes. Manhein signed a handwritten release scrawled on a sheet of State Police letterhead and took the remains back to her laboratory at LSU.

On the driver's side floorboard of the pickup, beneath the victim's legs, sunk into the goo near the cell phone and the glass eye, McKey found one other interesting piece of evidence—a bullet.

It wasn't even an entire bullet, just the spent lead core, but it spoke volumes about what had happened inside the truck.

McKey needed to find out where the bullet had come from. To do that he needed answers to three questions about the dead man. Who was he? What had happened to him? And how had it happened?

TWELVE

The answer to the first question Detective McKey needed answered—who was the dead man?—was in the hands, so to speak, of the Louisiana State Police Crime Laboratory.

Identifying the body found inside the white Dodge pickup truck proved to be a fairly easy—if rather gruesome—task. Vicki Barbay, a State Police fingerprint examiner, had the victim's hands and the name and numerical identifiers of the missing person believed to have been driving the truck. What made it so easy was the fact that the missing man, Emile Anthony Jackson, was a convicted felon with a long rap sheet. His fingerprints were on file with the State Police, the Department of Corrections, as well as several other law enforcement agencies throughout the state.

Had the missing man been an honest citizen who'd never been in trouble with the law, it might have made the identification a little more difficult. The actual comparison was going to be easy. All Vicki Barbay had to do was take the dead man's fingerprints. To do that she smeared black ink across a plate of clean glass, then took hold of one hand at a time and rubbed the fingertips across the ink. Then she rolled the fingertips onto a print card. To be extra certain, she also inked the dead man's palms and pulled the print impressions off with a wide strip of 3M fingerprint tape.

When Barbay compared the prints of the victim found in the truck to those of Emile Anthony Jackson, she got a match. Without a doubt, the dead man was Emile Anthony Jackson, whose girlfriend, Dionne Chaney, had reported him missing on May 6, thirteen days before his body was discovered broiling inside the cab of the couple's Dodge pickup truck in the piney woods outside Jackson, Louisiana.

By coincidence, Emile Jackson also happened to be first cousins with Joe "Mooney" Reese, the thirty-year-old dope dealer gunned down outside Jesse's Speed Shop in December while entertaining a local crack whore.

The bone lady was working on the second question: What had happened to Emile Anthony Jackson?

At the FACES lab, Mary Manhein stretched the body out on an examination table. She recorded a detailed description of the remains and then photographed and X-rayed them from head to toe.

She then began a systematic examination of the body. In her report, Manhein later described the corpse as being in an "advanced state of decomposition with putrefactive soft tissue and extensive maggot activity."

In Jackson's right front pants pocket, Manhein found $295 in cash. Behind his right eye socket and sunken into what was left of his brain, she found the movement ball for his glass eye. In the X-rays of the head, Manhein saw traces of metal. She dug into the skull and pulled out more than a dozen bullet fragments, mostly pieces from a bullet's copper jacket.

The skull itself was heavily damaged. Using a scalpel and a jet of hot water loaded with detergents, Manhein removed the flesh and other soft tissue from outside and inside the cranium, a process that left the skull bleached white. She then examined, measured, and photographed the skull. The bullet that had struck Jackson in the head had punched a jagged entrance hole through the left temporal area, just above the ear, and blown out a corresponding, although much larger, exit hole through the opposite temporal area, slightly above and in front of the right ear. The skull was also fractured in several other places, including the brain vault, the left eye socket, and the lower jaw. One fracture ran along the top of the skull, just to the left of the centerline, from the crown, down through the forehead, and into the left eye.

After Manhein's examination, the answer to the second question was pretty obvious. Emile Anthony Jackson was dead because somebody had shot him in the head.

The third question—how had it happened?—was the key to the entire investigation. Discovering the answer to that question was the responsibility of Detective Don McKey, and how he answered it likely meant the difference between a murderer going free or going to prison.

The two labs had done the scientific part. Now it was time for some good old-fashioned police work. It was time to track down a killer, something a country boy like Don McKey, who'd spent half his life in the woods hunting game, was good at.

While McKey was still working the crime scene, word of Jackson's death spread quickly through the parish. Jackson had once lived in East Feliciana Parish, and many of his relatives still lived there. By early evening, some of those relatives began showing up at the crime scene.

Although Don McKey needed to wait for a positive

identification, members of Jackson's family were already sure whose body had been left to rot inside that white Dodge pickup truck. Some of them were even sure who was responsible for putting it there.

Bird did it, they said.

Bird was Joseph Flowers Jr., a nineteen-year-old petty thug from Clinton who had been staying down in Baton Rouge with his sister. Bird's sister lived at 2326 Riley Street, the same address Emile's girlfriend had discovered was the source of the mysterious 11:45 p.m. call to her boyfriend's cell phone on the night she last saw him.

It was also the same address the Baton Rouge police had been dispatched to on May 8—five days after Jackson disappeared—when residents complained that two carloads of Jackson's friends and family had shown up and accused them of concealing information about the missing man's whereabouts. In their report, the Baton Rouge cops had noted the presence at the house on Riley Street of one Joseph Flowers Jr.

Joseph "Bird" Flowers's record showed only one arrest. In 1996, deputies in East Feliciana Parish had arrested him for illegal use of a weapon, carjacking, and distribution of cocaine. Flowers had been picked up on March 21 and released the same day after posting a $7,500 bond.

While McKey was still processing the crime scene and trying unsuccessfully to hold down the contents of his stomach, Detective Joel Odom, who'd recently been promoted from Patrol, started talking to Jackson's relatives.

Curtis Jackson, Emile Jackson's cousin, told Odom that during the last couple of weeks he had heard that Bird had been talking about how he'd shot someone in the head. Word had also reached Curtis that Bird had been seen flashing a lot of money around since Emile Jackson disappeared. Curtis Jackson knew that Bird and Emile hung together. Emile sometimes sold dope to Bird.

Mitch Jackson, another cousin, told Odom that at

around 2 a.m. on May 4, a little more than two hours after the late-night telephone call that sent Emile Jackson on his mystery trip, Bird called his seventeen-year-old cousin, Maurdel Flowers, and said that he "blew a nigger's head off." Bird described to his cousin how he had clubbed the guy with the pistol and then shot him in the head.

A couple of days later someone asked Maurdel why his cousin Bird was jumping from house to house. According to Mitch Jackson's handwritten police statement, Maurdel's answer was that Bird was on the run because he had "blowed a nigga's brains out."

Rumor was that Bird was supposed to meet Emile Jackson the night he disappeared to buy cocaine from him.

On May 21, McKey and Odom talked to Maurdel Flowers about his cousin Bird. Maurdel, who was still in high school, had turned eighteen on May 11. Four days later he managed to get himself locked up in East Feliciana Parish for public intoxication. The detectives also talked to nineteen-year-old Draper Campbell and to Bird's former girlfriend, twenty-three-year-old Tonika Collins. All three lived in East Feliciana Parish.

According to his former girlfriend, Joseph Flowers showed up at her apartment in Jackson sometime during the early morning hours of May 4. His pants and shoes were muddy, he wore no shirt, and he had grass and twigs stuck in his cornrowed hair. Flowers said he needed a shirt and a ride to Baton Rouge. Tonika told him she didn't have a shirt for him, nor did she have any way to drive him to Baton Rouge, but he could use the telephone if he wanted. Over the next couple of hours, Flowers made a few phone calls. He never explained to his former girlfriend how he'd gotten to her apartment or what he'd been doing that had left him shirtless and dirty.

Maurdel Flowers told McKey and Odom that his cousin Bird had called him at his grandmother's house in Clinton early on the morning of May 4. Bird asked if Maurdel would

find someone to pick him up at Tonika's apartment and give
him a ride to Baton Rouge. Maurdel said he would try. A few
minutes later, Maurdel stepped outside of his grandmother's
house and spotted his friend Draper Campbell cruising down
the street in a van. Maurdel flagged Campbell down and
asked if he would give Bird a ride to Baton Rouge. Campbell
dropped his stepdaughter off at school and then came back
and picked up Maurdel. The two of them then drove west a
dozen or so miles on Louisiana Highway 10 to Jackson.

Once they got to Jackson, it took a couple of calls from
a pay phone and some better directions to narrow the location down, but Maurdel and Draper finally found Tonika's
apartment building. When they drove into the parking lot,
Maurdel spotted Bird standing outside. Bird climbed into
the backseat behind Maurdel. When Maurdel asked his
cousin what happened to his shirt and why he was all dirty,
Bird told him the police had stopped him and his boys and
he had to take off running. He said he'd hidden under a
house until the cops quit searching for him. Bird also admitted that he'd smacked a guy in the head with a pistol
and stolen his cocaine.

Draper drove Maurdel back to Clinton and dropped him
off at school; then he took Bird to his sister's house in
Baton Rouge.

A couple of days later, Bird showed up at Maurdel's
grandmother's house in Clinton.

Maurdel told the detectives that while Bird was outside
talking on a cell phone, he overheard his cousin say that he
needed his friends to pitch in and put a lot of cash together
for him. He wanted someone to drop it off at his sister's
house in Baton Rouge. Bird told the person he was speaking with that he needed the money because he'd gotten into
trouble, that he'd hit someone in the head with a gun and
"knocked his brains out," that he'd stolen the guy's cocaine. He mentioned a truck and said he'd wiped his
fingerprints off of it.

Maurdel told Detective McKey that he heard Bird tell the person on the other end of the telephone, "I think I killed the dude."

On May 21, just two days after the discovery of the body in the pickup truck, Detective Don McKey got a warrant from State District Judge George H. Ware Jr. for the arrest of Joseph Flowers Jr., aka Bird, for the first-degree murder of Emile Anthony Jackson.

Word spread quickly through the piney woods telegraph that the cops in East Feliciana Parish were looking hard for Bird. No dummy, Bird made it his business to stay out of the parish. He just didn't stay out far enough.

On Sunday night, July 1, Bird was driving around Baton Rouge when the police pulled him over for a traffic violation. The cops tossed Bird's car and found a .40-caliber pistol with a filed-down serial number. Possession of a gun with an obliterated serial number is a felony under both state and federal law. The cops arrested Bird for the gun charge and ran his name through NCIC, the National Crime Information Center, a nationwide database of criminal records, wanted persons, and stolen property, maintained by the FBI.

Information about Bird's murder warrant from East Feliciana Parish flashed across the top of the dispatcher's screen: "WANTED PERSON . . . NAME: JOSEPH R. FLOWERS JR . . . CHARGE: FIRST-DEGREE MURDER."

Bird's troubles were just beginning.

THIRTEEN

The morning after Bird was arrested in Baton Rouge, East Feliciana detectives Don McKey and Joel Odom sped south in a plain-Jane sheriff's sedan to the East Baton Rouge Parish Prison, located next to the Baton Rouge Metropolitan Airport.

One hour and a stack of forms later, they took custody of nineteen-year-old Joseph R. "Bird" Flowers Jr. and drove him to Clinton.

The East Feliciana Parish Sheriff's Department operates out of two offices. The administrative division is housed in an ancient, single-story, redbrick building that sits beside the 160-year-old courthouse in downtown Clinton. The Communications, Patrol, and Detective Divisions are a couple of miles away at the parish prison.

As with most correctional facilities, the amenities at the parish prison are spartan, even for those who aren't locked up there. Inside the glass front door of the building is the lobby, complete with a painted concrete floor, a rack of molded plastic chairs, and a Coke machine. Opposite the

front door is the communications office, separated from
the lobby by metal-reinforced bulletproof glass. To the
right are the restrooms and to the left is the detective office. There is no interrogation room, no two-way glass, no
darkened observation room, no hardwired audio or video
monitoring equipment.

Suspect interviews usually take place inside the detective office, with the suspect sitting in a cushioned metal
chair pushed back against the wall between a couple of
desks. For important cases, the detectives record the interview with a video camera set up on a desk or mounted on
a tripod.

At 8:30 a.m., Don McKey and Joel Odom sat Bird down
in a chair in their office. They turned on a tape recorder
and read him his Miranda rights. McKey explained to Bird
that he had the right to remain silent, the right to have an
attorney present during questioning—at state expense if he
couldn't afford his own attorney—that he could stop the
questioning at any time, and that anything he said could be
used against him in court.

"Do you understand these rights?" McKey asked.

Bird said he understood.

"With these rights in mind, would you be willing to answer questions or make a statement at this time without a
lawyer present?" McKey asked.

Bird said okay.

On the night of May 3, sometime around eleven o'clock,
Bird called Emile Jackson to set up a dope deal. Bird
wanted to score some cocaine. He had bought dope from
Jackson before. A little while later, Jackson showed up at
Bird's sister's house on Riley Street in Baton Rouge driving a white Dodge pickup truck. Jackson said he had the
cocaine with him. Bird glanced up and down the street,
then told Jackson to pull around to the back of the house.

That's when things went awry.

According to Bird, his friend Alvin "JJ" McManus

rushed up to the driver's side of the truck, stuck a pistol through the open window, and pressed it against the side of Jackson's head.

McManus forced Jackson to push over to the middle of the seat.

Bird said he climbed into the cab from the passenger side, and he and McManus sandwiched Jackson between them. McManus handed Bird the gun and Bird held it on Jackson while McManus backed the truck into the street and headed north to East Feliciana Parish.

Once they got into the woods, Bird said, to the spot where the pickup truck was later found, he handed the gun back to McManus, who shot Emile Jackson in the head. They stole his dope and ran away.

As far as confessions go, from an investigator's standpoint, Bird's was pretty good. It not only put him at the scenes of both Emile Jackson's kidnapping in Baton Rouge and his murder in East Feliciana Parish, it also put a gun— the murder weapon—in his hand as he held it on the victim for the entire forty-five-minute-or-so ride from Baton Rouge to Jackson. In addition, it gave McKey and Odom the motive—armed robbery. The murder left Bird on foot in the backcountry in the early morning hours of May 4, thirty or forty miles from home and badly in need of a ride.

Bird's statement corroborated what the detectives had learned from several witnesses. Dionne Chaney said the last call to her boyfriend's cell phone had come from Bird's sister's house at 2326 Riley Street. Curtis Jackson said his cousin Emile sold dope to Bird. Mitch Jackson heard that Bird had called his cousin Maurdel Flowers two hours after Emile Jackson disappeared claiming he "blew a nigger's head off." Bird's former girlfriend, Tonika Collins, said Bird showed up at her door in Jackson early on the morning of May 4 with no shirt, muddy pants and shoes, and with grass and twigs stuck in his hair. Maurdel Flowers, Bird's cousin, said his friend Draper Campbell gave Bird a ride from East Feliciana to Baton Rouge on the morning of May 4. Bird said he'd been running from the cops. A couple of days later, Maurdel said, he overheard Bird telling someone on the telephone that he'd knocked a guy's brains out, stolen his cocaine, and wiped his fingerprints off of a truck.

The problem was that not one witness had mentioned Alvin "JJ" McManus, or anyone, for that matter, as being with Bird in East Feliciana Parish the morning after Emile Jackson disappeared.

The discrepancy left McKey and Odom in a bit of a dilemma. On one hand, Bird was confessing to kidnapping, robbery, and murder. It didn't even matter that he denied pulling the trigger; the fact that he'd been there, that he'd participated, that he'd held the gun on Emile Jackson was enough for the state of Louisiana to stick a needle in Bird's arm. On the other hand, Bird was trying to shuck some of the blame off onto someone the cops had never heard of.

Who the hell was Alvin "JJ" McManus?

A quick computer check showed that McManus was a twenty-three-year-old wannabe gangster with previous arrests for drug and weapons violations. His most recent arrest had been May 21—two days after Emile Jackson's body was found and the same day McKey and Odom were interviewing Maurdel Flowers—when Baton Rouge police picked him up for possession with intent to distribute marijuana, possession of stolen property, and carrying a firearm while in possession of narcotics. McManus lived in Baton Rouge, three miles from Bird's sister's house on Riley Street.

McKey and Odom knew that in his statement Bird might already be doing a little bit of jailhouse lawyering by trying to diminish some of his own responsibility.

I was just there. I didn't kill the dude. JJ done that.

But a suspect's confession isn't a buffet; you don't get

to pick out what you like and leave the rest. It is what it is. Juries tend to either believe it or not believe it—in toto.

On the afternoon of July 2, McKey got a warrant for Alvin McManus for first-degree murder.

Baton Rouge police pulled McManus out of a car twelve days later after stopping him for a traffic violation and running him through NCIC. Again the flashing header across the dispatcher's screen: "WANTED PERSON . . . NAME: ALVIN J. MCMANUS . . . CHARGE: FIRST-DEGREE MURDER."

To the Baton Rouge cops it must have seemed like everyone with a connection to East Feliciana was wanted for murder.

On July 16, it was McManus's turn in the hot seat. He acknowledged that he understood his rights under *Miranda*, but denied any involvement in the murder of Emile Jackson. McManus told McKey that he knew Bird. He and Bird recently had a beef and Bird had threatened revenge. He said he didn't see or talk to Bird on May 3.

Judge George Ware ordered McManus held without bail.

Nine days later, McManus asked to meet with the detectives again. This time he brought a lawyer. He asked for a polygraph exam. He failed.

In a second round of questioning after the failed polygraph, McManus admitted that he had heard from Bird sometime in early May. Bird called him, he said, and asked him for a ride. Bird said he'd just killed someone. He didn't mention any names. McManus told McKey that he didn't give Bird a ride because he was afraid Bird would kill him. The beef he and Bird had gotten in was over money, money McManus had stolen from Bird.

McManus volunteered a blood sample for DNA testing. A few days later, McManus was cleared, and the district attorney released him.

The killing of Emile Jackson fell on Bird's head alone, and he went down for it.

FOURTEEN

Nearly a year after the discovery of Genore Guillory's mutilated body, the investigation into her brutal murder was stalled. Steve Williams was the primary suspect—actually he was the only suspect—but there wasn't enough evidence to take the case to a grand jury. And Williams wasn't talking. Since he'd asked for a lawyer the day of his polygraph, McKey hadn't had any contact with him. The law simply forbade McKey from initiating any further questioning, and Steve Williams knew it.

Without direct evidence linking Williams to the murder, and without a confession, McKey knew there was no case. District Attorney Charles Shropshire, the parish's first black DA, wasn't going to prosecute a Baton Rouge policeman for a murder based on circumstantial evidence alone.

For most prosecutors, the single most important criteria for deciding whether to take a case to trial is the likelihood of winning it.

Strong cases, those with corroborated confessions or

near-incontrovertible physical evidence—the defendant's fingerprint inside the victim's house, where the defendant was never known to have gone, or the defendant's semen found inside the victim when the two didn't know each other—get taken to trial.

Decent cases, those with strong circumstantial evidence but weak direct evidence—the defendant did maintenance work at the victim's house, or the defendant and the victim were lovers—get plea-bargained.

Weak cases, those with flimsy circumstantial evidence and little or no direct evidence—there is no fingerprint and there is no semen—get declined.

Because most prosecutors view their win-loss record as their most vital statistic, few of them are willing to take on anything less than a strong, airtight, almost indefensible case. Fewer still are willing to take on decent, middle-of-the-road cases. And practically no prosecutor would even dream of teeing up anything he or she thinks is weak or that presents the possibility of a defense. Lame cases, like lame horses, get put down quickly and quietly.

In the Genore Guillory murder, there just wasn't much to work with, not yet.

"The case went cold," McKey says.

Then a telephone call turned everything around.

*Joel Odom had made detective in April 2001, replac-*ing Drew Thompson, whose personal life had spun out of control and crashed.

When Odom stepped into the detective office, he brought with him an innate sense of organization and order, but what he found when he first sat down at Thompson's old desk was chaos: incomplete reports, investigative notes scribbled on napkins, and evidence stuffed into drawers. In Thompson's locker, Odom found a kitchen knife. A patrol deputy had discovered it lying on a gravel road a mile and a half from Genore Guillory's house less than two weeks after her murder. Odom compared the knife to the crime scene and autopsy photos, and to Dr. Laga's description of the stab wounds on Genore's body, and thought there was a possibility that it might be one of the weapons they were looking for. It also looked a lot like the table knives found in Genore's kitchen utensil drawer. Incredibly, despite the similarities, Drew Thompson had never submitted the knife to the State Police Crime Lab for examination.

At the time Joel Odom was promoted, there were twenty-one open cold-case homicide investigations in East Feliciana Parish. Odom decided to take a look at each of the cases to see if a fresh pair of eyes might bring a new perspective to some of them. As soon as he started going through the cases, Odom realized that his predecessor's chaotic nature had not been limited to his personal life and his desk. It had spilled onto the investigative files, too. They were a jumbled mess. Reports, photos, interview notes, documents—everything was jammed into folders. To find any one piece of information on a case, Odom had to search the entire file.

Before he could investigate any of the old cases, Odom had to know what had been done before, so he began the painstaking task of taking each case file apart and organizing it. He divided the existing information into sections and identified them with tabbed, color-coded page separators. Then he put the file back together in a thick three-ring binder.

As he reviewed each file, he doubled-checked the physical evidence to see what had been submitted to the crime lab and what results had come back. In addition to a near-obsession with organization, Odom also had a keen interest in forensics—the science of criminal investigation. What he found was disappointing. "You're talking about a department, when I walked in, it was like stepping back

into the 1960s," Odom says. "Black fingerprint powder
was the extent of their forensics."

When Odom opened the Guillory case file, he discovered that the nail clippings taken from Genore during the
autopsy and sent to the State Police Crime Lab had not had
a DNA profile done on them. At that time, the crime lab
did not have the technology to identify a DNA profile. The
FBI lab offered the service for free to state and local law
enforcement, but it took months to get the results back. A
private lab in New Orleans, ReliaGene Technologies,
could do it a lot faster than the FBI, but they were expensive. They charged $1,500 for a profile. Odom persuaded
Sheriff Bunch to let him send the clippings to ReliaGene.

On Friday evening, July 27, 2001, McKey and Odom
were sitting in the detective office. Odom was going over
old case files. The Guillory case was open in front of him.
The file itself was jammed into a thick blue folder. Odom
hadn't yet created a binder for it. At about six-thirty that
evening, Odom's telephone rang. It was Detective Mark
Apperson from the Tangipahoa Sheriff's Office. Apperson
said he'd just wrapped up an interview with a twenty-
three-year-old woman who had information about an unsolved homicide in East Feliciana Parish.

"Do you have any open murders with a Miss G?"
Apperson asked.

Odom looked down at the file on his desk for a second.
The coincidence was almost too much to believe. Then he
glanced over at McKey and waved to get his partner's attention. "Yeah," Odom told the Tangipahoa detective. "I
do have an open murder on a woman called Miss G."

"The girl also mentioned an older black man who had a
lot of money and is missing," Apperson said.

Yvette Schexneyder had come into the Tangipahoa
Parish Sheriff's Office Domestic Violence Unit to file a
complaint against her boyfriend, Donny Fisher. The two of
them had gotten into a fight that had become a little too

physical for Schexneyder. While talking to a detective about the fight she and Donny had gotten into, Schexneyder mentioned a murder her boyfriend had told her about, a murder near Clinton, a murder involving a woman people called Miss G.

According to what Schexneyder told the Tangipahoa detective, she and Donny Fisher had moved into an old trailer on Phillip Skipper's property sometime in mid-July 2000. She already knew about the lady across the street who'd been murdered. At the time, Schexneyder worked with Phillip's mother, Isabella Skipper, at a nursing home. A day or so after the murder, Isabella told Schexneyder that her son's neighbor had been found shot, stabbed, and beaten to death. Phillip, his wife Amy, and their stepson John Baillio, referred to the lady as Miss G. Schexneyder said she heard that a policeman from Baton Rouge was the suspected killer.

Schexneyder had only stayed in the derelict trailer for a few weeks before she and Donny Fisher broke up. She moved out and he stayed for another month or so. They got back together in November and occasionally visited the Skippers. During those visits, Schexneyder noticed Fisher acting strangely when he was around Phillip Skipper or John Baillio. One day while Schexneyder and Fisher were driving in her car, she confronted him about it.

"What's going on, Donny?" she said. "Why are you acting so funny?"

Fisher stared at her for a long moment, then said, "If I told you that Phillip and them were the ones that killed Miss G, would you believe me?"

"What?" Schexneyder said.

"Yeah," Fisher insisted. "They're the ones who did it. They took me step-by-step through the house and told me where they did it and showed me how they did it."

Skipper had told Fisher he would kill him if he told anyone about the murder.

Schexneyder also told the Tangipahoa cops about another murder.

Phillip Skipper wanted Donny to help him rob and kill an old black man, who, rumor had it, kept a stash of money at his house. The Tangipahoa detectives wanted to know who the old man was and where he lived. Schexneyder didn't know much. "He's a black, old man," she said. "He lived in Clinton, I think. Supposedly, he had a lot of cash in his house. I think they said something about he walked with a cane. Couldn't see good. He was old, very old, and that supposedly they couldn't find his body."

More than ten months after the disappearance of Roosevelt "Buddy" Mack, Donny Fisher told his girlfriend, "That old man that Phillip and them had asked me to go help them kill, guess what, that old man is missing."

Schexneyder said she believed that Phillip Skipper, his brother-in-law Johnny Hoyt, and John Baillio were evil. "They are possessed with demons," she told Detective Mark Apperson. The three of them were into all kinds of weird stuff, she said. They were trying to form a group connected to the Aryan Nation prison gang. Baillio was a Hitler freak, and all three were Ku Klux Klan sympathizers. "They play with knives," Schexneyder said. "They throw knives at each other."

According to Schexneyder, Phillip told Donny that when they killed Genore Guillory they had pulled off "the perfect murder."

By the following Friday, August 3, 2001, McKey and Odom had managed to track down Donny Fisher. He was a skinny white kid, twenty-six years old, with hair trimmed just above his ears and a ratty goatee. A local troublemaker, Fisher was frequently on the wrong side of the law. He'd been picked up for armed robbery when he was eighteen, but the DA knocked it down to simple robbery.

Fisher pled guilty and got five years' probation. Early in 2000 he got popped for weed, and then in July 2001 cops in Tangipahoa Parish arrested him for simple battery and armed assault. Despite his legal problems, Fisher had managed to find steady employment at Wal-Mart in Livingston Parish.

He agreed to meet McKey and Odom at the Tangipahoa Parish Sheriff's Office, but when he showed up at the courthouse in Amite, he could barely speak. He'd just come from the dentist. He was goofed on painkillers and had both cheeks packed full of gauze.

Fisher was uncooperative at first as he sat across the table from the two detectives. He admitted that he knew Phillip Skipper, that he knew his stepson John Baillio, and that he knew his brother-in-law Johnny Hoyt, but claimed he didn't know anything about the murder of Genore Guillory.

McKey wasn't buying it. Yvette Schexneyder had been too specific. Fisher knew about the murder. McKey pulled the case file from his briefcase and thumbed through the crime scene photos. Fisher stared at him, not saying anything. McKey took his time as he picked out the most gruesome of the pictures. One by one, he laid them on the table. As if driving past a traffic accident, Fisher couldn't help but look.

McKey let the silence hang between them a little while longer. Then he broke it by pounding his fist on the table. "Did she deserve this!" he shouted.

Fisher swallowed hard. Then he broke.

He said he knew Phillip Skipper and Johnny Hoyt from junior high. They'd gone to school together in Livingston Parish. Hoyt had lived in a trailer down the street from Fisher's house. The two of them rode the same bus to school. None of them had graduated from high school, but Skipper and Hoyt had remained tight. Hoyt ended up marrying Skipper's sister Lisa.

After the collapse of their academic careers, Fisher

remained friends with Skipper but less so with Hoyt. "He just wasn't the same Johnny Hoyt that I went to school with," Fisher said.

Soon after Fisher and his girlfriend moved into the Skippers' junked trailer, Phillip Skipper asked Fisher if he wanted to make some extra cash by helping him and John Baillio, whom everyone called either John-John or Little John, clean up the murder scene across the street. Genore's family had hired Skipper and Baillio to help straighten up the house and get it ready for sale. They were also taking care of Genore's animals.

One day while the three of them were working at Genore's house, Fisher and Baillio found themselves alone. They were cleaning out an old tool shed while Skipper was off tending to something else on another part of the property. As they worked, Baillio surprised Fisher with a hypothetical question.

Would he like to know how the murder might have been committed if Baillio had been involved?

Sure, Fisher said.

Baillio took Fisher into the house and showed him step-by-step how the murder had taken place, or at least how it would have taken place had Baillio, Johnny Hoyt, and Phillip Skipper done it. Baillio described the initial attack, the pursuit into the house, the brutal beating, stabbing, and shooting, and the gang rape.

That night Fisher and his girlfriend heard shouting and screaming coming from the Skippers' trailer. Phillip was kicking the shit out of Baillio, yelling over and over, "You fucking idiot!"

FIFTEEN

John Baillio was a scrawny fifteen-year-old, close to five feet, ten inches but rail thin. He had a shaved head and sported a tuft of hair under his chin. He idolized Adolf Hitler and hated blacks. He thought of himself as an artist and doodled all the time, mostly sketching swastikas and other Nazi symbols. Baillio's goal was to become a tattoo artist, and he was well on his way to covering himself with ink.

Baillio grew up in a tiny camper trailer on Sallie Kinchen Road in Tangipahoa Parish, just outside the city of Hammond, Louisiana. Sallie Kinchen is a dead-end road, both literally and figuratively. It winds its way through cow pastures for a mile or so off of North Baptist Road, until it peters out next to a pond. The front half of the road is paved while the back half is gravel. It's as if the parish got halfway through with paving it and then decided they didn't give a shit. Sallie Kinchen is a neighborhood of rundown trailers, dilapidated houses, junk cars, and Confederate flags.

After Phillip Skipper dropped out of school in Livingston Parish, he moved to Sallie Kinchen Road. Skipper was seven years older than Baillio, but the two began palling around a lot. Skipper introduced his young friend to booze and drugs. Inexplicably, John Baillio's mom, Shawn Smith, thought Skipper was a positive male influence for her son since his own father was long gone.

By her own account, Smith wasn't a complete pushover when it came to raising her only son. She didn't let him do absolutely anything he wanted. There were limits. Smith had her own brand of Sallie Kinchen Road discipline. In certain areas she was a stickler for rules. For example, she didn't allow her twelve-year-old son to drink booze around her. "He may have smoked pot around me, but that was the extent of it," she says.

What her son did when he was out of her sight, though, was another matter, one that didn't seem to concern her too terribly much. "Phillip was taking him off in the woods, getting him drunk, getting him high," Smith says.

Phillip was also teaching Baillio other things, among them a deep-seated hatred for blacks. Smith later described it this way: "This white supremacy, skinhead mentality thing. That was just part of their little thing. That was just part of them. That's what they did. It was a race thing. Swastikas. It was just a race thing. Phillip's opinion about race was no secret to anybody."

No doubt Phillip's own upbringing played a key role in shaping his opinion about race. His father, Gilbert Skipper Jr., was reportedly a lifelong Klan member, who in 1986 was convicted of rape, aggravated sodomy, and murder in Georgia and sentenced to death. Although his death sentence was later vacated, the elder Skipper is currently serving a life sentence.

Besides the steady dose of brainwashing, there were other things that Phillip Skipper was doing to John Baillio, not all of them mental. Baillio later told his mother that sometimes after getting him drunk, Phillip would tie him to a tree and burn him with cigars.

Not surprisingly, Baillio's behavior changed radically under Phillip Skipper's influence. According to his mother, he went from saying "yes, ma'am" and "no, ma'am" to what she later described as cussing, ranting, and raving. "He went from a sweet kid to an angry kid," Smith says.

When Baillio was twelve, his mom caught him in a bedroom with a six-year-old girl. Both of them were naked. Smith later said her son was "about to get started fucking."

Not long after the incident with the little girl, a counselor who examined Baillio suggested that he might have been the victim of sexual abuse. The counselor recommended therapy. Smith says she never followed up on the recommendation because she couldn't afford it.

Later, Baillio got arrested for busting up heavy machinery at a construction site. Then he and some friends got caught stealing cars. The cops also arrested him for breaking into a house. After a brief stay at a boot camp for troubled youths, then a stint in a state-run juvenile detention facility, John Baillio returned to Sallie Kinchen Road, but his mother had had enough of him.

She gave him to Phillip Skipper to raise.

Skipper had already proven himself to be less than an ideal role model for young Baillio, but when he got the pubescent teen under his control full-time, things quickly went from bad to very bad.

According to Baillio, Skipper beat him frequently, sometimes with his fists, sometimes with a garden hose. Baillio says Skipper burned him with cigarettes and once used a cigarette lighter to heat up nails and then pressed them against Baillio's arm. Skipper said the brand made Baillio a part of his family.

Sometime during the late 1990s, while playing surrogate daddy to John Baillio, Phillip Skipper married a girl named Amy Sikes, a short, stocky girl with a high squeaky voice and a foul mouth. Not long after the nuptials, Skipper moved his bride and Baillio to Oakwood Lane outside Clinton.

Neither the marriage nor the move stopped the abuse, however. According to what Baillio later told investigators, when Skipper's wife wasn't around, he would hold a knife to Baillio's throat and make the terrified boy suck his penis. And whenever the mood struck him, Skipper would bend Baillio over and sodomize him.

Years later, a much thicker and much more hardened John Baillio denies that Skipper ever forced him to submit to anal sex. Skipper only made him perform oral sex, Baillio claims. "I'm not queer or nothing," he says. "He would just make me do it."

According to Skipper's friend Donny Fisher, Skipper completely dominated his so-called stepson. "He was cruel to him," Fisher says. "John Baillio—well—he was passive. He took it. He took the beatings. Phillip was strong. He was big, strong, very intimidating. He had that kid's mind messed up."

The night after John Baillio halfway admitted to Donny Fisher that he and Phillip Skipper and Johnny Hoyt had killed Genore Guillory, Skipper grabbed Baillio by the throat and started choking him while the two of them were standing outside Skipper's trailer.

"Do you want to see me go to the electric chair?" Skipper screamed at him, apparently unaware that several years earlier Louisiana had switched its method of execution from electrocution to lethal injection.

"No," Baillio gasped, maybe not knowing, but certainly not giving a shit at that point that the state had traded in Old Sparky for a hard table with straps and needles.

"Well, you better keep your mouth shut," Skipper said.

Baillio understood clearly the threat to his own life if he didn't keep quiet.

Five years after Genore Guillory's murder, John Baillio described his "stepfather," Phillip Skipper, in clear, simple terms: "He's a crazy, psycho son-of-a-bitch."

•   •   •

Donny Fisher told Don McKey and Joel Odom that the day after John Baillio's admission—an admission that had earned the teenager a severe beating—Fisher rode with Skipper to Baton Rouge. On the way back, Skipper pulled his green Ford pickup truck to a stop on a deserted gravel road.

Fisher tensed up, afraid he was about to be killed because of what Baillio had told him. Skipper turned toward Fisher. After a day of drinking whiskey, smoking weed, and popping pills, Skipper was wasted. "You don't trust me, do you?" he said.

Fisher swallowed hard. He knew Skipper kept a pistol under the seat. "Why wouldn't I trust you? Are you going to kill me?"

"No, I ain't going to kill you," Skipper said. "You just don't trust me no more, huh?"

"Do I have a reason not to trust you?"

Skipper shook his head. "No."

The two men stared at each other for a long moment. According to Fisher, Skipper then said, "What would you think if I told you I killed . . . if we killed G?"

"I wouldn't think nothing. You wouldn't trust me no more if I did."

"That's what I wanted to hear," Skipper said. "I trust you."

Skipper told his friend to get out of the truck. Fisher was terrified as he stepped out. He glanced up and down the gravel road. Not a soul in sight. A perfect place for a murder.

Skipper slid out of the truck behind him. Fisher glanced at Skipper's hands to see if he was carrying a weapon. Nothing.

They stood near the tailgate. "You want to know how I faked the cum?" Skipper asked.

Fisher shrugged. "Sure."

Skipper grinned just a bit at the cleverness of what he was about to say. "I hired a nigger to cum in a cup, and I put that in her to throw the cops off."

Fisher glanced around again at the emptiness surrounding them. Skipper was strong. Even without a weapon, he might still intend to kill Fisher. "Why couldn't you tell me that in the truck?"

Skipper gave Fisher a conspiratorial nod. "Because they might have some wires or other devices or something in there recording us."

Fisher wasn't buying it. He didn't believe for a minute that Skipper was worried about police listening devices. He knew Skipper. Skipper had been testing him. His old junior high school chum had driven them out to a deserted spot so that he could find out what kind of reaction Fisher was having to the news that two of his friends and a teenager had murdered Genore Guillory. Fisher knew that if his reaction hadn't been what Skipper had been looking for, if he'd voiced outrage or disgust, or if he'd tried to run away once they got out of the truck, Skipper would have snatched his gun from under the seat and shot him down like a dog.

As they climbed back into the cab of the pickup, Skipper looked across the seat at Fisher. "Just remember, if you ever tell anybody about this, God forgives, but the brotherhood doesn't."

It was clearly a threat, a warning to Fisher to keep his mouth shut about what he knew about the murder of Genore Guillory, and Skipper meant it. Across his back were tattooed the letters G.F.B.D.—*God Forgives, The Brotherhood Doesn't.*

Donny Fisher had known Phillip Skipper for more than a decade, since they smoked pot together in junior high and palled around with Johnny Hoyt. Fisher told McKey and Odom that he genuinely liked Skipper. "He's a great guy," Fisher said. "He got along with everybody, but it's like he would switch, like something in his brain would switch and he would just go off."

As the interview with Fisher dragged on, it got harder

and harder for McKey and Odom to understand what he was saying. Gauze and painkillers were degrading his speech. The two detectives kept having to ask him to repeat himself. Finally, Fisher pulled the wads of bloody gauze out of his mouth. It helped some.

Fisher said that after his confrontation with Skipper on the gravel road, Phillip drove him back to Oakwood Lane. Later that night, Skipper sucked down more whiskey and got even more trashed. He started talking shit about "The Brotherhood." Skipper pulled out a tattoo gun and tried to pressure Fisher into getting a G.F.B.D. tattoo on his back.

Skipper said Fisher could earn the tattoo, meaning earn the right to be a member of The Brotherhood if he would help him rob an old black man in Clinton. The old man kept a bunch of cash under his bed.

"We won't have to kill him unless he wakes up and starts fighting with us," Skipper said. "All you've got to do is hold him down while I reach under his bed and grab the money."

Helping steal the old man's money would get Fisher the tattoo on his back, Skipper said. The same one he and his brother-in-law, Johnny Hoyt, and John Baillio had.

Originally, the idea of the tattoo had been Johnny Hoyt's. He stole it from a 1991 B movie called *Stone Cold*, starring former NFL linebacker Brian Bosworth. In the movie, Bosworth plays an undercover cop who infiltrates a Mississippi biker gang called The Brotherhood. As part of his initiation into the gang, Bosworth's character, known to the gang as John Stone, is supposed to kill a rival gang member. During one scene, the gang's leader, who goes by the unlikely name of Chains Cooper—played by veteran actor Lance Henriksen—warns another character just before he shoots him: "God forgives. The Brotherhood doesn't."

Johnny Hoyt liked the movie so much he decided to use it as a model for the gang he and Phillip Skipper formed.

The difference was, instead of a biker gang, Hoyt and Skipper formed a skinhead gang whose single founding principle was the ideology of white supremacy.

Harleys cost money. Hatred is free.

Twenty-three-year-old Johnny Hoyt was definitely a product of Bubbaville. He grew up in Livingston Parish, where, until just within the past few years, saying someone lived in a trailer was a redundancy. At five feet, eight inches tall and 160 pounds, Hoyt was deceptively strong. He was also aggressive. He once jumped out of a pickup truck and punched a guy so hard he shattered several bones in the guy's face.

In just an eighteen-month stretch between August 1999 and March 2000, Hoyt racked up an impressive arrest record. In four separate incidents, Livingston cops charged him with three counts of aggravated battery, meaning a weapon was involved; two counts of simple battery, fists only; and one count of simple assault. He was also a dope fiend and a methamphetamine cook.

Like any good meth cook, Johnny Hoyt did most of his cooking in the woods. Baillio explains, "If the cops come, you can leave the woods, but you can't leave your house."

Cooking methamphetamine is a dangerous business not only from a legal standpoint but also for health and safety reasons. Plenty of aspiring cooks have been blown up by the volatile chemical mix needed to whip up a good batch of methamphetamine. "Only a dumbass does it in his house," John Baillio says. "That shit's got to be able to breathe."

Up until September 2000, when federal gun charges brought by the Bureau of Alcohol, Tobacco and Firearms (ATF) earned Hoyt a three-year stretch in federal prison in Oakdale, Louisiana, he and his wife, Lisa Skipper Hoyt, who was Phillip's sister, lived with their three children in a rented trailer in St. Helena Parish. In typical Bubba fashion, all three Hoyt children were known as "Little" something:

Little Johnny was five, Little Cody was four, and Little Angel was not yet one. Although Angel would celebrate her first birthday, she would not live to see her second.

St. Helena Parish lies just to the east of East Feliciana Parish and directly on top of Livingston Parish. The Hoyts' near-derelict trailer sat a quarter mile north of the Livingston Parish line on Highway 43, a two-lane ribbon of blacktop that slices through the scrub pine forest of the upper part of southeastern Louisiana.

Prior to ATF grabbing him on the gun charges, Johnny Hoyt had been a part-time roofer and a full-time scumbag. Most of his waking hours were spent as a half-assed hoodlum—stealing, scamming, and robbing. He was also an ardent racist. And he looked the part. Hoyt had a shaved head, pale blue eyes, a dark mustache, and a goatee that came to a sharp point about an inch and a half below his chin.

"Tell me he doesn't look like the devil," Don McKey said years later as he pointed to an old booking photo of Johnny Hoyt. "You can see the devil in his face."

Sometime around 1999, Hoyt and Skipper started making trips to a tattoo shop called the House of Pain in Ponchatoula, a town in Tangipahoa Parish, five miles south of Hammond. The owner, whom Baillio later described as a "dogfighting meth cook," inked the gothic letters G.F.B.D. across their backs. He also put a tattoo of a pit bull on Hoyt's leg and another on his arm. Skipper got a pit bull on his arm, too.

To Hoyt and Skipper, both of whom had grown up in the dogfighting subculture of the eastern Florida Parishes, where Bubbas ride around with stickers on the back glass of their pickups that say, "If you ain't pit, you ain't shit," the pit bull symbolized their bond to each other and to their fledgling racist gang. In their twisted little heads, to wear the pit tattoo and the letters denoting the gang's motto— "God forgives, The Brotherhood doesn't"—was quite an honor.

Donny Fisher, however, didn't see it that way. Although no stranger to violence or general scumbaggery, Fisher was already on probation for armed robbery and thought that perhaps his junior high school buddy had gone off the deep end.

Fisher told the drunk, stoned, and obviously unsteady Skipper that he wasn't interested in getting the tattoo or in helping rob some old black man.

"I don't believe I want to do anything like that," Fisher said. "It's not me."

Skipper responded by beating the crap out of John Baillio later that night.

The next morning, Fisher's girlfriend, Yvette Schexneyder, decided she had had enough of Phillip Skipper and of Donny Fisher. She was working twelve-hour days at the nursing home, and Fisher wasn't doing anything except cleaning up around Genore Guillory's house and getting stoned with Phillip.

Yvette packed up her meager belongings and the couple's baby daughter, Kylee, and went back to her husband. Although Kylee was really Fisher's baby, Yvette's husband didn't know that. Sometime during one of Yvette's frequent marital separations, Fisher got her pregnant. When Yvette went back to her husband and gave birth to Kylee, she simply passed the baby off as her husband's. They already had two. A few years later, Schexneyder and Fisher ended up getting married and had two more children.

Fisher told McKey and Odom that he stuck around Skipper's place for another month or so, and then he too bailed out. Skipper was becoming too much for Fisher to take.

SIXTEEN

Race.

In the South, especially in the deep South, it's always there. During good times it simmers quietly. The tension lies below the surface. When people are happy, they tend to get along. During bad times it boils over. The veneer of tranquillity explodes. When people are upset, they lash out.

Nigger this . . . nigger that . . . Fuck those niggers . . . Kill those niggers.

After the Civil War, Louisiana remained die-hard Democrat. That meant the party of segregation. That meant the party of what would soon become the Ku Klux Klan.

On Easter Sunday, April 13, 1873, more than one hundred black members of the nearly all-black Louisiana state militia took refuge in the parish courthouse in the tiny central Louisiana town of Colfax. By noon, the courthouse was surrounded by close to three hundred members of the White League, a Democrat-backed militia that acted as a shadow government and operated in opposition to the legitimate government of the newly elected Republican Governor William P. Kellogg.

The confrontation had begun with a dispute over local elections. A black Republican had challenged a white candidate in a run for sheriff. Another black Republican ran for district judge. In both races, each side claimed victory. The governor eventually stepped in and sided with the black candidates.

Meanwhile, in Washington, D.C., Republican President Ulysses S. Grant, fresh from a successful reelection bid, ordered federal troops to Louisiana to back the governor and to put down the anti-Reconstruction forces of the Democrats.

In Colfax, Columbus C. Nash, the white candidate who claimed victory in the sheriff's election, took charge of the assault on the courthouse. After ordering the black women and children who were camped outside to leave, he and his White Leaguers opened fire on the courthouse. The shootout produced few casualties until Nash managed to position a cannon behind the courthouse. The resulting explosions and flying cannonballs panicked many of the militiamen inside, prompting dozens of them to flee. Nearly sixty were shot down.

Later, a black turncoat set fire to the courthouse. With flames and smoke at their backs and rifles to their front, the rest of the defenders were forced to surrender. Once Nash and the White Leaguers disarmed the black militiamen, they shot most of them. Some of the blacks who survived were taken to the local jail and were executed later that night. Federal troops arrived in Colfax the next day. When the soldiers counted the dead, they found the bodies of more than a hundred black militiamen and three White Leaguers.

John G. Lewis, a black Louisiana teacher and state legislator called the Colfax massacre "the bloodiest single instance of racial carnage in the Reconstruction era."

Colfax may have been the bloodiest, but it was far from an isolated case.

*In New Orleans, at the time the state capital, the vi-*olent conflict between Republicans and Democrats threatened Governor Kellogg himself. During the long hot summer of 1874, the city became a skirmish ground, pitting the Republican administration's Metropolitan Police Force—which included several black officers—the several-thousand-man-strong, nearly all-black state militia against the newly formed, Democrat-supported Crescent City White League. Like its sister organization in Colfax, the Crescent City White League, which numbered some fourteen thousand, was an armed force mostly made up of ex-Confederate soldiers hell-bent on maintaining white rule.

On August 30, White Leaguers executed half a dozen Republican government officials. Governor Kellogg declared martial law. Two weeks later, the White League came after the governor.

At the time, the Statehouse was in the French Quarter, at the corner of Toulouse and Chartres streets, near City Hall and the Customs House. As the violence in the city spiraled out of control, the governor and several other state and city officials took refuge in the Statehouse and called on former Confederate General James Longstreet to defend them. Longstreet, once second in command of the Confederate Army and deputy to General Robert E. Lee, had moved to New Orleans after the war and taken a job as adjutant general of the state militia.

On September 14, 1874, the White Leaguers were expecting the steamship Mississippi to deliver to them an arms shipment at the Port of New Orleans. Approximately eight thousand White Leaguers assembled downtown to secure the off-loading of their weapons. Standing in their way were three thousand black militiamen and about six hundred policemen, all under the command of General Longstreet. As the aging ex-Confederate general sat astride his horse, he ordered his biracial force to form a defensive line from Jackson Square to Canal Street. He also dispatched a contingent of troops and policemen to the Customs House. Though outnumbered more than two to one, Longstreet had two Gatling guns and a battery of cannons.

With tension mounting, the White Leaguers demanded that Governor Kellogg, holed up in the Statehouse, resign. Longstreet ordered the White Leaguers, many of whom he knew personally, to disperse. Instead of complying, the White Leaguers' commander, General Fred N. Ogden, a former Confederate cavalry officer, launched an attack.

Despite their rapid-fire Gatling guns and battery of artillery, the Republican forces quickly folded under the onslaught of so many combat-hardened Confederate veterans. A reporter for the New Orleans *Times* chronicled the battle this way: "They [the White Leaguers] received the fire of the Metropolitans without flinching and kept straight on in their charge. Seeing this, the Metropolitans wavered, scattered, and rushed off toward the Custom House."

During the ensuing gun battle, General Longstreet was wounded slightly, knocked from his horse, and captured. Within an hour, the White Leaguers had routed the Republican forces. The clash claimed thirty-eight lives and left nearly eighty wounded. The White League seized control of the Statehouse, the Customs House, and the militia's nearby armory. They also captured the governor and installed Democrat John McEnery, who'd lost to Kellogg in the contested 1872 gubernatorial election, as the new and "legitimate" governor of Louisiana.

Three days later, federal gunboats and troops—sent by a shocked President Grant—arrived in New Orleans. They seized control of the city and put Kellogg back in the Statehouse.

To this day, a controversial monument erected in 1891

commemorating the White Leaguers' short-lived rebellion and paying homage to the eleven White Leaguers who died in what has become known as the Battle of Liberty Place stands near the foot of Canal Street next to the Mississippi River. The original inscription on the concrete obelisk-shaped monument read in part, "McEnery and Penn, having been elected governor and lieutenant governor by the white people, were duly installed by the overthrow of the carpetbag government, ousting the usurpers Gov. Kellogg (white) and Lt. Gov. Antoine (colored)."

During the 1980s and 1990s, as the population of the city and the makeup of its local government became predominately black, Liberty Monument, a dedication to white racists who slaughtered dozens of black city policemen and state militiamen, became quite an embarrassment, particularly when ex-Nazi and former Ku Klux Klan leader David Duke began using it as a rallying cry for his particular brand of contemporary racist politics.

The city removed the monument for a few years for "repairs" but was eventually forced to return it, although not to its original location. Instead of its once-prominent place at the foot of Canal Street, the monument now sits tucked into an obscure spot a block away. Sandwiched between a hotel and a floodwall, and sitting amid a network of electrical transmission line support poles, Liberty Monument is still there but well out of the view of most of the city's millions of yearly visitors.

The inscription has also changed and now reads, "In honor of those Americans on both sides of the conflict who died in the battle of Liberty Place." The names of the metropolitan policemen killed during the battle have also been engraved at the base of the monument.

From big cities to small towns, the issue of race permeated everything in post–Civil War Louisiana.

In October 1875, in the town of Clinton, ninety miles northwest of New Orleans, an armed mob of white Democrats, led by Dr. J. W. Saunders, stormed the town square and drove all of the black elected officials out of East Feliciana Parish. The mob threatened the officials with death if they ever returned.

One black official who initially refused to leave was Sheriff Henry Smith. He was shot and wounded for his troubles and immediately forced to resign. The mob booted a white Republican judge from his post as well. A few days later, Dr. Saunders's black maid, Babe Matthews, slipped poison into the doctor's dinner. Unfortunately for her, the potion had less than the desired effect and Saunders survived. When Babe Matthews's culpability was discovered, Dr. Saunders's friends dragged the maid into the courthouse square and strung her up by her neck. Just another dead Negro.

A newspaper in neighboring Tangipahoa Parish, the Amite City *Democrat*, declared its support for the coup against the black elected officials: "The insolent, ignorant, negro Sheriff Smith of East Feliciana has at last resigned." The newspaper made no mention of the details surrounding the sheriff's "resignation."

Charles Kennon, a Democratic Party organizer in the Florida Parishes during Reconstruction, said, "We can never control the Negro vote for the simple reason that it involves social equality, which we can never accept."

Sometimes oppressed blacks fought back but often without success. Just north of Clinton, in the tiny hamlet of Pinckneyville, Mississippi, a group of angry armed blacks clashed with white Democrats. In the resulting fray, fifty blacks were killed, and another half dozen were later lynched. Soon after, the Republican government of Mississippi collapsed and the black-hating Democrats regained control of the state.

Although most of the violence in Louisiana involved race, some was the result of blood feuds between families.

The bloodshed got so bad in the newly created Tangipahoa Parish—which Republicans had cobbled together in 1869 from parts of the parishes of Livingston, Washington, St. Helena, and St. Tammany—that to this day the parish's nickname is "Bloody Tangipahoa."

In *Politics and Pistols*, Samuel C. Hyde Jr. wrote that on the eve of the 1876 presidential and gubernatorial elections, "Chaos prevailed throughout the Florida Parishes."

The New Orleans newspaper *The Daily Picayune* declared that Louisiana was in "a complete state of anarchy."

The editor of a Tangipahoa newspaper, the *Kentwood Commercial*, said that proportionately more people carried guns in the Florida Parishes than anywhere in the United States. By 1879, the racial and blood feud violence was so bad that several newspapers were calling for the state legislature to step in and put a stop to the carrying of concealed handguns.

And the chaos continued. By the 1890s, a secret organization called the Whitecaps had become a powerful force in the Florida Parishes. "Whitecaps . . . typically functioned as racial regulators, keeping the blacks down and assaulting the interests of economic competition," Hyde wrote.

Like their ideological brothers in the Ku Klux Klan, the Whitecaps operated in the shadows. Members kept their identities hidden. One of the main goals of the Whitecaps was to keep blacks from getting high-paying jobs and to drive out those blacks who already had them. In the Florida Parishes, especially in the piney woods of the eastern parishes, the good-paying jobs were in the sawmills. The Whitecaps wanted black workers out of the sawmills and back in the field where they belonged.

In June 1895, a group of Whitecaps gathered at a sawmill in central Tangipahoa Parish and told the black mill workers to leave. Those blacks with a sense of self-preservation did just that.

The next day, Whitecappers Peter Kemp and Jim Wilkinson waylaid a mill worker who hadn't gotten the message.

A mile from the mill, Kemp and Wilkinson, both armed with pistols, stopped Monroe Buchanan as he walked to work. Kemp asked the black man if he'd heard them the day before when they told him and the other black workers not to come back. No Negroes were allowed at the mill anymore.

Buchanan, no fool, tried to talk his way out of the ambush. He told the two Whitecappers that he had misunderstood them the day before and he would be happy to give up his job at the mill now that he was clear about their message. But it was too late. Kemp pulled his pistol and fired. The ball tore through Buchanan's lunch bucket and entered his right side just below his rib cage, lodging beneath his bladder. Kemp tried to fire at the defenseless Buchanan again, but Wilkinson stopped him. The two Whitecappers walked off, leaving Buchanan lying in the road.

A fellow mill worker who witnessed the shooting helped Buchanan to a doctor in the town of Kentwood, but the wound was too severe. Buchanan died three days later. Later that month, a coroner's jury issued their findings: "We, the jury, find that Monroe Buchanan came to his death from internal hemorrhage from a pistol ball in the hands of Peter Kemp, entering the right side just below the ribs and ranging downward . . . causing slow hemorrhage and death."

After the murder of Monroe Buchanan, newspaper editor C. T. Curtis of the *Kentwood Commercial* had had enough. In a blistering editorial he blasted the lawlessness and violence of Tangipahoa Parish. Within days of Curtis's verbal attack on Democrats, Whitecaps, and Klansmen, two letters were delivered to the newspaper's office threatening Curtis's life. The editor, no fool either, backed off. In a series of follow-up editorials, Curtis apologized to those he may have offended. However, within a few weeks, Curtis vanished, never to be seen or heard from again. Whether the editor got scared and left on his own, or something more sinister happened, no one was ever sure.

In the October 1, 1895, edition of the *Commercial*, an

unidentified writer commented rather offhandedly that "Mr. Colvert . . . has been in charge of the office since Mr. Curtis disappeared."

Samuel Hyde made the point in *Pistols and Politics* that Whitecaps operated as a quasi–law enforcement entity, often with the loose approval and under the semi-protection of local officials. "Whitecaps frequently attacked prostitutes, wife beaters, and the like but also whipped, murdered, and generally terrorized blacks, driving scores from the region," he wrote.

But Whitecaps weren't the only thing that blacks and Republicans had to worry about in south Louisiana during the second half of the nineteenth century. In 1866, a group of Confederate veterans in Tennessee founded an organization they called the Ku Klux Klan. Within two years, several local Klan groups, called klaverns, were operating in Louisiana's Florida Parishes. In 1867, a group of Louisiana "gentlemen" founded the Knights of the White Camelia. The Knights were more political organization than terror group, but their goal was the same as that of the Whitecaps and the Klansmen—white supremacy.

Camelia Knights were members of the Old South's aristocracy. Because membership in the organization was not a secret, most Knights were content to fight their battles with words, money, and votes. If things needed to get dirty, the Knights used the Klan.

According to Hyde: "The Klan combined an unqualified commitment to white supremacy with a murderous contempt for aspiring blacks and white Republicans. Terror served as the weapon of choice for Klansmen. Murder, arson, and intimidation all played an integral role in the Klan's nightly adventures."

In the Florida Parishes, Hyde wrote, "unrestrained violence remained a fundamental component of everyday life." The constant carnage, Hyde argued, created what he described as "a culture of violence."

SEVENTEEN

If anyone thought a new century would bring a new attitude toward race relations in the South, they were wrong.

The twentieth century had indeed dawned on a new world. The United States was on the threshold of emerging as an international superpower. During the preceding century, the young nation had defeated powerhouse England a second time, pushed its borders westward to the Pacific Ocean, battled and beaten Mexico and avenged the massacre at the Alamo, held together after fighting the bloodiest war in history (a war fought against its own citizens), been forced to overcome aging world power Spain in Cuba and elsewhere in the Caribbean and Pacific, and by the close of the century had completed its transformation from an agrarian-based economy into a true industrial heavyweight.

In the South, race relations had changed since the Civil War, although not necessarily for the better. Legally, blacks were free, but free to do what? The South was caught in transition between the Old South and what would eventually become known as the New South. At the turn of the century, Southern aristocrats and poor whites, who never before had much in common, found themselves united in their fear of emerging black power. Blacks were in the labor force and competing with whites for good-paying jobs. They were opening their own businesses. They were voting. They were even being elected to public office.

To many Southerners, the new order represented madness. It was the world turned upside down. The Thirteenth Amendment to the United States Constitution had abolished slavery, but in the hearts of many in the South it had also transformed blacks from mere property into an insufferable enemy, an enemy who had to be defeated.

To defeat an enemy you need an army. In the South, that army went by the name Ku Klux Klan.

By the mid-1870s, the original Klan was dead. Republican President Ulysses S. Grant had smashed it using as his hammer the Civil Rights Act of 1871, also known as the Ku Klux Klan Act.

In its original manifestation, the Klan, under the leadership of its first grand wizard, ex–slave trader and ex–Confederate general Nathan Bedford Forrest, was dedicated to opposing so-called carpetbaggers, a derogatory term for white Northerners who moved to the South during Reconstruction looking for a quick buck, and punishing scalawags, Southern whites who joined the Republican Party and supported integration. The Klan also used terror tactics against blacks to keep them from getting an education, from getting decent jobs, and from voting. The white sheets of the Klan were themselves meant to play on the cultural superstitions of blacks and were supposed to give the impression that Klansmen were the ghosts of dead Confederate soldiers.

When first told of the creation of the original Klan, General Forrest is reported to have remarked: "That's a good thing. That's a damn good thing. We can use that to keep the niggers in their place."

To his credit, two years after being installed as the Klan's leader, Forrest, who grew uncomfortable with the organization's increasingly violent tactics, resigned his position and called for the organization to disband. His call went unheeded, and the Klan happily carried on its reign of terror for several more years before being crushed under the boot of President Grant.

Unlike the Confederate South, which many Southerners promised would rise again but which never did, the Ku Klux Klan did undergo a resurrection. In 1915, at a secret meeting on top of Stone Mountain in Georgia, the Ku Klux Klan was reborn. In its second manifestation, the Klan pledged to continue its violent opposition to Republican scalawags, Yankee carpetbaggers, and freed blacks, but it also added to its hate list a few new groups: immigrants, Catholics, and, of course, Jews.

Like its predecessor, the new Klan quickly found supporters and a home in Louisiana. Because membership was a closely guarded secret, verifiable numbers are impossible to come by, but reasonable estimates put nationwide Klan strength in the mid-1920s at four to five million members, mostly in the South and Midwest.

In Louisiana, the Klan continued its terror campaign. In his 1995 book *Race & Democracy: The Civil Rights Struggle in Louisiana*, historian Adam Fairclough wrote that "lynching was commonplace." According to Fairclough, between 1882 and 1952, 355 blacks were murdered in Louisiana, giving the state the dubious distinction of being second only to Mississippi in the number of race-related murders. Many were committed with at least the tacit approval of local law enforcement. "Blacks were usually lynched because the sheriffs allowed them to be," Fairclough wrote.

Nationwide, the number of lynchings was staggering. A

study by the Tuskegee Institute concluded that between 1882 and 1968, nearly 3,500 blacks were lynched in the United States. And that number represents only those cases for which documentation exits. Certainly there were many lynchings between those years that went unrecorded. There were also plenty of lynchings that occurred outside of those years, particularly between 1865, the year the Civil War ended, and 1882, the first year of the study.

Blacks weren't the only victims. Whites, too, were lynched, usually for supporting fair treatment for blacks and, ironically enough, for opposing lynching, but the same Tuskegee study found that roughly 75 percent of lynching victims were black. A 1930 study by Dr. Arthur Raper supports that figure. Of the 3,724 lynchings he was able to document that were committed between 1889 and 1930, 80 percent of the victims were black. Although lynchings occurred in nearly every state, the vast majority of them took place in just five: Mississippi, Georgia, Alabama, Texas, and Louisiana.

Of the top five states, Louisiana ranked number four in the number of lynchings, with 335 blacks and 56 whites lynched between 1882 and 1968.

Although hanging is certainly the most common form of lynching, and in the minds of many the two are nearly synonymous, it isn't the only form. According to most sources, including the Tuskegee Institute (now Tuskegee University) and the NAACP, lynching is generally defined as an illegal public execution carried out by a group of three or more people with the killers claiming to have committed the act in the service of justice or tradition.

The word itself is most commonly associated with either William Lynch, a late–eighteenth century bounty hunter from the Commonwealth of Virginia who made a deal with the Virginia Legislature to pursue and capture suspected criminals without due process; or with Colonel Charles Lynch, a Revolutionary War–era Virginia magistrate who used extralegal steps to track down British sympathizers on behalf of what was called the Virginia Vigilance Committee.

Regardless of its origins, lynching became a common practice in the United States, particularly after the Civil War, particularly in the South, and particularly against blacks. Most lynchings involved hanging, although shootings, beatings, burnings, and mutilations were also used. Photos were often taken afterward, usually with the mob standing around the dead man or woman and mugging for the camera. (Although not as frequently as men, black women were sometimes the victims of lynchings.) The photographs were often turned into postcards and sold. In recent years, many of those cards have been collected and published in books and used in documentary films as grim reminders of one of the ugliest chapters in American history.

Typical of Louisiana lynching cases is that of Jerome Wilson. In July 1934, a stock inspector showed up at the Wilson farm in Washington Parish and demanded access to the family's livestock. Jerome and his brother told the inspector to come back after their father returned. The inspector left but soon came back with three sheriff's deputies. A scuffle broke out and the deputies shot both Wilson boys. With his brother dead, James dashed inside the house and grabbed a shotgun. As he stepped back onto the porch, James shot and killed Deputy Delos C. Wood. The other two deputies disarmed James and arrested him. Later, the sheriff ordered the arrest of James's parents, John and Tempie Wilson, and his sisters, none of whom were at home at the time of the shooting.

A Washington Parish jury later convicted James Wilson of murdering Deputy Wood, but the Louisiana Supreme Court overturned the conviction and ordered a new trial. On the night of January 11, 1935, before the new trial had begun, a mob of angry white men broke into the jail and beat James Wilson to death in his cell with hammers.

Talking to reporters later, Washington Parish Sheriff J. L. Brock said: "There wasn't any lynching. There wasn't any mob . . . just about six or eight men who were going about their business."

Commenting on the death of James Wilson, U.S. Senator Huey Long, the former governor of Louisiana, said, "That nigger was guilty of cold-blooded murder."

As the United States struggled through the Great Depression and fought World War II, sacrificing hundreds of thousands of its soldiers, sailors, and airmen to bring freedom to Europe and Asia, freedom in America still eluded many of its own citizens. Even in the military, race played a huge role in assignments.

In the U.S. Navy, blacks usually served as cooks and mess stewards. Army units were segregated by race. There were black units and white units. Combat unit assignments, although certainly the most dangerous, were given almost exclusively to white soldiers. A common perception held at the time was that black soldiers couldn't be trusted in battle. As in the Navy, blacks who served in the Army were relegated to service roles, in military parlance— cooks, bakers, and candlestick makers.

As the war dragged on, however, and more and more troops were needed to fill combat roles, the Army formed all-black combat units and many black soldiers distinguished themselves as heroes.

Vernon Baker led his platoon against a dug-in German position. During the attack, he and his troops destroyed six German machine guns and killed twenty-six enemy soldiers. In 1997, President Bill Clinton awarded Baker the Medal of Honor, the nation's highest award for military heroism.

The famed Tuskegee Airmen flew more than fifteen hundred bomber escort missions over Germany without losing a single bomber.

Navy messman Dorie Miller served on the battleship U.S.S. *West Virginia*. During the surprise Japanese attack at Pearl Harbor, he rescued his wounded captain and shot down at least two Japanese planes.

At the 1997 Medal of Honor ceremony at the White House for Vernon Baker and six other black American heroes, Baker, who was forced to serve in an all-black unit, said: "As a black soldier, I fought a war on two sides. I was an angry young man, and all of my soldiers were angry. We were all angry, but we had a job to do and we did it."

In congratulating the men for their service to the country and granting them their long overdo recognition, President Clinton said: "These heroes distinguished themselves in another, almost unique way: In the tradition of African-Americans who have fought for our nation as far back as Bunker Hill, they were prepared to sacrifice everything for freedom—even though freedom's fullness was denied to them."

Despite having sacrificed and fought for their country, when black servicemen from the South—even those swathed in medals and glory—returned home, Jim Crow was there to greet them.

They lived in black neighborhoods. They toiled at low-paying, black-only jobs. They rode to work in the back of the bus. They ate at separate lunch counters. They drank from "Colored" or "Negro" water fountains. Their children went to second-rate black schools.

A state law in Louisiana made it a crime for anyone to rent an apartment or any part of a building to a "Negro person or a Negro family when such building is already in whole or in part in occupancy by a white person or white family." Violations of the law carried a minimum sentence of ten days in jail and a maximum of sixty days.

Up to two months in jail for renting an apartment in a "white" building to a black family.

Welcome home, black veterans of World War II,

members of the "Greatest Generation." Thanks for a job well done.

While a class action lawsuit filed by thirteen parents on behalf of their children against the Topeka, Kansas, Board of Education was grinding its way through the legal system on its way to the U.S. Supreme Court, individual black Americans were fed up and many were taking a stand against forced segregation.

In 1953, the Reverend T. J. Jemison of Mount Zion Baptist Church in Baton Rouge challenged the city's ordinance requiring whites to sit in the front of city busses and blacks to sit in the back. On June 13, Jemison, a black preacher, boarded a city bus and took a seat in one of the clearly marked whites-only front seats. When the bus driver told him to move, Jemison refused. The bus drivers went on strike for four days. When the strike ended, Jemison organized a bus boycott—the first of its kind in the nation—and forced the city to pass a new ordinance allowing integrated seating in all but the first and last two rows, which remained reserved for whites and blacks, respectively.

It wasn't victory, but it was progress.

Two years later, Rosa Parks refused to give up her seat to a white passenger on a Montgomery, Alabama, city bus. Her act of civil disobedience resulted in her arrest and prompted the Reverend Martin Luther King Jr. to organize a boycott of the Montgomery bus system. Before King launched the boycott, he called his friend, the Reverend T. J. Jemison, to ask his advice.

In his book, *Stride Toward Freedom: The Montgomery Story*, King wrote that Jemison's "painstaking description of the Baton Rouge experience proved invaluable."

In 1954, the U.S. Supreme Court dropped the hammer on Southern segregationists. In its landmark decision *Brown v. Board of Education*, the court ruled that "separate but equal" was no longer good enough and ordered the desegregation of all public schools. The following year, in what has become known as the Brown II decision, the Supreme Court ordered that schools be desegregated "with all deliberate speed."

The *Brown* decision didn't sit well with many in the South, particularly white Democrats. In Arkansas, Democratic Governor Orval Faubus called out the National Guard to block the entrance of nine black students into Little Rock Central High School. The next day, Republican President Dwight D. Eisenhower sent twelve hundred paratroopers from the U.S. Army's 101st Airborne Division to the school to ensure the students, who became known as the "Little Rock Nine," could attend classes. The nine students spent the entire school year accompanied by the soldiers. The next year, Little Rock public schools closed to avoid integrating.

In 1962, James Meredith, a nine-year U.S. Air Force veteran, was the first black person to enroll at the University of Mississippi. Ole Miss, as the school is called, is very proud of its Confederate heritage and has as its mascot a Confederate officer known as Colonel Reb. The university's sports teams are known as the Ole Miss Rebels, and Confederate battle flags are always seen at the school's sporting events. During the Civil War, the university closed down because the entire student body and much of the faculty left school to join the Confederate Army.

Meredith's court-supported enrollment at Ole Miss infuriated Democratic Governor Ross Barnett, who proclaimed that Mississippi "will not surrender to the evil and illegal forces of tyranny . . . [and] no school will be integrated in Mississippi while I am your governor."

President John F. Kennedy sent more than one hundred deputy U.S. marshals to make sure that Meredith got to class on time. When Meredith and his escorts arrived at the university on the afternoon of September 30, they were confronted by armed state troopers and hundreds of angry students. As night fell, many of the students were replaced by a hodgepodge of hate mongers, including Klansmen and other anti-integration forces. The riot that followed began with protesters throwing rocks, then hurling chunks of concrete, then firing gunshots. By morning, two protesters had been killed and almost eighty deputy marshals had been wounded, thirty of them from gunshots.

Meredith went on to graduate from Ole Miss, and in 1966 he organized what he called a March Against Fear, a civil rights protest march from Memphis, Tennessee, to Jackson, Mississippi, designed to encourage blacks to register to vote. During the march Meredith was severely wounded by a shotgun blast from a sniper. He recovered and went on to become a staunch Republican. He made a few unsuccessful bids for a seat in Congress and worked for a while on the staff of U.S. Senator Jesse Helms, a Republican from North Carolina.

In Louisiana, the *Brown* decision received a similar reception. The Supreme Court ruling and subsequent order to integrate public schools "with all deliberate speed" prompted one St. Helena Parish School Board member to say, "We'll never be integrated . . . until there are a lot of dead niggers around here."

The *Brown v. Board of Education* decision was a boon to at least one organization—the Ku Klux Klan. When people saw what was coming, Klan membership surged.

In his seminal work, *Race & Democracy*, Adam Fairclough wrote, "By 1965 [Bogalusa, La.] boasted the largest and most powerful Klan organization in Louisiana, committed to perpetuating segregation through harassment, boycotts, beatings and murder."

EIGHTEEN

The Pearl River divides southeast Louisiana from southwest Mississippi. At the edge of the river's western bank sits the Washington Parish city of Bogalusa. Two brothers, Charles and Frank Goodyear of Buffalo, New York, founded the city in 1906 as part of their lumber empire. The two brothers built, named, and owned the town. It was there for one reason, to support the Great Southern Lumber Company, then the largest pine sawmill in the world. Bogalusa was a company town. The houses, the stores, the ships, the streets, and most importantly, the local government—all were owned by the lumber company and, by extension, the Goodyear brothers.

By the mid-1960s, Bogalusa's population was 40 percent black. The biggest—really the only—employer in town was the sawmill, yet blacks were forced to accept only low-paying, menial jobs there and weren't even allowed to apply for the better-paying supervisory positions. Tensions ran high. The 1954 *Brown* decision requiring the desegregation of all public schools and the 1964 Civil

Rights Act outlawing segregation in most other aspects of American life were gasoline poured on a smoldering fire.

On May 30, 1965, less than a year after President Lyndon B. Johnson signed the landmark Civil Rights Act into law, eight hundred people gathered in Bogalusa to support a Klan-sponsored rally. Fully half of those present wore the sheets and white hoods of the Klan. During the rally, Klansmen burned two crosses.

In *Race & Democracy*, Fairclough wrote, "With the tide of the civil rights movement lapping at the door, whites in Bogalusa began to join the Ku Klux Klan."

Fairclough went on to describe race relations in Bogalusa this way: "In a rough, violent, frontier environment that made the Wild West seem tame, black lives were cheap."

An FBI agent sent to Bogalusa reported, "Klavern meetings are filled with talks about dynamiting, guns, and violence."

Historian Lance Hill, in his 2004 book *The Deacons for Defense: Armed Resistance and the Civil Rights Movement*, wrote, "By 1965 the Ku Klux Klan had, through a well-organized terrorist war, carved out a virtual 'Klan Nation' in southwestern Mississippi and neighboring southeastern Louisiana—often with the compliance of state and local law enforcement agencies."

Several city officials, including City Attorney Robert Rester and nearly the entire Bogalusa Police Department, were members of the Klan.

According to several sources, during the mid-1960s, Washington Parish had more Klan members per capita than anywhere else in the United States. In 1965, journalist Paul Good, in an article in *The Nation* magazine, called Bogalusa "Klantown U.S.A."

Bogalusa Mayor Jesse Cutrer was caught in the middle, stuck between a rock and a hard place. On one side was the Klan, armed, secret, and terrifying. They represented the majority vote in Bogalusa and had put Cutrer in office. On the other side was the all-black Bogalusa Civic and Voters League, advocates for the new law of the land. They demanded that the mayor drag Bogalusa, kicking and screaming if necessary, into compliance with the recently enacted Civil Rights Act of 1964.

When the mayor and members of the City Council met with representatives of the Voters League, Klan members surrounded City Hall. Cutrer promised reforms. After the meeting, Klansmen circulated a flyer that read "Who Bought Jesse Cutrer?"

During a radio address a few days after the meeting, the mayor announced that he was ordering the desegregation of city facilities and accommodations. He also pledged to pave roads in black neighborhoods and hire black police officers.

Just days later, a group of black children and adults showed up at Cassidy Park, traditionally and "legally" a whites-only park. The white park goers left, and within minutes a carload of armed Klan members showed up. The Klansmen attacked and began beating the blacks in the park. Soon, they were joined by city police officers and state troopers, who participated in the beatings. A white FBI agent and a white New Orleans *Times-Picayune* newspaper photographer were also beaten when they tried to intervene.

On the night of June 2, 1965, black sheriff's deputies O'Neal Moore and Creed Rogers, the only two black sheriff's deputies in Washington Parish, were cruising in their patrol car on Highway 21 just north of Bogalusa. As the deputies approached the town of Varnado, a beat-up black pickup truck sporting a Confederate flag sticker on its front bumper came up behind them. The truck swung into the oncoming lane and started to pass the deputies. When the pickup pulled even with them, a shotgun barrel emerged from the passenger window and started firing.

The first shot blew apart the back windshield of the patrol car. Then two more blasts hit the front seat. Deputy Moore was shot in the head and killed. Shotgun pellets struck Deputy Rogers in the shoulder and face and blinded him in one eye. Despite his wounds, Rogers managed to call in a description of the truck.

Less than an hour later, police officers at a roadblock in Mississippi stopped a truck matching the description—even down to the Confederate flag bumper sticker—trying to sneak across the state line. The truck was headed to Tylertown, Mississippi. The driver and lone occupant was forty-one-year-old Ernest Ray McElveen from Bogalusa. McElveen, a Klan member, had two pistols with him but no shotgun.

Two nights later, six bullets struck the home of the Washington Parish Sheriff's Office's chief deputy, Doyle Holliday. Chief Deputy Holliday had been assisting the FBI and the State Police with their investigation into the slaying of Deputy Moore and the wounding of Deputy Rogers. The attack on Holliday's home came while he and his wife were inside. The bullets narrowly missed both of them.

McElveen was charged with the murder of Deputy Sheriff O'Neal Moore but the charges were later dropped.

On October 20, 1965, Bogalusa police attacked a group of black protesters marching in the city's small business district. The officers beat and then dragged dozens of adults and children to a waiting police bus for the short ride to the jail. Just before the bus drove away, Bogalusa Police Chief Claxton Knight and Washington Parish Deputy Sheriff Vertress Adams stepped aboard the bus. Chief Claxton announced to the battered and bloody prisoners, "I'll show you who runs this town."

Deputy Adams looked at them with undisguised contempt. "You niggers ain't gonna rule this town," he said.

A press account of the police riot, a day that became

known as "Bloody Wednesday," proclaimed, "Bogalusa, La. Police 'Run Wild'; Beat, Jail Negroes in 'Night of Terror.'"

The violence just wouldn't stop.

On March 10, 1966, Bogalusa resident Thomas Bennett needed to use a pay phone. The nearest one was in use. A black U.S. Army officer named Donald R. Sims was talking on it. Bennett tried to get Sims to hang up. When that failed, Bennett went home and got a rifle. He came back and found Sims still on the phone, so he shot the Army officer three times in the back.

Clarence Triggs was a twenty-four-year-old bricklayer from Bogalusa. He worked hard and just wanted to be treated fairly. He attended town meetings in Bogalusa sponsored by the Chicago-based Congress of Racial Equality, also known as CORE. On July 30, 1966, after attending one such meeting, Triggs was found lying in a ditch outside Bogalusa. He'd been shot in the head. A couple of Klansmen were later arrested for his murder but were eventually released. No one was ever convicted.

Although three decades had passed since a mob broke into the Washington Parish jail and beat Jerome Wilson to death with hammers back in 1935, decades during which the U.S. Supreme Court had ordered all of the nation's public schools desegregated, and the U.S. Congress had passed, and the president had signed, landmark legislation "guaranteeing" equal treatment for everyone in the country regardless of race—away down south in Dixie, not much had really changed at all.

During the 1960s and into the 1970s, the entire state of Louisiana, particularly the southern half, and even more particularly the piney woods of the eastern Florida Parishes, was a hotbed of Klan activity. Fairclough wrote that St. Helena Parish, like its neighbor to the east, Washington Parish, "was regarded as a stronghold of the Ku Klux Klan."

Likewise, just south of St. Helena, the Klan was very active in Livingston Parish, a place that attorney John Martzell, a member of Governor John McKeithen's so-called Bi-Racial Committee, described as "the Klan country of all Klan country."

It was in that Klan country of Livingston Parish where Johnny Hoyt, Phillip Skipper, and Phillip's sister Lisa—Hoyt's future wife—spent their formative years.

The South's culture of racial violence certainly didn't end in the 1960s. Although by the end of that decade, the country's growing unease and increasingly militant protests over the war in Vietnam gradually began to replace the civil rights movement and incidents of racial violence on the front pages of newspapers and on the evening news broadcasts, their diminished prominence in no way signaled that the nation had turned the corner on racism and the race-related carnage it spawned, or that all there was left to do to rid the country of them was to mop up a few isolated cases of extremism.

On the contrary, in the decade of the 1970s, racial hatred was alive and well, especially in places like Livingston Parish, Louisiana. The only difference was that it had become less blatant. It had moved underground.

Johnny Hoyt was born and raised in Livingston Parish. Locals call it "the free state of Livingston," a name meant to reflect the parish's legacy of nonconformity and noncompliance with the laws and traditions of the rest of the country. Modern Livingstonians have their own spin on the nickname, attributing it to what at least one official parish Web site refers to as the area's "philosophy of independence and self-reliance."

Probably more than any other parish in Louisiana, Livingston clings to its history of racial hatred and violence. In a state whose current population is nearly 40 percent black, le[...] [pa]rish residents are black [...] Parish, 40 percent of t[...] [i]n Tangipahoa Parish, [...] [ar]e black. To the north, St. [...] [is] [mo]re than 50 percent black; and to the south of Livingston, black residents make up more than 20 percent of Ascension Parish's population.

Up until the area's housing boom of the mid-1990s, a boom that brought a host of new people into the parish who were in search of less expensive homes, Livingston was viewed regionally as one giant trailer park. Many of the parish's more urban neighbors in Baton Rouge thought of Livingston residents as backwoods trailer-trash wife beaters and cross-burning racists. Local folklore pegged Livingston Parish as the modern-day home of the Ku Klux Klan. Even black law enforcement officers from surrounding parishes were afraid to go there. Alvin Jackson, a black investigator with the East Baton Rouge Parish District Attorney's Office, said in 1988 that he didn't mind going into Livingston Parish during the daytime, but he was afraid to stay there past dark.

An urban legend at the time told of a sign posted beside an unnamed highway somewhere on the parish line that read, "Any nigger found here after dark will be found here in the morning."

The message was clear. Livingston Parish had always been, and was trying to remain, even as late as the last quarter of the twentieth century, "whites only."

The reason there are so few black residents of Livingston Parish has as much to do with geography as with history. The Livingston soil was just not suitable for sprawling cotton plantations. Unlike several of its neighboring parishes, timber, not cotton, was the number one cash crop in Livingston Parish. Timber harvesting didn't require an army of black slaves. What fertile cotton-friendly soil there was in the parish was confined to its relatively few miles of riverbanks.

According to the U.S. Census taken in 1860, just before the start of the Civil War, only one of Louisiana's sixty-plus parishes had fewer slaves than Livingston. There was just no need for slave labor there.

Asked why there were still so few black people in Livingston Parish, one longtime resident said, "We picked our own cotton."

Although geography is certainly an important factor in Livingston Parish's racial mix, it's not the only factor. Culture can't be ignored. Livingston Parish is filled with undereducated rednecks, otherwise known as Bubbas. Confederate flags, single-wide trailers, junked cars, and chained up pit bulls blanket the landscape. A drive through Livingston Parish is like a scene from a metal recycler's wet dream. It's hard to tell which there's more of, working or nonworking automobiles. At least half of the vehicles on the road seem to be pickup trucks. Young men wear ball caps, dip tobacco, and leave their shirttails hanging over the waistbands of their dirty jeans. Gun racks are popular. So are missing teeth.

Johnny Hoyt's father, Johnny Hoyt Sr., lives off of an interstate service road in a ramshackle wood-framed house near the Livingston Parish town of Holden. His front yard is decorated with three junked cars, a couple of broken bicycles, and a rusted out lawnmower. Two more broken-down cars sit beside the house. A rusty basketball hoop with no net is nailed to a tree. The front porch was built around an oak tree and is furnished with a tattered sofa, recliner, and love seat—all intended to be used indoors, away from the rain. A white picket fence with chicken wire added to the top separates the front yard from the circular asphalt and gravel driveway. A pit bull lives behind the fence, a thick chain running from its neck to a post stuck in the ground. Behind the house sits a dilapidated trailer home.

All of the streets in Hoyt Sr.'s subdivision are named after lakes, Lake this, Lake that, but the only lake to be seen is a muddy, rain-filled borrow pit from which the state long ago dug dirt to build the interstate. Most of the homes are trailers. Only about 20 to 25 percent of the vehicles in the neighborhood appear to run. In Mr. Hoyt's subdivision, chained up pit bulls outnumber working automobiles.

NINETEEN

Johnny Mitchell Hoyt Jr. was born in 1978. Two years later, David Duke of nearby Metairie, Louisiana—arguably the United States' best known racist—founded the National Association for the Advancement of White People. Twelve years later, as Hoyt hit puberty, Duke was at the height of his notoriety. In the next parish over from Hoyt, in the state capital, as well as across the country, David Duke had become a household name.

Duke was born in Tulsa, Oklahoma, in 1950. Soon afterward, his parents moved to the Netherlands for a short stay before settling in New Orleans. Duke attended Louisiana State University in Baton Rouge, where he gained notoriety for goose-stepping around campus in a Nazi uniform and for holding birthday parties for Adolf Hitler. While at LSU, Duke formed an organization called the White Youth Alliance. He graduated in 1974 and that same year was elected grand wizard of the Louisiana Knights of the Ku Klux Klan.

One of the first things Duke did as the new grand wizard

was trade in the Klan's bedsheets and pointy white caps for business suits and salon haircuts. More than perhaps any other Klan leader in history, Duke was determined to change the image of the Klan. The message, however, remained the same: *The white man rules.*

In an April 1975 interview with *The Wichita Sun* newspaper, Duke said, "White people don't need a law against rape, but if you fill this room up with your normal black bucks, you would, because niggers are basically primitive animals."

In 1976, perhaps in his own twisted celebration of the nation's two hundredth birthday, Duke ran an unsuccessful campaign as a Democrat for a seat in the Louisiana State Senate.

In 1988, Duke—who'd since dropped out of the Klan in favor of his own, less baggage-laden organization, the National Association for the Advancement of White People—ran in the Democratic presidential primary. His miserable showing as a presidential candidate for the party that a hundred years before had embraced the Klan, forced Duke to switch to the Populist party in time for the general election. Duke's name didn't appear on every state ballot, but it appeared on enough of them that he received nearly 50,000 votes.

In 1989, Duke ran as a Republican for the Louisiana House of Representatives—and won!

Duke won 51 percent of the vote against fellow Republican John Treen, the brother of former Louisiana Governor Dave Treen. As the first Republican governor elected in Louisiana since the end of Reconstruction, Dave Treen was widely regarded as one of the state's most honest governors.

Duke's ascension from the gutter of the political fringe to a seat at the State Capitol was a black eye to Louisiana, a state that was desperately trying to reshape its image from that of a banana republic dominated by corrupt political potentates to one governed by democracy and the rule of law. The Republican Party disavowed any connection to

Duke just as the state was trying to lock him in the basement like an embarrassing half-wit relative.

Infamy is its own brand of fame, and Duke's election made him a star. In 1990, shortly after being sworn in as a state representative, Duke—who surely had to cross his fingers behind his back when he took the oath of office and swore to uphold the Constitution of the Unites States of America—challenged longtime incumbent U.S. Senator J. Bennett Johnston for his senate seat. Although Duke lost the election, he managed to ride the crest of Republican and conservative disaffection enough to garner 45 percent of the general vote and 60 percent of the white vote.

Riding high, and with Klan dollars pouring in from around the country, Duke didn't waste any time. Always much more interested in campaigning for political office than in actually serving his constituents, Duke ran for governor in 1991, challenging incumbent Governor Buddy Roemer. Roemer had been elected as a Democrat but switched parties halfway through his four-year term. Also in the race was Democratic candidate and former three-time governor Edwin W. Edwards.

Edwards was the stuff of political legend. Regardless of what he did in his personal or professional life, the people of Louisiana liked him and kept voting him back into office. Edwards was a charmer, a master politician, and the undisputed king of the political one-liner.

During his third run for governor, after a state constitutionally mandated one-term layoff, and the day before the election in which he crushed incumbent Republican Governor Dave Treen, Edwards quipped, "The only way I can lose this election is if I'm caught in bed with either a dead girl or a live boy."

While campaigning, Edwards had fired zinger after zinger at Governor Treen, once describing him as "so slow it takes him an hour and a half to watch *60 Minutes*."

During a debate, Treen tried to fire back and attacked

Edwards's habit of contradicting himself by telling people whatever they wanted to hear. Treen asked the former governor, "How come you talk out of both sides of your mouth?" Edwards didn't miss a beat as he fired back, "So people like you with only half a brain can understand me." The barb didn't really make much sense, but it was funny and it was classic Edwin Edwards. Afterward, it was all anyone remembered about the debate.

During Edwards's third term as governor, he was indicted by a federal grand jury in New Orleans for his political shenanigans and crooked deals, specifically mail fraud, obstruction of justice, and public bribery. A defiant Edwards stood trial twice and was eventually acquitted, but the daily grind of revelations of corruption and the nightly newsreels of the governor and his team of criminal defense lawyers going in and out of federal court made it seem that Edwards's star had finally fallen. Proof of that seemed to come in 1987 when the charismatic and flamboyant governor suffered a stinging reelection defeat at the hands of an obscure U.S. congressman from north Louisiana named Charles "Buddy" Roemer III.

After the election, a reporter for the *Shreveport Journal* declared Edwards's political career dead when he wrote that the only way the former governor could ever be elected again would be to run against Adolf Hitler.

In 1991, four years after his first political defeat, Edwards was back on the campaign trail, challenging one-term incumbent Governor Buddy Roemer. Roemer's father had been a top aide to Edwards during one of his previous administrations and had ended up in federal prison following a conviction for public bribery. Although the feds also investigated Edwards himself, the cagey governor had managed to avoid the federal indictment that landed his friend and political confidant behind bars.

In addition to Roemer, the three-term former governor also found himself up against if not Adolf Hitler himself, certainly his self-styled protégé.

The 1991 Louisiana governor's race was about personality. Edwards had one. Roemer didn't.

Edwards was a coonass from south Louisiana. He was quick with a joke for a friend and quicker with a barb for an enemy. He gambled, he drank, he had left his wife of forty years for a blond secretary less than half his age, he'd been investigated by the FBI a dozen times and taken to trial twice. He was crooked and everybody knew it.

Roemer was from solid, dependable, sturdy north Louisiana stock. He was a product of the Bible Belt. Known as a reformer, Roemer had few, if any, vices, and certainly none of the type flaunted by his predecessor and current electoral rival. Roemer's flaw was his reputation for being hard to get along with. He had managed to woo enough voters in 1987 to pull off a remarkable come-from-behind victory over a politically wounded Edwin Edwards—Roemer supporters called it the Roemer Revolution—but during his term as governor the sometimes cantankerous Roemer was not able to muster enough friends in the state legislature to pass many of his reforms.

Duke was the wild card. He didn't have a personality so much as a personality problem. Yet more than any other modern racial demagogue, Duke made racism seem almost logical. He made it seem palatable. If it is true that timing is everything, then Duke the politician was a product of good timing. He came along at just the right moment to tap into a wellspring of white disaffection and dissatisfaction.

Duke's home city of New Orleans was a welfare state within a welfare state. Poverty, unemployment, and hopelessness had become mainstays of its culture. In 1991, the percentage of New Orleans residents who were living in public housing was higher than that of any other American city. The city itself was in the throes of an orgy of violence, mostly black on black. Many of the residents of the city's ten sprawling, crime-infested housing projects slept on their floors with their children in hopes of avoiding any bullets that came ripping through the walls during the night.

So when David Duke talked, when he argued that the welfare system in the United States was broken and should be done away with, when he proclaimed that Lyndon Johnson's three-decades-long "Great Society" experiment had failed, when he pointed out that the answer to Martin Luther King's plea for a raceless society was not reverse racism—Black Entertainment Television; Miss Black America; jobs, test scores, and scholarships based strictly on race—people listened.

And they prepared to vote.

Louisiana has a unique electoral process. The state uses an open primary system, something engineered by Edwin Edwards himself way back during his first term as governor. In the open system, as many candidates as can qualify get on the ballot for the primary election, regardless of their political party. Voters cast ballots for whichever candidate they want.

After the primary, if no candidate has collected more than 50 percent of the vote, a runoff election is held a month or so later between the top two finishers. Almost all political contests in Louisiana result in a runoff.

The 1991 governor's race was no exception. Not surprisingly, charismatic ex-governor Edwin Edwards led the field of twelve candidates, finishing first with 34 percent of the vote. Duke came in a strong second with 32 percent, while incumbent reformer Buddy Roemer finished a distant third with 27 percent, worse than he'd done in the primary four years before.

The pending runoff election, pitting Edwin Edwards, a career politician widely regarded as one of the most corrupt in the country, against David Duke, a former Ku Klux Klan leader and neo-Nazi, focused national and international attention on Louisiana and did nothing to dispel the common perception that the state was indeed nothing more than a banana republic whose culture and politics were more akin to those of some third-rate South American dictatorship than to the rest of the United States of America.

In Louisiana, many residents did what they always do when faced with humiliation—they laughed about it. Across the state bumper stickers popped up that read: "VOTE FOR THE CROOK. IT'S IMPORTANT."

During the runoff campaign, as the nation watched, an aging Edwards showed that he still had it when it came to hurling political zingers. During a debate in front of a group of senior citizens, Duke criticized Edwards for raising state taxes by a billion dollars during his previous administrations. Edwards glanced over at his opponent and said a more accurate figure was something like $600 million in new taxes. Then he quipped: "I don't know why you worry so much about taxes. Until they [the IRS] caught you, you didn't even file income tax returns." Turning back to the crowd, the former governor continued, "Three years in a row he didn't pay his income taxes, and then he didn't pay his property taxes . . . until they caught him and made him pay."

Caught off guard, Duke tried to defend himself by claiming that for three years he hadn't earned enough money to meet the minimum threshold to owe federal income taxes and that he'd only been late in paying his local property tax bill.

Some of the old-timers in the crowd booed Duke's dodgy explanation.

In the November runoff, Edwards trounced Duke 61 to 39 percent. The smooth-talking, barb-tossing ex-governor showed that he still knew how to win a race.

Yet in Duke's failed bid for the governor's mansion, the former Klansman collected almost 700,000 votes and took 55 percent of the white vote statewide. He carried nineteen of the state's sixty-four parishes, including Livingston Parish, which he won by a landslide 60 percent.

TWENTY

In the mid-1990s, Phillip Skipper, his wife, Amy, the couple's young son, Phillip Jr., whom they of course called Little Phillip, and their "stepson," John Baillio, moved into the rundown trailer on Oakwood Lane across from Genore Guillory and her longtime live-in boyfriend, Eddie Dixon.

Genore and Eddie got along fine with their new neighbors. Eddie worked at Georgia-Pacific in West Feliciana Parish and Genore worked at BlueCross BlueShield in Baton Rouge. Both spent long hours away from home. Phillip didn't have a steady job and Amy didn't work, so both of them were home a lot of the time. Genore counted it a blessing to have someone around, particularly a nice young family man like Phillip Skipper, to keep an eye on her house while she and Eddie were gone.

A couple of years later, Eddie died in a car crash and Genore's neighbor's were there for her. Without Eddie around, taking care of her property and her animals would have been near impossible for Genore had not the Skippers been there to help. Genore's closest family members were a good two hours away in Eunice. Phillip cut the grass, performed minor maintenance work, and fed the dogs and horses. Amy sometimes cleaned the house. Even Little John Baillio helped out.

"When Eddie died, Genore became more dependent on Phillip and Amy's help," says longtime coworker and friend Ann Fendick.

As she saw more and more of her neighbors, Genore felt increasingly bad about the their living conditions, particularly the dilapidated trailer home the couple was forced to live in with their baby boy and adopted teenage son.

Not long after Eddie's death, Genore lent the Skippers $8,000 to help them buy a better trailer. When Little Phillip's birthday came around, Genore sprang for a party at a pizza restaurant in Denham Springs, the biggest town in Livingston Parish. Because the Skippers didn't have a telephone, Genore gave Amy a key to her house so she could use the telephone.

Amy frequently used her neighbor's phone to call Genore at work to ask her to pick up things from the store, particularly food and diapers for Little Phillip. In addition to groceries and baby items, Genore sometimes gave the Skippers money for their utility bills, and she always bought gifts, especially birthday and Christmas gifts for Little Phillip.

She also named Phillip and Amy as beneficiaries on a $25,000 life insurance policy she had with the JCPenny Life Insurance Company. Genore had several insurance policies listing family members as beneficiaries. She also had one in Eddie's name. When Eddie died, she transferred the policy into her neighbors' names and continued to pay the $7.95 monthly premium. If something happened to her, Phillip and Amy would get a little money. It wasn't much, but it would help them take care of their baby. They were good neighbors and good friends.

It was typical Genore.

But behind Genore's back, and out of earshot of his wife, who genuinely liked Genore, Phillip Skipper referred to his neighbor as a "nigger whore."

Johnny Hoyt had a violent temper that he couldn't control. In November 1998, while at his father's house near Holden, Johnny got into a beef with his sister-in-law Jina Skipper. Like Johnny, Jina was a dope fiend. There is no telling what they argued about, but Johnny Hoyt got so mad at his wife's little sister that he punched her in the chest.

Even by the standards of Livingston Parish's white trash subculture, where beating up women is a tradition, sort of a rite of passage into manhood, Johnny's violent outburst against Jina—who died of a drug overdose a few years later—was enough for someone in the family to call the police. When sheriff's deputies arrived, they threw Johnny Hoyt in jail and charged him with one count of simple assault and one count of simple battery.

He later posted a $1,000 bond to get out of jail and then asked the state to pick up the tab for a defense lawyer. On his public defender worksheet, Hoyt listed his occupation as roofer and his monthly income as $2,050. For assets, he listed only his ten-year-old pickup truck. As for liabilities, he said he paid $250 a month for his rented trailer home, $400 a month for food, and $150 a month for utilities.

Hoyt eventually pleaded guilty and was sentenced to six months in the parish prison. The judge suspended the sentence and placed him on probation for two years. In Bubbaville, beating up your sister-in-law was bad, but it wasn't *that* bad.

Six months after the Livingston cops arrested Hoyt for knocking Jina Skipper around, they picked him up again and charged him with simple battery after he beat up someone else.

Nine months later, in March 2000, the Livingston Parish Sheriff's Office sent Deputy Bobby Dillion on a disturbance call—copspeak for a fight—at a house on Milton Road outside the small Livingston Parish town of Walker.

When Deputy Dillion arrived at the house, resident Vernon Pierson and his buddy, forty-three-year-old Donald Tibbitts, were there. Tibbitts was bleeding from a cut on his head and holding on to some busted ribs. To Deputy Dillion, Tibbitts seemed drunk or stoned or both. He said he lived on Milton Road but claimed not to know his own address and said he didn't have a telephone. Pierson also appeared to have suffered some injuries. His face was puffy and red and he complained of a broken nose, and, as the deputy observed, Pierson had the makings of one hell of a black eye.

Deputy Dillion called for an ambulance to take Tibbitts to the hospital to get his head injury checked out. While waiting for the medics to arrive, Dillion tried to find out what had happened. All Tibbitts and Pierson would say was that their neighbor Johnny Hoyt, who was also living on Milton Road at the time, came into Pierson's home and attacked both of them. Neither claimed to know why Hoyt had done it. Tibbitts said he wasn't sure what Hoyt had hit him with. Pierson said he thought Hoyt had clobbered him while clutching a roll of pennies in his hand.

Dillion went to a judge and got a pair of arrest warrants for Hoyt charging him with two counts of aggravated battery. The judge agreed with Dillion that under Louisiana law a roll of pennies constituted a dangerous weapon. Four days later, deputies picked Hoyt up at his home on Milton Road.

Meanwhile, Hoyt's young wife, Lisa, was entangled in her own legal troubles.

At 10:15 on the night of March 26, 2000, Livingston Parish Sheriff's Deputy Ken McMorris stopped Lisa Hoyt for running a stop sign as she turned off of Rodeo Drive

The front of the Hoyt trailer on LA 43. Ed Roberts was killed here.
Photo by Chuck Hustmyre

The comfortable home of Genore Guillory would be the site of her vicious murder. *Photo by Chuck Hustmyre*

John Baillio, Philip Skipper's "stepson." Taken shortly before his release from prison in 2005. *Photo by Chuck Hustmyre*

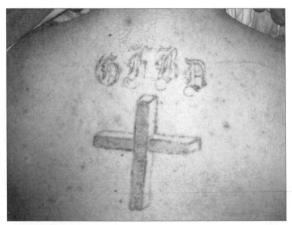

John Baillio's tattoo. GFBD stands for "God Forgives, the Brotherhood Doesn't." *Photo by Chuck Hustmyre*

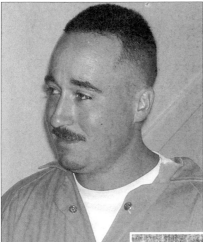

Johnny Hoyt, a founder of the Brotherhood. Everyone who knew him was scared of him.
Photo by Chuck Hustmyre

Lisa Skipper Hoyt, Johnny's wife and Philip's sister.
Courtesy of the East Feliciana Sheriff's Department

Philip Skipper's mug shot. He was Genore Guillory's neighbor and "friend"—until the day he killed her. *Courtesy of the East Feliciana Sheriff's Department*

Grave vaults at St. John's Cemetery. They were broken into and jewelry was stolen. *Photo by Chuck Hustmyre*

Detective Dennis Stewart displays the weapon
used to kill Ed Roberts.
Courtesy of Sgt. Dennis Stewart, Louisiana State Police

David Duke speaks at
a Klan rally in a country music
auditorium in Livingston Parish,
Louisiana.
Courtesy of James Minton

Detective Don McKey of the East Feliciana Sheriff's Department chased the killers of Genore Guillory for nearly five years. *Photo by Chuck Hustmyre*

Former Detective Joel Odom of the East Feliciana Sheriff's Department. *Photo by Chuck Hustmyre*

The 167-year-old Clinton courthouse where Johnny Hoyt, Philip Skipper, and Lisa Skipper Hoyt were finally convicted of Genore Guillory's murder.
Photo by Chuck Hustmyre

Mary Manhein, known to cops as the "Bone Lady," and director of LSU's FACES Lab. *Courtesy of Mary Manhein*

When Sam D'Aquilla was elected DA of East Feliciana Parish, he promised to prosecute the Guillory case. *Courtesy of Sam D'Aquilla*

onto Woodland Street in Denham Springs. In the passenger seat beside Lisa sat her seven-week-old daughter, Angel. Little Angel was the third child in the Hoyt brood—the couple also had five-year-old Little Johnny and four-year-old Little Cody—but Angel's paternity was subject to debate and remained an open, festering sore between Lisa and her husband.

When Deputy McMorris asked to see Lisa's driver's license, he found out that she didn't have one. The state had suspended it. McMorris got out his ticket book. Running a stop sign, no license plate light, no child safety seat, driving under suspension. The violations were piling up. But Lisa wasn't done. She couldn't stop running her mouth. Finally, sensing there was something else going on, McMorris asked where Lisa was coming from. Why had she been out so late at night with a two-month-old baby?

"I was buying crack for a friend of mine," Lisa said.

Buying crack for a friend.

McMorris must have thought he was hearing things. The deputy asked Lisa to step out of her vehicle. He patted her down and searched the car. He found two rocks of crack cocaine.

After arresting Lisa for felony drug possession, McMorris ran her name through the Sheriff's Office's computer system and discovered that she also had a warrant out for her arrest for two misdemeanors: simple assault and simple battery. Under Louisiana law, assault is threatening to use physical force against a person; battery is actually using it. The crimes are covered by two different statutes and thus are separate violations of the law. The adjective "simple" means that no weapons were used. Both crimes are misdemeanors and carry a maximum penalty of six months in jail and a $500 fine.

The charges stemmed from an argument Lisa had gotten into two weeks before with a female neighbor on Milton Road. Lisa decided to settle the dispute with blows instead of words. It seemed that like her husband, Lisa, too, had quite a temper.

Lisa's mother, Isabella Skipper, picked up Little Angel from the Sheriff's Office, and between Isabella and Johnny, the two of them managed to post a $50,000 appearance bond to get Lisa out of jail. She later pleaded guilty to the drug charge and got a six-month suspended sentence plus two years' probation. It was the same sentence Johnny got for beating up Lisa's sister.

Among his hobbies, Phillip Skipper liked to raise pit bulls. He traded them, he sold them, he fought them, he bet on them. Skipper had more than a dozen dogs, mostly pits, penned up at his trailer compound on Oakwood Lane. In the spring of 2000, one of his dogs, not a pit but one of his other mutts, was causing problems among his fighting dogs, so he asked Genore to keep it at her house. She agreed.

One day in May, the dog escaped from Genore's kennel and ran back home to Skipper's trailer. There, the mutt found a goat tied up in the yard. True Bubbas are very fond of what they consider to be exotic pets—boa constrictors, ferrets, chinchillas, mongooses . . . goats. For some reason, Phillip and Amy had recently picked up a goat as their newest "exotic" pet.

When the mutt came back home, he killed the goat.

Genore was at work and had no idea what had happened, but Amy blew a gasket when she saw the dead goat lying on the ground. Amy stormed over to Genore's house, used Genore's key to let herself in, used Genore's telephone to call her at work, and then proceeded to chew Genore's ass out.

After several minutes of listening to Amy Skipper rant and rave and curse at her, Genore was livid. She told Amy to leave the key behind and get out of her house. Friend and coworker Ann Fendick was there when Amy called. "I think it upset Genore that she had done so much for Amy and Phillip and their child and to have them act so ugly about the goat and dog incident," she says.

Of all those who've heard about the goat incident, John Baillio alone claims the goat wasn't killed, only mauled. He says that after the dog attacked the goat, Phillip told him to catch the dog and bring it back to their trailer home so they could punish it. Acting on Phillip's instructions, Baillio says he threw the dog into a pen with a pit bull and let the pit chew on the mutt for a while. Then he let the mutt out of the pen and watched as it hobbled back to Genore's house. He says Phillip did it to upset Genore.

From Genore's point of view, the friendship she'd shared over the last couple of years with Phillip and Amy Skipper was over. That meant no more parties, no more gifts, no more money, no more trips to the store for diapers and baby food on the way home from work, no more key to her house, no more free telephone, and no more life insurance policy.

In Genore's mind, it was finished. And she was right. The friendship was finished. What she didn't know, what she had no way of knowing, was that something else was just beginning.

TWENTY-ONE

At about the same time that the mutt escaped from Genore's dog kennel and was either killing or mangling the Skippers' pet goat, Johnny Hoyt and Phillip Skipper decided to take young Baillio on a ride to the House of Pain in Ponchatoula. It was time to man up and join the club, time to become a member of The Brotherhood.

At the tattoo parlor, Hoyt and Skipper watched like proud papas as the tattoo artist/methamphetamine cook, inked a three-dimensional wooden cross between the fifteen-year-old's shoulder blades and etched the letters G.F.B.D. in gothic print across the top of it. The tattoo man also put the image of a pit bull on the inside of Baillio's right forearm.

When the tattoos were finished, Hoyt and Skipper looked approvingly at the fresh ink on John Baillio's back. They saw their matching tattoos as symbols of their bond with one another, of their faith in one another, and of their loyalty to one another. As members of The Brotherhood, they were inseparable and unbreakable. At least that's what they hoped.

Baillio was proud, too. He finally felt like he belonged

somewhere, to something, and to someone. Other than this fledgling racist gang, the teenager had no one else. His mom hadn't been able to control him and had, in essence, given him to a neighborhood friend. His grandmother, whom he adored, was in prison for vehicular homicide. For John Baillio, Phillip Skipper, for all of his problems, his rage, and his abuses, was it, the only parental figure in the boy's entire fucked-up life.

So with inked symbols in place, the three founding members of The Brotherhood piled into Phillip's green Ford pickup truck and headed back to Clinton. They had business to take care of, business that carried with it the near certainty of making some real money.

*Johnny Hoyt wasn't as lazy as his one-lung brother-*in-law, Phillip Skipper. Hoyt worked part-time for a roofing contractor, hauling fifty-pound stacks of shingles up a ladder in the sweltering south Louisiana heat. John Baillio sometimes worked with him. Baillio would do almost anything to get a break from Skipper's sexual assaults.

Skipper on the other hand was a wannabe quick-buck artist. He got a monthly Social Security check from the government and listed his occupation as disabled. The only work he ever really performed was diddling around Genore Guillory's house, taking his time cutting her grass and feeding her animals. The rest of the time he spent trying to figure out ways to scam money.

One day as he drove his pickup truck along Rist Road, just before turning onto Oakwood Lane, Skipper rumbled past a cemetery and it suddenly occurred to him that the dead might have more than the living. In their grief, people often buried deceased family and friends with gifts and expensive jewelry. A cemetery might literally be a gold mine. All any enterprising soul had to do was simply pluck the gold from the ground.

The cemetery sat on the east side of Rist Road a quarter mile from Louisiana Highway 961, a thinly traveled two-lane blacktop. The cemetery backed up to a patch of woods and, beyond that, to a strip of water called Sandy Creek. There were a few dozen graves, mostly of the cement vault type, inside a chain-link fence with an open gate.

Rist Road itself was a half-dirt, half-gravel trail that wound its way in a generally northerly direction through piney woods and pastureland for three or four miles until it butted up against Highway 67. There were few homes and no lights. At night it was pitch dark.

According to John Baillio, one night Skipper and a friend crept down Rist Road to the cemetery. They carried a shovel and a couple of prybars. Grave vaults are cement liners placed in the ground. The vaults are buried so that the open tops are level with the surface. Once a casket is lowered into them, a heavy cement lid is placed on top of the vault, sealing it, presumably for eternity.

Unless someone attacks it with a prybar.

Phillip Skipper and his friend did just that. Baillio said they muscled open the lids of several vaults and then reached down inside them and pried off the lids of the caskets underneath. Among the decomposed remains they found watches, rings, and necklaces. When they forced open the mouths of the corpses, they discovered gold teeth. They took those, too.

The raid on the Rist Road Cemetery wasn't a huge financial boon—there weren't enough graves, and besides, it was hard work—but it was successful in the sense that it opened up a whole new revenue stream for the usually cash-strapped Phillip Skipper, and he was eager to share his new moneymaking scheme with the other members of his skinhead brotherhood.

Not long after Skipper's midnight foray to the graveyard on Rist Road, he took another aspiring Brotherhood member, a young guy everyone called Junior, on a nocturnal visit to the St. John Baptist Church Cemetery on Gilead Road, Baillio says. Like the cemetery on Rist Road, the one at St. John was deep in the woods, about two miles behind Slaton's General Store on Highway 10, just east of Clinton. You had to look hard just to find it.

The main building at St. John Baptist was a single-story, rectangular, red brick church with a high peaked roof running the length of the building and an imitation bell tower built over the main door. The long axis of the church ran perpendicular to the street. To the left, a sheet metal building with a brick facade served as a Bible school. To the right, about fifty feet away from the main building, stood a whitewashed brick storage room.

Behind the church was a cemetery holding dozens of graves, mostly burial vaults. A fence across the front of the cemetery was designed to keep out cars, not people.

Skipper and Junior used crowbars to unseat the lids from two or three of the vaults and then broke open the caskets. Inside they found a valuable collection of jewelry, including an ornate mother's ring wedged tightly onto the finger of a dead woman.

As the two grave robbers went about their grim task, they discovered that some of the vaults were flooded. They needed something to get the water out. Skipper eyed the nearby storage shed. He broke in and found a sump pump, but couldn't figure out a way to power it. He stole it anyway, along with a couple of weed eaters.

Before they left, Skipper and Junior replaced the vault lids so that they did not appear to have been disturbed. A rash of grave robberies was bound to attract the attention of the authorities. There was nothing to be done about the storage building—Skipper had caused some damage getting into it—or the missing equipment, but that would likely be written off as a simple burglary.

Back at home, Skipper and his grave-robbing partner separated their loot by type. Gold in one pile, silver in another. They pried the stones from the jewelry and formed a third pile. Then they dropped each of the precious metals into a steel cooking pot and blasted the bottom with a blowtorch until it got so hot the jewelry melted. A few days later they sold the two lumps of melted metal and the stones to a pawnshop operator. Apparently in Bubbaville, no one was too interested in questioning where a broke loser like Phillip Skipper managed to put his hands on shapeless lumps of melted gold and silver.

The only thing that didn't go into the homemade smelter was the mother's ring. Phillip decided to keep it, perhaps to give to his darling wife, Amy.

Grave robbery was dirty, disgusting work at best, but it wasn't the only work available to Phillip Skipper and the boys in the piney woods. Although not as daring, or as gruesome as digging up dead bodies and stripping them of their valuables, there was another way to make money from rural churches: straight-up burglary. The trip to St. John's had given the ever resourceful Skipper a new idea.

The landscape of the Florida Parishes is dotted with rural churches. Many of them are so far out in the sticks that it would take the cops half an hour just to get there if someone set an alarm off. Most rural churches don't even have alarms. At night there's no one there. There was almost no risk.

In the early summer of 2000, Skipper broached the subject with Hoyt. When they couldn't rob graves, they'd burglarize churches. Hoyt liked the idea. He also had a place in mind. It was a rural church on Highway 961, not far from Skipper's trailer. Hoyt had recently done some roofing work there and knew the schedule of the church's services and other activities. He also knew how far away the pastor lived.

Skipper brought Baillio along to help. Baillio said they smashed out a window in the back of the church and climbed through. They looted the church of a public address system, an amplifier, and a drum set. Some of the stuff was so bulky the thieves had to stash it outside the church and come back to pick it up the next night.

Not long after the church burglary, Junior got picked up by the police and thrown in jail. Skipper got nervous. He was worried his buddy might rat on him, the secret code of The Brotherhood notwithstanding. Besides, Junior wasn't even a full-fledged, tattoo-sporting member of The Brotherhood, so there was no telling how much the others could count on his silence. Skipper chucked the mother's ring he'd pulled from the dead woman's finger at St. John Cemetery into the Amite River. He also ordered his "stepson" to cut up the drum set and throw it, the PA system, and the amplifier into the river as well.

TWENTY-TWO

On Saturday afternoon, June 24, Phillip Skipper and John Baillio drove Skipper's pickup truck to Johnny and Lisa Hoyt's rented single-wide trailer on Highway 43 in St. Helena Parish, just north of the Livingston Parish line. When they arrived, Hoyt had bad news for them. That morning, he'd found their first pit bull, the female pit that had gotten them all into dogfighting, dead on the highway. A car had run her over. The news was hard to take. Those dogs were their life. Each of the three Brotherhood members bore a huge tattoo of a pit bull somewhere on his body. Skipper and Baillio helped Hoyt bury the dog, and then the three of them grieved in true Bubba fashion, by drinking whiskey and smoking weed. They also popped a couple of Valiums each.

After the doggie wake and after everyone was good and fucked-up, Hoyt decided to go over to the Skippers' place for a visit. That way they could keep the party going. Hoyt piled his three kids, the Little brood—Little Johnny, Little Cody, and Little Angel—into the cab of his brother-in-law's truck. Then he, Lisa, and John Baillio crawled into the open bed of the pickup with a bottle of whiskey and a couple more joints.

During the ride to Clinton, Hoyt decided to have some fun. He pulled out a long-barreled .22-caliber revolver, chrome plated with wooden grips, and started firing it from the back of Skipper's moving truck. Fueled up with weed, whiskey, and Valium, Hoyt took potshots at anything that struck his fancy—road signs, trees, whatever.

Hoyt looked over at Baillio. "How would you like to kill a nigger?"

Baillio thought he was probably joking, although with Hoyt it was hard to tell. "Sure," he said. "Sounds good to me."

"No, I'm serious," Hoyt said. "We're going to kill a nigger."

Lisa Hoyt shook her head. "Shut up, Johnny."

But Hoyt kept on shooting and talking about the killing they were going to do.

It was dark by the time they got to the Skippers' trailer in Clinton, and Hoyt and Baillio had smoked all the weed and nearly polished off the whiskey. Baillio didn't feel too good. When he stood up to climb down from the truck, he toppled over the side and crashed to the ground. He was so drunk and stoned the fall didn't even hurt. It made him laugh. A few minutes later, as he struggled to stand, he threw up next to Skipper's truck.

"I gotta go to bed," Baillio told the others.

He disappeared into the Skippers' trailer and crashed on the sofa. Within minutes he passed out.

Sometime after midnight, Hoyt shook Baillio awake. "It's time to earn that tattoo on your back."

Lisa sat across the room stuffing marijuana into a cigar wrapper.

As Baillio shook his head to clear it, Phillip walked into the darkened room carrying a MacGregor baseball bat made of silver aluminum.

"What's going on?" Baillio asked.

"We're going to kill that nigger across the street," Hoyt said. He clutched the .22 revolver in one hand. "And you're going to help us."

Baillio sat up. He looked at his feet. He still had his shoes on. He'd been so drunk when he got home he'd forgotten about them.

"Take your shoes off so you don't leave no footprints and let's go," Hoyt said.

They filed out the door quietly, careful not to wake Amy or the trailer full of kids. Outside, Skipper handed Baillio a length of rope. "For the dog," he said. Baillio knew what dog he was talking about. Cleo. The vicious tan chow. Miss G, Skipper, and Baillio were the only people who could even get close to that dog without getting bit.

As they walked across the gravel road, Baillio looked at Johnny's feet. He had them jammed into a pair of white high-top Reebok sneakers that were a couple of sizes too small. Baillio recognized the shoes. They belonged to Phillip and Lisa's mom, Isabella.

Why in the hell would he be wearing Isabella's shoes? Baillio wondered.

As they drew near Genore's house, Phillip explained what was going to happen. Baillio just nodded. He knew not to argue with Phillip. To challenge anything Phillip said always resulted in a beating, sometimes worse. Sometimes cigarette burns, sometimes rape.

All the lights were off inside Genore's house. Baillio guessed it was close to two o'clock. Lisa walked up the short flight of wooden steps to the side door and knocked. Baillio and Skipper crouched out of sight on either side of the steps. Hoyt stood a few feet away, hidden around the front corner of the house. Lisa knocked again. Baillio saw the glint of steel in her hand. She was holding a knife. The faint glow from an interior light suddenly shone across the backyard. Genore had turned on a light in her bedroom.

Inside the house a dog barked. Baillio looped the end of the rope into a noose.

A moment later the carport light flashed on. Then the solid wooden door opened just a crack. Genore's face appeared through it. She looked surprised.

A second later, the door opened the rest of the way. Genore stood in the doorway dressed in a green slip-on nightshirt, her thick black hair a tangled mess. It was obvious she'd been asleep. Her face showed surprise. "Lisa?" she said. Cleo's snout poked out from behind her legs. The dog growled.

Lisa spoke quickly, nervously, her words tripping over each other. "I need money for some diapers for the baby."

Genore blinked her eyes open. She looked groggy. "Your baby or Amy's baby?"

Hoyt stepped around the corner and approached Lisa, strolling casually as if he'd been just a minute or so behind her and was just now catching up. Cleo let out a menacing bark.

Lisa glanced at her husband then turned back to Genore. "Both."

Genore hesitated. Some type of internal alarm, some base instinct must have been ringing inside her head. Money for diapers at 2:00 a.m.? Where were Lisa and Amy going to find diapers this late, or this early, depending on your perspective?

"Okay," Genore said. "Just a second."

Hoyt reached the top of the steps. Just as Genore began to turn away, he stepped in close and punched her hard in the face. Genore staggered backward. Phillip Skipper and John Baillio sprang from their hiding places and rushed up the wooden steps. Cleo lunged at them, but Baillio grabbed a handful of the chow's thick mane and lifted its forelegs off the ground. With his other hand, Baillio slipped a noose around the dog's neck and cinched it tight. As Cleo's front paws thrashed the air, the dog's nails dug into Baillio's and Skipper's arms.

To Genore, the situation may have had a certain dream-like quality, perhaps even a temporarily paralyzing effect. Here was her neighbor's sister, Lisa, knocking on her door at two o'clock in the morning asking for diaper money. Here was Lisa's husband, Johnny, popping out of nowhere and punching her in the face. And here was her neighbor, Phillip, and his adopted son, Little John, stringing her dog Cleo up by the neck.

What in the hell could possibly be going on here?

If Genore was paralyzed, it could not have lasted more than an instant because almost as soon as Hoyt's punch crashed against her face, instinct took over. Standing before her was a threat. She may not have understood why it was there, but she surely understood that she was suddenly and unexpectedly facing very real danger. Fight or flight. Nature's most basic survival instinct.

In front of her stood a woman, a teenage boy, and two grown men, one suddenly holding a bat. Fighting was out of the question. Genore turned and ran.

From behind her came a sharp popping sound, like a small string of firecrackers going off. It was Hoyt opening fire with the .22-caliber revolver he'd brought from the Skippers' trailer. One of Hoyt's bullets hit Genore in the upper right portion of her back and blew apart her shoulder joint. Another struck the left side of her butt.

Genore must have sensed that the close confines of her house were a death trap. Just a few steps away stood the locked front door. A set of keys hung from the deadbolt. When Genore reached the front door, she stopped and tried to open it. She fumbled with the keys, but before she could get the lock to turn, Hoyt was on her, slamming his fist into her face and head. Genore broke free and ran again, leaving her blood smeared across the door handle, the dead-bolt, and the keys.

She ran toward the kitchen. There was a telephone in there. Maybe she could reach the police. Maybe they could help her. As Hoyt chased after her, Phillip and Lisa scurried across the living room and into the hallway to cut her off. John Baillio followed behind Phillip and Lisa, struggling with Cleo and trying to keep the chow's front feet off the ground.

In the kitchen, Genore grabbed the handset for the old-fashioned wooden box phone mounted on the wall, but Hoyt knocked it out of her hand. He punched her again and again and clubbed her with the long-barreled .22 revolver in his hand. Genore spun away and tried to cover her face. She found herself standing in front of the kitchen utensil drawer. Inside were knives. She jerked the drawer open and reached inside, but Hoyt unleashed a torrent of blows that sent her staggering toward the hall. Her empty hand fell away from the drawer.

Genore stumbled into the hallway. Phillip and Lisa were already there. They stood between her and the living room. The only place left was her bedroom. Beside her bed was a telephone. Her last chance to call for help.

They chased her into the room. Genore grabbed the telephone from the nightstand with her left hand and turned to face them. Someone started shooting. Baillio says it was Lisa, that somehow she'd gotten the gun from her husband. More likely it was still Hoyt doing the shooting. One .22-caliber bullet tore completely through Genore's left ring finger. Another hit her left wrist. A third buried itself in her upper left arm. The telephone slipped from her hand. She was trapped.

They came at her like a pack of wild dogs. Her neighbor and handyman, Phillip Skipper, swinging his aluminum bat like Babe Ruth. Johnny Hoyt, slamming her with his fists. Lisa, a crazed look plastered on her face, stabbing her with a knife, the long blade biting deep, once, twice, three times, four times, five times, into Genore's chest and abdomen. Baillio standing in the doorway, holding Cleo's neck stretched as high as he could raise it.

Genore fell to the ground beside her bed. She was still conscious. Lisa stood over her, breathing hard. Through smashed and bloody lips, Genore gasped out one final plea. "Lisa, please make them stop."

Phillip dropped the bat and snatched a heavy lamp from the nightstand. He smashed the ceramic lamp base down on top of Genore's upturned face. Still, she wouldn't die. So Phillip picked up the bat once again and swung it as hard as he could at Genore's head. The blow landed just behind her left ear. It cracked her skull and severed her brain stem. Finally, she was dead.

"She fought all the way to the end," John Baillio says.

Lisa started laughing, cackling really, as she ransacked Genore's jewelry box and dresser for valuables. She took Genore's pearl collection, some gold chains, the diamond engagement ring Eddie had given her, a gold earring collection, and Genore's graduation ring from the Eunice High School class of 1975.

"It was crazy," Baillio recalls as he describes the gruesome scene. "It was supposed to be my initiation into The Brotherhood."

Then, according to Baillio, Skipper and Hoyt, took turns raping Genore's dead body.

Baillio claims he didn't take part in the rape. He says he just held the dog. He says Skipper and Hoyt wore condoms. Skipper later bragged to a friend that he injected semen he got from a black man into Genore's vagina to "throw the cops off." Baillio says he doesn't remember Skipper doing that. He says Lisa stood and watched while her husband and brother raped her dead friend. Every once in a while she would laugh. At one point, Baillio heard Lisa say, "I never thought it would be this much fun to kill somebody."

On the way out of Genore's house, Baillio tied Cleo to the step railing outside the side door. Then the four murderers walked home in silence.

Back at the Skippers' trailer, they took their bloody clothes off and hid them in a junked school bus on the property. Skipper washed off the baseball bat and stashed it in an old car behind his trailer. Then they went inside to get drunker and more stoned.

TWENTY-THREE

The next morning, Isabella Skipper, Phillip and Lisa's fifty-three-year-old mother, showed up for a Sunday visit. She worked as an attendant at a nursing home and had gotten off work at 6:00 a.m. Friday. She didn't have to be back at work until 6:00 p.m. Monday. Isabella played with her grandchildren and chatted with her son and daughter and their spouses.

Across the road, everything remained quiet at Genore's house.

Later that day, Phillip, Johnny, Lisa, John Baillio, and Isabella climbed into Phillip's truck and went to Isabella's house on Sallie Kinchen Road in Tangipahoa Parish. Before Isabella had moved into the house, Johnny and Lisa used to live in it and they still had an old freezer stored there. Isabella says they loaded the freezer into Phillip's truck and hauled it to Johnny and Lisa's trailer in St. Helena Parish.

Years later, Isabella claimed that they moved the freezer on Saturday afternoon—before Genore's murder—but

John Baillio clearly remembers that Isabella arrived at the Skippers' on Sunday morning, and that they moved a kitchen appliance—he recalls moving a stove—to the Hoyts' trailer in St. Helena Parish that afternoon, the day after they murdered Genore. What no one disputes is that Phillip dropped the Hoyts off at their trailer Sunday afternoon and that Isabella spent Sunday night at Phillip and Lisa's. Isabella later admitted that her white Reebok sneakers were missing that weekend and that she never found them.

Monday morning, when Genore didn't show up for work, her coworkers got worried about her. They called, but the line was busy. According to a telephone company operator the phone was either out of service or off the hook. At ten o'clock, Genore's friend Ann Fendick called the East Feliciana Sheriff's Department and asked them to check on her.

*Deputy Ronald Johnson was patrolling on U.S. High-*way 61 in the far southwest corner of East Feliciana Parish when he got the call from the Sheriff's Department dispatcher. It was a welfare check. A woman named Genore Guillory hadn't shown up for work at her office in Baton Rouge. Her coworkers were worried. The dispatcher told Johnson to check it out. It was 10:05 a.m.

Johnson had been on welfare checks before. There was almost never anything to them. Someone was running late. Someone didn't call in on time. Someone partied a little too hard over the weekend and couldn't make it in to work. On a Monday morning that was very likely to be the situation.

The address was 11856 Oakwood Lane in Clinton, but Johnson knew the location was really several miles past Clinton to the northeast. A good twenty-mile drive for him. Odds were the lady would show up at work or call in before Johnson even got to her house, but still he pushed the accelerator down on his Jeep Cherokee so it wouldn't take all morning to get there.

Oakwood Lane runs off of Rist Road. Rist is mostly dirt—mud when it rains—with a smattering of gravel to give it just a bit of traction. It meanders through woodland and cow pastures between two blacktop highways, Louisiana Highway 67 and Louisiana Highway 961.

Midway between the two highways, Oakwood Lane branches off and angles to the east for about half a mile. Oakwood is a narrow dead-end gravel road with more rocks and less dirt then Rist.

When he turned onto Oakwood Lane, Deputy Johnson started scanning the mailboxes, looking for Genore Guillory's address. As he got near the end of the lane, Johnson spotted the number on a mailbox near an old mobile home on the south side of the road. Outside the mobile home a small child chugged around on a tricycle. The deputy pulled his patrol vehicle into the driveway and watched the kid scurry inside.

There was nothing to this welfare check, Johnson thought. The people were home. Probably just a bad telephone line.

There was a second trailer on the property, also a run-down camper parked close to the main trailer, and an old school bus. There were a couple of other junked cars around and a dilapidated storage shed that was halfway attached to the main trailer. The yard was strewn with trash.

A man stepped through the door of the big trailer. He took a step or two down then stopped. He was skinny, early twenties, with a shaved head and a goatee. He had a bunch of tattoos. A short, dark-haired woman stood in the doorway behind him.

"Is this the Guillory residence?" Johnson shouted through the open window of his cruiser.

The man shook his head and pointed across the street. "That's her house over there."

Johnson nodded. "Thanks." He gave the couple a long look then put his Jeep in reverse and backed out of their driveway.

When Deputy Johnson pulled into the gravel driveway across the street, he crossed into a different world. The contrast between the Guillory residence and the trailer and junkyard combo across from it was like night and day. Ms. Guillory's house was a raised, wood-framed, two-story Acadian-style home with dark wooden siding and an attached carport. The house sat on several acres of well-manicured property.

A small Toyota pickup was parked near the house. A dark Toyota Camry sat just behind it. No grass grew around the vehicles and they appeared to Johnson to be in running condition. Behind the house was a dog kennel holding at least a couple dozen barking dogs. Stacks of bagged dog food and bales of hay stood under the carport. The house looked neat, lived in, and had the feel of a working ranch or maybe a home for wayward animals.

From his Jeep, Johnson could see a short set of wooden steps leading up from the carport to a side door. The door was wide open. Wooden railings ran along both sides of the steps.

With several cars at the house and the side door open, Johnson was sure someone was home. He tapped his hand against the horn of his patrol car a couple of times. Then he waited.

The dogs kept barking but no one came outside.

She's probably out on the property, Johnson thought.

He flipped on his police lights and tooted his siren.

No response from the house or the property. Johnson waited. He'd been a sheriff's deputy for more than a decade. His instincts were telling him that something wasn't right.

He hit the siren again, this time giving it a long yelp.

Nothing.

The house in front of Johnson sat dark and still. No sound came from it, no movement could he see inside it. The whole place was eerily silent except for the barking of the dogs in the kennel behind the house.

Deputy Johnson started to tense up.

He radioed the dispatcher and told her he had an open door at the house and no one was responding. "Something might be wrong," Johnson said. "I'm going to take a look."

Just across the street, Deputy Johnson saw the couple from the trailer peeking through the bushes that ran along the front edge of their property.

Johnson stepped out of his Jeep. He approached the open side door, stepping lightly. It was a beautiful Monday morning, the sky bright, with no hint of the storm that was brewing for later that afternoon. The temperature was warm. With the vehicles still parked outside and the house standing open, it seemed like a great day to skip work and get in some spring cleaning.

Everything here will turn out fine, Johnson told himself.

But his gut was saying something else. Despite the beauty of the morning, despite the warm sun shining down on him, Johnson knew that everything wasn't fine. In fact, his gut was screaming at him that something was terribly wrong.

As Johnson neared the steps that led up to the open side door, a ball of snarling tan fur and teeth jumped out at him from under the steps. Johnson's heart leapt into his throat as he backpedaled away. He reached for his pistol, but a rope looped around the dog's neck and tied to the nearest step railing pulled the dog up short.

Johnson had to take a couple of deep breaths to steady his nerves. While he did, he looked at the dog. It was a tan chow with a thick mane of fur around its head. And it was vicious. It snarled as it strained to reach him. The sound the dog made, and the intensity with which it tried to reach him, terrified the deputy and forced him to retreat back to his Jeep to grab his flashlight.

The second time Johnson approached the house, the chow charged him again, but this time Johnson was prepared. He swung the flashlight over his head in wild exaggerated motions and took short, lunging steps at the dog. The chow backed off and scampered under the porch just long enough for Johnson to dash up the steps and slip through the open door.

Inside, the house was quiet. As he crossed the hardwood floor of the den, Johnson glanced briefly around the room. It had an old-fashioned feel.

Just inside the door, to his right, stood a six-foot-tall wooden display case. Behind the glass front were a dozen collectible dolls. A grandfather clock hung on one wall, while directly across from the door stood a floor-to-ceiling bookcase that spanned the entire wall. Books, figurines of horses, more dolls in elaborate dresses, and knickknacks covered its shelves. Rugs covered much of the space around the neatly arranged reproduction antique chairs and floor lamps.

The silence screamed at Johnson. To break it, he called out, "This is the Sheriff's Department. Is anyone home?" The house swallowed his words, leaving nothing but the silence.

Johnson crept toward the kitchen. He passed the front door. A set of keys hung from the deadbolt. Blood was smeared across the inside handle.

Deputy Johnson pulled his pistol.

The smell hit him as soon as he crossed into the kitchen. He tried to ignore it. He saw an old-time wooden box phone mounted to the wall next to the side-by-side refrigerator. The handset was off the hook. It dangled at the end of its cord, almost touching the floor. On the counter next to the sink, clean dishes were stacked in a large metal pot. More dishes stood piled in the right-hand side of the double sink. Beneath the kitchen counter, a drawer had been pulled open. Inside was a plastic tray packed with utensils.

A couple of knives were out of place, their ceramic handles smeared with blood. Another blood smear stood out against the rose-colored countertop.

The smell got stronger as Johnson pushed deeper into the house. It washed over him and turned his stomach. It choked him. Johnson knew what it was. He had smelled it once before, on a suicide call. It was a smell you never forgot. It was the smell of decaying human flesh. It was the smell of death.

TWENTY-FOUR

On Wednesday, June 28, just seventy-two hours after he helped slaughter Genore Guillory and rape her still warm corpse, Johnny Hoyt got busted by the Livingston Parish Sheriff's Office for one count of simple possession of marijuana. The charge, a misdemeanor under Louisiana law, indicated that the amount of marijuana was small enough that the police believed it was for personal use and not for sale.

Hoyt's booking photo, shot the day of his arrest, shows him staring steely-eyed and cocky into the camera. His sharply pointed goatee gives him a slightly demonic look.

Branded for life with letters that symbolized the motto "God Forgives, The Brotherhood Doesn't," a motto that served as an unambiguous warning to members of Hoyt's fledgling skinhead gang—a motto he himself selected— not to take any actions that might bring dishonor upon the gang. Hoyt saw himself, and certainly wanted to be seen by others, as a stand-up guy. Here was a guy who could be counted on not to crack under pressure.

Because cooperating with the police would clearly bring dishonor and discredit to the gang, any self-respecting tough guy like Hoyt could certainly be counted on to keep his mouth shut when confronted by the cops and to take his misdemeanor marijuana charge like a man. But he didn't.

Although Hoyt demanded absolute loyalty from everyone around him, and insisted that those closest to him tattoo themselves with a reminder that disloyalty would be neither forgotten nor forgiven, when he got caught by the cops, he squealed like a little girl.

Hoyt told Detective Stan Carpenter of the Livingston Parish Sheriff's Office about a guy named Little Jamie who drove loads of weed into Livingston Parish from Texas. Not long after Hoyt passed the information on to Carpenter, the cops stopped Little Jamie on the highway. According to Baillio, they knew right where he hid his dope—thanks to Hoyt. They pulled eight pounds of weed out of the car and threw Little Jamie in jail. Five pounds of that load was supposed to have been for The Brotherhood. In exchange for ratting out his own gang's supplier, the marijuana charge against Hoyt was dismissed. Detective Carpenter also promised Hoyt a cash reward.

As soon as word spread that Little Jamie had gotten popped and that the eight pounds of weed had been seized, everyone knew that someone had ratted. Hoyt blamed the bust on another local weed dealer named Eddie Roberts. Hoyt and Roberts had done business before, and Hoyt claimed that Roberts still owed him some money.

Just like legitimate markets worldwide, the illegal drug market is subject to the law of supply and demand. In the murky world of Livingston Parish dope peddlers, a guy could be your customer one week and your supplier the next. It depended on the amount of dope available and the vagaries of the police, on who got busted and who didn't, and on how much product the cops seized.

To be fair, Johnny Hoyt may not have snitched on Little

Jamie strictly to get out of a misdemeanor marijuana charge for which he was very unlikely to get any jail time. Cops know it, prosecutors know it: If you apply the right amount of pressure and offer the right deal, anyone will snitch.

Mafia hitman Sammy "The Bull" Gravano admitted to committing at least fifteen murders and still managed to get what amounted to a get-out-of-jail-free card from the feds because he helped put Gambino family crime boss John Gotti in prison for life.

In Hoyt's case, however, Detective Stan Carpenter didn't have much pressure to apply or much of a deal to offer. In Louisiana, simple possession of marijuana carries a maximum sentence of six months in jail and a $500 fine. Usually, the sentences, especially for a first offense, are a lot less, more along the lines of a "don't do it again" lecture from the judge, a few months of probation, and referral to a rehab program.

So Hoyt likely had other reasons for becoming an informant.

Besides helping themselves out of a criminal charge, people snitch for a lot of reasons, but mostly they boil down to variations or combinations of just a few: to make money, to get revenge, to eliminate their competition, and to curry favor with law enforcement. The latter is particularly helpful as a hedge against a snitch's own future arrests. Cops frequently go to bat for their informants to keep them out of jail, and often overlook a good informant's minor, and sometimes even major, transgressions.

A few days after the murder, and at the request of Genore's family, Phillip Skipper and John Baillio were cleaning up the bloody crime scene that they—unbeknownst to the Guillory family—had created. As they washed down the walls and pulled up the carpet in Genore's bedroom,

Baillio found a gun sight under her bed. It looked familiar. It looked like the rear sight from the .22 revolver they'd shot Genore with. Baillio showed it to Skipper.

"That's not from that gun," Skipper said.

"Where'd it come from then?"

"It's from Eddie Dixon's gun," Skipper said. "I was in here cleaning it one time and the sight popped off. I looked for it but never could find it."

Baillio knew Skipper was lying. He would never have been in Genore's bedroom cleaning a gun. She wouldn't have allowed it. But Baillio also knew better than to question Skipper.

Skipper held out his hand and Baillio dropped the sight into it.

Later that day they retrieved all of their bloody clothes from the junked school bus behind Skipper's trailer and brought them back over to Genore's. Behind her house they'd started a burn pile to get rid of the bloody carpet. Skipper and Baillio built a fire and then tossed their clothes and Isabella's blood-soaked sneakers into it.

A few days later, Skipper, Hoyt, and Baillio went on a canoeing and camping trip. As they drifted down the Amite River, they used a screwdriver to take apart the .22 revolver, then tossed the pieces into the water.

As unschooled and as unsophisticated as your average Bubba is in legal matters, particularly as they apply to criminal law, he's smart enough to know that no evidence means no case.

Just a couple of miles from Sallie Kinchen Road, west of the city of Hammond, stuck out in the middle of the woods at the end of a winding gravel road called Entropy, lies Gatlin Cemetery. The private cemetery dates back well over a hundred years and serves as a well-maintained final resting spot for at least seventy-five or eighty departed souls, all of whom are in some way loosely affiliated with the Gatlin family.

Going back several generations, a great uncle of John Baillio, a man named James S. Gatlin, who died in 1885, is buried there. Gatlin's grave site, marked with a faded white marble headstone and surrounded by an iron fence, occupies a place of honor at the back of the cemetery. Several more of Baillio's relatives are buried nearby.

On a hot night in early July 2000, half a dozen or so of the souls resting at Gatlin Cemetery had their rest disturbed.

Phillip Skipper had told Johnny Hoyt about his forays into rural boneyards and about the loot he was able to mine from the dead. Hoyt liked the idea. Hoyt liked any idea that had the potential to make him money and to keep him off of those hot rooftops.

A little more than a week after they murdered Genore Guillory, Phillip Skipper, John Baillio, Johnny Hoyt, Lisa Hoyt, Johnny Hoyt's "stepbrother" Little Ricky (who wasn't really related to Hoyt) rode dirt bikes and four-wheelers to Gatlin Cemetery in the middle of the night. They carried flashlights, crowbars, whiskey, and guns.

Like a band of ghouls, they attacked the graves with the crowbars and pried off the vault lids, Baillio says. Then they busted open the caskets and robbed the dead of everything they could take from them: rings, watches, necklaces, pendants, earrings, bracelets, souvenirs and mementos of any potential value, and gold and silver teeth.

Most of the vaults were sealed tightly enough to keep out the rainwater, but some weren't. Some had leaked. Baillio opened one grave and found the casket inside under water. When he reached down into the water and opened the casket, it flooded.

In another water-filled vault, Baillio and Little Ricky were struggling to lift the casket out when it slipped from Ricky's fingers. When the casket plunged back to the bot-

tom of the vault, it splashed rancid grave water all over
Baillio.

Some bodies smelled worse than others. Some were
dried up and looked like well-dressed mummies. Others
that had been in the ground longer had turned into skele-
tons, their burial clothes nothing but rags. Rings were the
hardest to take from the bodies. In one casket, Baillio spotted a ring he wanted and tried to pull it off the corpse's
hand, but the dead man's finger came off instead. Sitting
beside the open grave, Baillio had to work the rotten finger loose before he could get the ring off.

Most of the dead had died old, but not all of them. In one
grave, they found a young man with a caved-in skull. Baillio figured he must have died in a car wreck. By Baillio's
estimation they got about $2,500 in jewelry off of him.

As they moved from grave to grave, John Baillio, who
says he spent most of that night in a drunken stupor, clinging
to a Smith & Wesson .45-caliber semiautomatic pistol that
belonged to Johnny Hoyt, claims he threatened to kill Little
Ricky when he tried to open the grave of an infant girl.
Ricky, who may not have been as frightened by the threat as
Baillio thinks, shrugged it off and moved on to another
grave.

Eventually, Baillio sat down on a vault lid and took a
swig from his half-empty bottle of whiskey. He spent the
rest of his time in the cemetery that night staring through
bloodshot eyes at the dead end of Entropy Road, on the
lookout for cops or other interlopers. Years later, he swears
he would have shot anyone who came up the road.

"That whole night was just fucked-up," Baillio says.

The entire gang—Phillip Skipper, Johnny and Lisa
Hoyt, John Baillio, and the rest—do nothing but disgust
East Feliciana Parish Sheriff Talmadge Bunch. "They were
taking people's teeth and making necklaces out of them,"
he says.

Unlike Skipper's previous grave robberies, this time,

when he and the others carted their swag away from Gatlin Cemetery, they made no effort to hide that they'd been there. They left the tops off of the vaults they'd opened and the busted lids sprung wide on the caskets they'd robbed.

It was already the beginning of the end for The Brotherhood.

TWENTY-FIVE

On the afternoon of July 6, Johnny Hoyt showed up unexpectedly at Phillip Skipper's trailer. He met John Baillio in the yard. "I want you to go get me that forty-five," Hoyt told him. "I got some business I need to take care of. Somebody's been ratting on me."

Baillio wove his way through the piles of junk behind Skipper's trailer to an old pickup truck bedliner lying under some bushes. From beneath the liner he pulled out a black nylon case. It was about a foot long, padded, and had two strap handles and a zipper. Inside was the same blue steel .45-caliber pistol Baillio had had with him at Gatlin Cemetery and two fully loaded magazines.

After Baillio handed the case to Hoyt, Hoyt made a couple of telephone calls from his cell phone. About an hour later Little Ricky pulled up to the Skippers' trailer in Hoyt's white Chevy van. Johnny Hoyt climbed in the van and the two of them drove away.

• • •

Sometime during the afternoon of July 6, Lisa Hoyt ran into Eddie Roberts in the parking lot of the L&W Quick Stop in Holden. Lisa had walked over from Johnny Hoyt's grandmother's house, which was right next door to the Quick Stop. The L&W was a mom-and-pop convenience store with a couple of gas pumps outside. Roberts, decked out in a new pair of overalls and a new Harley-Davidson T-shirt that he'd just pulled the tag from, was pumping diesel into his pickup truck, a red Ford with an extended cab. When Roberts finished at the pump, he went inside to pay and to pick up a couple of things. Lisa followed him.

The forty-nine-year-old Roberts was a local marijuana dealer who also worked as a driver for a produce company. He pushed a delivery truck back and forth between Texas and Louisiana. In addition to legitimate produce, Roberts also hauled marijuana in from Texas.

When he wasn't working, Roberts hung around stores like the Quick Stop so people could find him. He was like the ice cream man for weed.

Roberts had recently gotten into a jam with his marijuana supplier when he ruined thirty pounds of weed the guy had sold him on credit by storing it in a leaky shed and letting it get wet during a storm. At somewhere around $1,000 a pound, it was a big financial hit for his supplier. After that, Roberts got cut back to just four of five pounds at a time. Because he didn't have much of a supply, he had to turn over what he had quickly so he could order more. He was hanging around the parking lot of the Quick Stop looking to make a deal.

Linda Stewart, who owned the L&W Quick Stop along with her husband, Wayne, saw Lisa Hoyt trailing Roberts around the store talking to him, but Stewart couldn't hear what they were saying. Lisa was twenty-one years old and attractive in a Bubba-girl sort of way. Roberts was pushing fifty. The two of them had gotten it on a few times when

Johnny wasn't around. It was true romance, Bubba style: pussy for pot.

Lisa had once confided to Johnny's "stepsister" Carrie Keen—who wasn't really Johnny's stepsister at all—that she had been a crack whore before she started dating Johnny and that he had "straightened" her out.

In the tangled web of Bubba relationships, which often resemble not so much family trees as they do family hedges, trying to figure out who really is related by blood or marriage can be a challenge. Carrie Keen's mother, Alice Young, who was also the mother of Ricky Young, aka Little Ricky, spent several years shacked up with Johnny Hoyt Sr.; and although the couple wasn't legally married, all of their children considered themselves siblings, which may explain why there were so many explanations of how Johnny Hoyt and Ricky Young were related. Some of their friends and relatives have described them as brothers, others as half brothers, still others as stepbrothers, and some as mere cousins, but the fact is that they weren't really related at all. And neither were Johnny Hoyt and Carrie Keen. They just thought of themselves as brother and sister.

Not long after Johnny and Lisa started dating, they ran into Carrie on Sally Kinchen Road. When Johnny gave Carrie a hug and a kiss, Lisa wanted to "jump on" her, meaning a cat fight—slapping, hair pulling, nail scratching—which is how Bubba-girls protect the sanctity of their relationships. Lisa calmed down as soon as Johnny explained that Carrie was his "sister."

Before Johnny and Lisa met in 1995, Lisa had been peddling her pussy for crack cocaine on Cafe Line Road, a notorious doper hangout that straddles the parish line between Livingston and Tangipahoa. A few years after Lisa got together with Johnny, she met Eddie Roberts and occasionally hooked up with him for much the same reason—sex for drugs. But Edwards started to like Lisa. He suggested that she ditch Johnny for him. He had a trailer a

few miles north in Roseland, in Tangipahoa Parish. Lisa
and the kids could move in.

Roberts already had a girlfriend living with him part-
time, but he'd recently confessed to a neighbor that he
wanted the woman to move out but didn't know how to tell
her. If Lisa and her brood moved in, it would certainly
bring matters to a head with his other girlfriend.

Johnny Hoyt knew about the affair his wife was having
with Eddie Roberts, and he'd come up with a plan to not
only end it but to profit from it.

In addition to selling weed and screwing other men's
wives, Eddie Roberts had another dangerous habit. He
usually carried a lot of cash on him, and he had a tendency
to flash it around. Rumor was that in addition to the thousand dollars or so he kept on him, Roberts had a zippered
bank bag in his truck with even more cash in it. He also
kept a stash of weed in his truck.

Roberts was no stranger to trouble, but he wasn't a violent man. His brother, John Roberts, had been murdered
back in the late 1980s after a stint at the Louisiana State
Penitentiary. While John had been in prison, someone told
him his wife was screwing someone else. When John got
out, he confronted the man but wound up dead.

According to Estelle Colkmire, who says she was Eddie
Roberts's stepmother but really wasn't, just a close friend
(another example of how in Bubbaville "step" relations are
rather vague), John Roberts's accused killer was arrested
but never prosecuted. "He got out of it," Colkmire says.
"They didn't do him nothing. If you got political pull in
Livingston Parish, you can kill and do what you want to."

Colkmire met Eddie Roberts through his brother and
liked him so much she started calling him her stepson. "He
was a fine fella," she says. "He liked to drink his beer and
have a good time, and if he could help anybody, he would
go out of his way to help them."

When Johnny and Lisa got home the night of July 6 to

the trailer they rented in St. Helena Parish, Johnny told Lisa that he wanted her to page Eddie Roberts. When Roberts called back, she was to tell him that she was ready to take him up on his offer. She was going to leave Johnny and move in with him.

Lisa was ready to do whatever Johnny said. Carrie Keen, Lisa's "sister-in-law," said Johnny regularly beat Lisa, and not always with just his fists. Once Keen had seen Johnny beating Lisa with a board and another time, while she was pregnant, with a coat hanger.

At about eight o'clock, Johnny called his brother Mark Hoyt and asked him to come pick up his kids for a while. Mark was at their grandmother's house, next door to the L&W Quick Stop. Mark had a small pickup truck but needed more room to haul Johnny's three kids around, so he borrowed his girlfriend's car, a dark blue, four-door Mercury Tracer, and drove north on Highway 43 past the town of Albany into St. Helena Parish. He picked up his brother's kids and brought them back to his grandmother's house in Holden.

After Mark and the kids left, Lisa paged Eddie Roberts several times. When he finally called back, she told him exactly what Johnny had told her to say. She asked Roberts to come get her and the kids that night. Johnny wasn't going to be home for a couple hours, she said. It was a perfect time for her to escape.

A short time later, Eddie Roberts pulled his Ford pickup into Hoyt's front yard. Johnny and Lisa lived in a shabby fourteen-by-sixty-five-foot trailer that sat about fifty feet from the east side of the highway. Scrub pine woods enclosed the right-hand side and back of their trailer. On the left side stood the remains of a dilapidated house. Discarded car parts and other odds and ends littered the yard. Someone had built a wooden deck with a set of steps outside the front door and another one at the back door. Johnny had a gas grill on the back deck.

When he saw headlights flash across the front of the trailer and heard Eddie's pickup truck, Johnny ducked inside a bedroom down the hall, just a few steps from the back door. He had his .45 automatic with him.

Eddie knocked on the front door and Lisa let him in. Stuffed inside Eddie's pocket was a small pistol. He had been selling marijuana to Hoyt for a while and knew his explosive temper. He also knew a thing or two about stealing other men's wives.

Lisa told Eddie that her clothes were packed in a bag and sitting on the back porch. She asked him to get it for her. As Lisa led Eddie down the narrow hallway, he may have been surprised that Lisa's kids weren't there, but if he asked about them, Lisa probably just told him the truth. They were staying at Johnny's grandmother's house.

Lisa opened the back door and Eddie stepped outside. As he bent down to grab Lisa's bag, Johnny Hoyt slipped out of the bedroom door and crept across the hall. He stepped through the open back door, the big blue steel pistol clutched in his hand and extended out in front of him. Eddie may have sensed something was wrong, because when he stood up with Lisa's bag in his hand he turned to look at her. Just then, a gunshot shattered the silence and a bullet blasted through Eddie's brain.

Lisa later described it to a friend this way: "My clothes hit the floor and the world went quiet for a couple of seconds. Then the body hit the floor. I never even heard the gunshot."

Hoyt pulled Roberts's pickup truck around behind the trailer and dragged his body off the back porch. Then Johnny and Lisa dumped Roberts facedown into the backseat of the extended cab.

Johnny got a bucket and a mop and washed the blood off the back deck. Then he made another call to his brother Mark. He told Mark to bring the kids back. He also told Mark to stop on the way and buy several gallons of gasoline.

Mark packed the kids into his girlfriend's four-door sedan and brought Little Ricky Young along with him. They stopped at the Junior Food Mart in Albany and filled up a gas can. Then they drove north on Highway 43 to Johnny's trailer. When Mark arrived, he set the gas can on the front porch and brought the kids inside.

Johnny took the gas can around back. Ricky followed him. In the backyard he saw a red Ford pickup. Ricky peeked inside. Stuffed down inside the backseat he saw a man's body. When Ricky climbed the steps to the trailer's back door, he noticed that the deck was soaking wet.

Everyone waited inside for Johnny. When he came in, he was bathed in sweat. Mark thought he looked shaken up.

"I need you to follow me," Johnny told Mark.

"Where are we going?" Mark asked.

"Over to the Big Gravel."

"Why?"

"Don't worry about it. Just follow me over there. When you see me pull off the road into the woods just stop and wait. I'll come out in a few minutes."

Johnny told Lisa to ride with Mark.

"What about me?" Ricky asked.

"You watch the kids," Johnny said.

Mark and Lisa got into his girlfriend's Mercury. A few minutes later, Johnny came bouncing around the side of his trailer in a red Ford pickup that Mark had never seen before.

They followed Johnny fifteen miles south on Louisiana 42 to Highway 442. They turned west and drove about four miles. Then they turned north onto Highway 441. Locals called the gravel-covered stretch of 441 that began at Highway 442 and ran up to the St. Helena Parish line the "Big Gravel." A paved portion of the highway continued north for a couple of miles past the parish line until it ended at the town of Montpelier.

Unlike most Louisiana highways, 441 is nearly arrow straight. There are no lights and few homes, mostly just trailers scattered among a sea of pine trees. It was a good place to dump a body.

An eighth of a mile past the parish line, Johnny turned off the road to the right and onto a thin dirt path hemmed in on both sides by trees and thick underbrush. About a hundred feet back he stopped next to an old dairy barn.

Out on the highway, Mark drove past the dirt path and turned around in a driveway. He eased back to a spot near where Johnny had turned off the road and coasted to a stop. He and Lisa sat in the car and waited.

Hoyt gave the inside of Roberts's truck a last-minute going over. He'd already taken Roberts's cash and marijuana and he'd found the little pistol in his former dope supplier's pocket. Hoyt slipped the fuel can out of the cab and then doused the interior of the truck and Eddie Roberts's body with gasoline. He soaked the outside of the driver's side door and then poured a trail of gas several yards down the dirt path toward the highway. He struck a match and tossed it on the ground.

The match ignited the gas, and the flames raced toward the pickup. When they reached the end of the trail, they scrambled up the door and rolled through the open window.

The air inside the pickup truck exploded in a giant *woosh* as flames erupted through the open windows and shot toward the sky.

Hoyt sprinted down the dirt path to the highway. He jumped into the waiting Mercury and he and his wife and his brother sped south.

TWENTY-SIX

Near midnight, July 6, 2000. Leland Vernon—his friends called him Lucky Vernon—was getting ready for bed when he heard an explosion outside his house. Seconds later, he heard a series of smaller explosions. Vernon stepped outside onto his front porch to see what was going on.

Vernon lived with his wife, Peggy, on Louisiana Highway 441, practically right on top of the line between St. Helena and Livingston parishes. The house sat on the Livingston side. Vernon's old dairy barn, across the highway and less than a hundred yards north, was on the St. Helena side.

Standing outside, Vernon looked northeast across the highway. The sky over the pine trees glowed orange. Fire. He thought it was his barn burning. It had only been two days since the Fourth of July. He worried that some late celebrant might have launched a bottle rocket and set his barn on fire. It hadn't rained in a while. The ground was dry. Vernon hoofed it down the highway toward the barn.

The old dairy barn sat back about a hundred feet off the highway at the end of a brush-choked dirt path. From the road, Vernon could see the flames through the brush. It had to be the barn that was on fire.

Only after he made it to the end of the path did Vernon discover that it wasn't his barn that was burning. It was a pickup truck. It sat right beside the barn, completely engulfed in flames.

Vernon raced back to his house and yelled for Peggy to call the fire department. Then he ran back to the barn. The flames spewing from the truck seared the nearby vegetation. There was a serious danger that the fire could spread. A spark could send his weather-beaten barn up in flames. Vernon grabbed an old garden hose and spun the tap on a spigot beside the barn. He got as close as he could to the burning truck and shot water on it. When he got too close, the heat pushed him back.

Bryan Dykes, fifty-three, the mayor of Montpelier, was at home asleep when the he got the call about the fire at Lucky Vernon's dairy barn. In addition to being town mayor, Dykes was also one of town's volunteer fireman. He also owned the local feed store. "The mayor does all kinds of things in a small town," Dykes says.

The mayor rolled out of bed and threw on his firefighting clothes. He drove the quarter mile or so to the fire station and within minutes was barreling through the night with the big truck, lights blazing and siren wailing.

Meanwhile, the Montpelier town marshal, sixty-six-year-old Gerald O'Malley, arrived on the scene. O'Malley had been elected by a majority of the town's 279 registered voters the year before, which meant he had had to tackle the Louisiana State University's Basic Police Training Academy in his mid-sixties. In addition to academic work, classes had included close-quarter combat, pistol marksmanship, felony traffic stop techniques, and a grueling physical fitness course.

When O'Malley beat his way through the brush and made it back to the dairy barn, the pickup rested on its rims, the heat from the fire having turned the tires into globs of melted goo. The interior of the cab was an inferno. Lucky Vernon's old hose had a dozen leaks and wasn't putting nearly enough water on the fire to do much damage to it.

O'Malley had seen this before. Three or four times recently along this same dark stretch of highway, car thieves, joyriders, whatever you wanted to call them, had run stolen cars off into the woods and set fire to them. The flames licked the cars clean of fingerprints and any of that fancy DNA evidence people were always talking about on the television. O'Malley knew of at least two other stolen vehicles that had been burned up on other highways not too far from Montpelier.

In the distance, a siren wailed. The town fire truck was lumbering closer.

Mayor Dykes had trouble getting the fire truck down the dirt path that led from the highway to the barn. By the time he and fireman Louis Warren finally made it to the barn and got a hose charged, the pickup truck was completely gutted. As they beat down the flames, the heat turned the water into steam, and a cloud of vapor swallowed the truck.

Vernon was just glad his old barn had survived. He no longer used it for dairy farming, but it was good for storage.

O'Malley, Dykes, and Vernon tried to peek inside the truck with flashlights, but the smoke was so thick they couldn't see anything. The only way to figure out what had happened was to wait until morning and run the truck's tag number. O'Malley or the State Police would contact the owner and find out when the truck had been stolen and where it was last seen.

It was sometime after midnight when tow truck driver Raymond Sibley made it to the scene. The fire department was still pouring water on the smoldering pickup. Sibley had driven over from Pine Grove, a speck on the map about ten miles from Montpelier. He owned Pine Grove Auto Parts, which, in addition to selling auto parts, operated as a gas station, convenience store, hardware store, mechanic shop, and junkyard.

Sibley was a burly man with thick, graying hair. He often wore a camouflaged baseball cap, and sometimes for close-up work, he perched a pair of reading glasses on the end of his nose. And he absolutely hated late night calls, especially for smelly, burned-up cars.

After the volunteer firemen finished drowning the pickup, Sibley pushed his flatbed tow truck through the tangle of brush and finally got it back beside Lucky Vernon's barn. Because of the way the pickup was pushed off into the bushes and the way Mayor Dykes had positioned his fire truck, Sibley couldn't get the right angle he needed to pull the burned-up truck onto the back of his tow rig. He had to wrap a chain around the pickup's axel and drag it out some. Then he hooked it up and winched it onto his flatbed.

While he stood on top of his flatbed making sure all his chains were set right, Sibley peeked inside the smoking cab of the pickup truck. The inside was a smoldering ruin. The thick smoke burned his eyes and forced him to look away. But he'd seen something in rear of the cab, a lump wedged onto the floorboard between the front and back seats.

"What's this back here?" he hollered.

Either Marshal O'Malley or Mayor Dykes yelled back, "It looks like the console melted."

Sibley wasn't sure who said it, but what he was sure about was that it was late and he wanted to get home. Whatever was inside the truck was ruined anyway. Besides, it wasn't his problem.

When Sibley reached Pine Grove, he drove past his shop on Louisiana Highway 16. Another mile down the road and he reached his house. There was no sense pulling into the shop and unloading the pickup. Very little of Sibley's business came from his tow service. He knew he wasn't going to get another call that night. He parked the flatbed in front of his house, and went inside, and climbed into bed.

The next morning, Raymond Sibley woke up and ate breakfast and drank some coffee. Around ten o'clock, he drove his truck to the shop. With his flatbed parked beside the blue sheet metal building that housed his mechanic shop, Sibley climbed up onto the back of the truck and unhooked the chain from the front axel of the burned pickup. Then he glanced inside the cab. With the smoke cleared away and the sun out, he could see clearly. And what he saw wedged between the front and back seats didn't look anything like a melted console. Not unless the truck had come with a set of bones.

"I thought someone had put a damn hog back there," Sibley recalls.

Then he saw the sole of a burned up leather shoe wrapped around the end of a long white bone. Sibley had grown up in the country. Hogs don't wear shoes.

He called the Sheriff's Office.

Leland Vernon woke up the morning after the fire and went to check on his barn. He found the area around the barn ringed off with bright yellow tape. Sheriff's deputies, state troopers, and lab technicians were scurrying all over the place. Overnight, Leland Vernon's old dairy barn had become a crime scene.

The man in charge of the scene and of the investigation was Louisiana State Police Detective Dennis Stewart.

Stewart was a hometown boy. He had grown up in St. Helena. In addition to knowing all the law enforcement officers in the parish, he also knew all the firemen. Stewart had served as a volunteer fireman in the town of Greensburg, the parish seat, for more than a dozen years. Shortly after Raymond Sibley reported the body he'd found in the backseat of the burned out pickup truck, St. Helena Parish Sheriff Ronald "Gun" Ficklin had called Dennis Stewart at home and woke him up. The sheriff asked Stewart to help with the investigation.

On the way to the crime scene, Stewart ran the truck's license plate and found that it was registered to Edward Roberts Jr., with an address in Springfield, Louisiana.

Although the body found in the backseat of the truck was burned beyond recognition—it looked like a gob of melted meat with bones sticking out of it—Edward Roberts's "stepmother," Estelle Colkmire, told the coroner later that day that Roberts had a steel plate in his right arm that ran from his elbow to his wrist, the result of an industrial accident years before when he'd worked at a plywood plant in the town of Tickfaw, in Tangipahoa Parish, just north of Hammond.

"That's the way they identified him and knowed that it was his body," Colkmire says.

That identification was later confirmed when the State Police Crime Lab matched the fingerprint impressions from two fingers, the left middle and ring fingers, which had been cut from the body during the autopsy, with fingerprints on file for Edward Roberts Jr., who had a criminal rap sheet stretching all the way back to the mid-1960s.

Also during the autopsy, State Police crime scene techs recovered a .45-caliber Winchester silvertip hollow-point bullet from inside the victim's skull. An analysis later determined that the bullet was fired from a gun barrel with six lands and grooves and a right-hand twist. One of the half dozen or so manufacturers of .45-caliber pistols with those characteristics was Smith & Wesson.

The investigation into the murder of a dope dealer, even a relatively harmless weed peddler like Eddie Roberts, is rarely easy. By the very nature of their chosen profession, dope dealers make enemies.

They sometimes short customers on how much product

they deliver to them—few dope fiends carry portable scales to ensure they're getting everything they pay for. That can piss people off.

Although they are ostensibly businesspeople, dope dealers are generally not the most financially responsible people in the world, and that means they sometimes "forget" to pay their suppliers. Again, a situation that can piss people off.

As they become more successful and sell more product, dealers have a tendency to horn in on other dealers' territory. It makes their competitors mad.

When dope dealers get arrested, they tend to rat on everyone they know. That definitely makes people mad.

Then there's the money. Dope dealing is an all-cash business. Dealers, as in the case of Eddie Roberts, carry cash, sometimes a lot of cash. They tend to flash it around. They buy expensive stuff. They usually stash their dope in their cars and in their homes. They don't call the police if they get ripped off.

Within the first few hours of his investigation, State Police Detective Dennis Stewart discovered that in the Roberts case, as in many homicide cases, there was also a romance angle, or at least a sex angle.

For the three months prior to his death, Eddie Roberts had been living on and off with a forty-five-year-old truck stop waitress named Rose Story. Before taking up with Roberts and more or less moving into his trailer home outside Roseland, just a few miles across the Tangipahoa Parish line from where his body was discovered, Rose had lived for twenty-three years with her husband, Larry. When Rose broke it to her husband that she was leaving him and going to shack up with Roberts, Larry hadn't taken the news all that well. Larry Story knew Eddie Roberts and knew where he lived.

To complicate matters further, the Storys had two grown sons, John and Matthew, who also knew Roberts. They knew what kind of vehicle he drove and where he lived. In fact, Roberts had recently bought a car for Matthew. Detective Stewart had to consider Larry Story and his two sons as possible suspects.

The night Roberts disappeared, Rose Story had worked the night shift at the truck stop. Roberts was supposed to call her that night. When he didn't, she got worried and paged him repeatedly until she got off at two the next morning. Rose caught a ride home after her shift and then called the truck stop to find out if Roberts had called or come by after she left. She was told he hadn't.

By early afternoon on July 7, just as Detective Stewart was beginning his investigation, a rumor spread among Roberts's friends and associates that he had been involved in a traffic accident. That evening, Rose, her son Matthew, and two friends went to Roberts's trailer and cleaned out his marijuana stash. They also took a scale, a pistol, a knife, and a cellular telephone. Matthew Story took the dope, weapons, and accessories to his father's house in Amite. Then he called his uncle for help. Later, Matthew and his uncle hid everything in the woods near the Tangipahoa River. Matthew later claimed he didn't know Roberts was dead and that he was just trying to protect him in case the cops searched his trailer.

By the night of July 7, everyone knew that Roberts had been murdered. The Bubba network was humming with speculation about who killed Roberts. Two months before his death, someone saw Roberts and another guy arguing. On the afternoon after the murder, someone saw that same guy cruising near the crime scene. A doper from Holden owed Roberts money. Instead of paying him, maybe the doper killed him. His supplier may have killed him over the $30,000 worth of weed Roberts let get wet.

Gossip swirls around every murder, particularly a dope-related murder, but the real break in the Roberts investigation came from the killers themselves. Johnny and Lisa Hoyt just couldn't keep their mouths shut.

TWENTY-SEVEN

Johnny and Mark Hoyt both worked for the same roofing contractor. The day after he killed Eddie Roberts, Johnny didn't show up for work. Later that afternoon he turned up at Mark's house and handed his younger brother the Smith & Wesson .45 pistol. "Do something with it," he said.

Mark recognized the pistol. Johnny had bought it about three months before for $100 from a guy who'd stolen it from a trailer in Walker. When Johnny bought it, the pistol was in good condition and came with a black nylon zippered case and a couple of spare magazines. Now the gun looked like someone had tried to burn it.

"What am I supposed to do with it?" Mark asked.

"Throw it in the river."

That night, Mark drove his truck down a logging trail toward a pond off of James Chapel Road near Holden, but he got stuck in the mud about four hundred yards from the road. He rocked his truck back and forth and tried to wedge branches and limbs under the trapped wheel, but he couldn't get enough traction to pull himself out. He tossed the .45 into a nearby mud hole and walked home. The next day his cousin helped him pull his truck out. Mark didn't mention the gun.

"Three can keep a secret if two are dead."

Benjamin Franklin is credited with saying it first. Then, more than a century and a half later, the Hell's Angels motorcycle gang decided they liked the axiom so much they adopted it as their official creed. The Sicilian Mafia has their own version. They call it *Omerta*, the code of silence. The U.S. War Department pounded the same message into the minds of Americans during World War II with the slogan "Loose lips sink ships."

The message is as simple as it is timeless. If you want to keep out of trouble, keep your mouth shut.

Evidently, Johnny and Lisa Hoyt had never heard of Ben Franklin, the Hell's Angels, the Sicilian Mafia, or maybe even World War II, because they couldn't stop talking.

Eddie Roberts's body was barely cooled off from the funeral pyre Hoyt set for him when Lisa told her best friend, Tonya Nienstedt, who lived next door to Hoyt's father in Holden, that she and her hubby had put a .45-caliber bullet through Roberts's brain and set him on fire. The way Lisa told it, she's the one who pulled the trigger. Lisa also told Tonya about the murder and rape of Genore Guillory and about robbing graves at Gatlin Cemetery. Lisa bragged that she'd pulled some cash from a corpse at the cemetery and that the money had crumbled into dust in her hand.

Tonya Nienstedt repeated Lisa's story to her brother and a cousin, both members of the wide-ranging Garrett clan. It wasn't long before a lot of people in Livingston Parish were talking about how Johnny and Lisa Hoyt had killed Eddie Roberts.

But it wasn't just Lisa who didn't get the Ben Franklin

memo about keeping quiet. Johnny was flapping his gums, too.

Not long after the Roberts murder, Johnny Hoyt was sitting on his dad's porch in Holden, hanging out with his drinking and weed-smoking buddies, kicking back shots of vodka and talking shit. Baillio was there and so was Hoyt's so-called stepbrother, Little Ricky. Phillip Skipper and another Hoyt brother named Earl were also there. Hoyt started bragging about killing Eddie Roberts. He said he did it because Roberts was about to turn snitch and rat on him. Hoyt didn't mention setting the truck on fire, but he claimed he'd killed Roberts up near the Big Gravel.

Little Ricky started telling people that he and Mark Hoyt had been there, too. Ricky claimed he had reached into Roberts's blown open skull and touched his brains. He touched them, he said, because he wanted to find out what brains felt like. Ricky didn't mention that what he'd really done was stay at Johnny's trailer and babysit his kids.

Lisa eventually heard that Little Ricky had been bragging about his part in Eddie Roberts's murder, and she wanted to set the record straight. It was she and Johnny who did it, Lisa told Johnny's "stepsister" Carrie Keen. Ricky hadn't even been there. According to Keen, Lisa told her that Roberts had it coming. "Ed was a thief and a nasty old perverted fat man who deserved to die," Lisa said.

Meanwhile, Johnny Hoyt admitted to a fellow dope dealer named Steven Johnson that he'd killed Roberts because he'd been trying to take Hoyt's wife and kids away from him. Later, when Johnson showed up at Hoyt's trailer with $1,200 he owed him for a pound of weed, Lisa confirmed that Johnny had killed Roberts over the affair she had with him.

Hoyt also confessed to roofing contractor Bejay Butters that Roberts had been trying to steal his wife. Butters had sold Hoyt the white Chevy van Little Ricky had picked

him up in at Phillip Skipper's house the day Hoyt got the
.45 pistol from John Baillio. Butters had also seen Hoyt
with the same pistol several times before that.

When the subject of the Roberts murder came up, Hoyt
posed a hypothetical question to Butters. "What would you
do if someone flirted with your wife and flashed a lot of
money and offered her a better life?" Then without waiting
for a reply, Hoyt answered his own question. "Kill him, put
the money in your pocket, and go on down the road."

Hoyt's bragging seemingly knew no bounds.

Fifteen-year-old Brok Hodges had been selling marijuana and methamphetamine for Hoyt for about a year,
maybe a year and a half. In the fall of 2000, Hoyt, Lisa,
Brok Hodges, and a couple other guys were sitting around
Hoyt's trailer snorting crank and smoking weed. Hoyt was
complaining that one of his dealers, a guy named Mike,
owed him money. "I'll send him and his family to hell before their time just like I sent Ed to hell before his time,"
Hoyt said.

Hodges asked Hoyt what he was talking about. Hoyt
told him he'd killed Eddie Roberts and burned his body inside his pickup truck. Hodges knew Roberts. He'd met him
a few months back at Hoyt's trailer. The three of them had
smoked some weed together.

Lisa, who was sitting with Hoyt as he described killing
Roberts, admitted that she had been there when it happened.

But Johnny Hoyt still wasn't done bragging.

He told Hodges about how he, Phillip Skipper, and Lisa
had murdered a black woman in Clinton. They shot her,
stabbed her, and beat her, Hoyt said, then added, "Phillip
raped that nigger bitch."

The Roberts murder was big news, and Mark Hoyt
wasn't happy that his brother had involved him in it. A few
days after the murder he confronted Johnny, demanding to

know why he'd killed Eddie Roberts, who everyone knew was Hoyt's marijuana supplier.

"He was hitting on my old lady and I dealt with it," Johnny said. He explained that he had told Lisa to invite Roberts over to their trailer. When Roberts got there, Johnny shot him. End of story.

With all the talk going on, it didn't take long before word filtered back to Detective Dennis Stewart that a lot of people knew about Eddie Roberts's murder. Stewart and St. Helena Sheriff's Detective Cade Blades, a retired State Police narcotics agent, started tracking down and interviewing anyone who'd been talking about it. Several of the people they interviewed admitted that they'd bought weed at one time or another from Eddie Roberts.

Not long after the murder, a rumor made the rounds that Roberts had been carrying five pounds of weed and $5,000 the night he was killed. A local dope dealer named Stacy Dale Stringer said he heard it was more than that. He claimed Phillip Skipper had confided to him that Roberts had been killed because he had twenty-three pounds of marijuana and $12,000 in cash in his truck that night.

In the early days of the investigation, almost everyone Dennis Stewart and Cade Blades talked to—members of the Garrett family, Linda and Wayne Stewart, who owned the Quick Stop, Tonya Nienstedt, and several of Hoyt's dope-dealing buddies—said they'd heard that Johnny and Lisa Hoyt had killed Eddie Roberts.

But rumor and innuendo don't lead to convictions and Dennis Stewart knew it. He and Cade Blades needed hard evidence that linked the Hoyts to the murder. Without it, they had no case.

On July 14, Cade Blades and St. Helena Chief Deputy Nat Williams paid Hoyt a visit at his tumbledown trailer on Louisiana Highway 43. Detective Stewart had checked with Eddie Roberts's pager company and gotten a list of all of the numbers that had appeared on his pager on July 6. Hoyt had paged him seven times that night.

As soon as Hoyt opened the trailer door, a cloud of marijuana smoke billowed out and engulfed the two St. Helena detectives. They pushed their way into the trailer and asked Hoyt for permission to conduct a search. Hoyt agreed and signed a consent-to-search form that Detective Blades pulled out of his briefcase.

Had Hoyt not signed the consent-to-search form, the detectives had enough probable cause, based on the odor of freshly burned marijuana, to secure the trailer and get a search warrant. Officially, Blades and Williams were just looking for marijuana and related paraphernalia. Unofficially, they were also looking for money and guns, specifically for a .45-caliber semiautomatic pistol, one whose barrel markings matched those from the bullet that had ripped through Eddie Roberts's head.

Surprisingly, Lisa helped the detectives find the marijuana. There was just under an ounce of it and she showed them right where it was. What she didn't show them, but what they found anyway, were Johnny's three sawed-off shotguns. They were hidden in the trailer's tiny laundry room, really an alcove off the kitchen just big enough to squeeze in an economy-sized washer and dryer. One of the shotguns was a single-shot 12-gauge with a sawed-off barrel and shoulder stock, wrapped in black electrical tape. Another was a Winchester model 1400 12-gauge with a partially obliterated serial number, also with a cut-down barrel and stock. The third gun was a 20-gauge, the serial number of which had also been scratched off.

Both federal and state law require that shotguns have a barrel length of at least eighteen inches and an overall length of not less than twenty-six inches. Those with dimensions less than that are not banned outright but are subject to a pile of restrictions and registration red tape. In the case of the federal statute, the law dates back to the 1930s, the era of gangsters like Al Capone, John Dillinger, and Baby Face Nelson, and was an attempt on the part of Congress to control the use of so-called gangster weapons, loosely defined as sawed-off shotguns and machine guns like the tommy gun.

The single-shot shotgun Blades and Williams found behind Hoyt's washing machine had the barrel chopped down to ten inches and had an overall length of nineteen inches. The Winchester had a fourteen-inch barrel and was twenty-four inches long overall. Both were clearly illegal. The 20-gauge had a nineteen-inch barrel and was twenty-six inches overall. It was legal.

The detectives arrested Hoyt on a state charge of possession of unregistered sawed-off shotguns in the hopes that getting him out of the way would be enough to loosen up Lisa's tongue. It was a good plan, but it didn't work. On subsequent visits that Blades and Stewart made to the Hoyts' trailer, Lisa was polite but unhelpful. She remained uncooperative even when the detectives threatened to throw her in jail and have her kids hauled away to foster homes.

The only link they had between Hoyt and Roberts, other than the eyewitness testimony that Lisa Hoyt had been talking to Roberts at the Quick Stop—no one could recall having actually seen Lisa get into Roberts's truck—was telephone company records revealing that Hoyt's telephone had been used to call both Roberts's telephone and his pager several times just before he disappeared.

On July 21, 2000, Stewart and Blades dragged Johnny Hoyt into an interrogation room at the St. Helena Sheriff's Office, where he was being held until he could arrange to bond out on the gun charges. The detectives confronted Hoyt about the repeated calls. Why had he paged Roberts seven times on the day he was murdered?

Hoyt was polite but not very helpful. He said he had met

Roberts about five months ago through Tonya Nienstedt, who lived next door to his father in Holden. Hoyt said his wife talked to Roberts on July 6 at the L&W Quick Stop. She was trying to score some weed from him. Roberts gave Lisa his pager number and told her to give him a call later.

That evening, Hoyt said, his wife paged Roberts several times. She was trying to get in touch with him to ask him to deliver some weed to her. Roberts called back once, but the connection was bad. He and Lisa couldn't understand each other. Roberts didn't call back. Hoyt denied ever buying marijuana from Roberts, but he admitted he knew that Roberts sold weed in the Holden area.

Stewart asked Hoyt why he hadn't picked up his snitch money from Detective Carpenter in Livingston Parish on July 7, the day Roberts's body was discovered. Stewart found out from Carpenter that Hoyt had called him on July 6, before Roberts went missing, to ask him if he had any money for him for the marijuana bust he'd helped orchestrate. Carpenter told him to come by the next day. He said he'd give Hoyt $100 or $150 for the case. Hoyt never showed up.

Now why would a broke-dick bastard like Johnny Hoyt not jump at the chance to pick up a yard, maybe even a yard and a half of cash? the detectives wanted to know.

The reason he didn't show up to get the money, Hoyt said, was because he was busy and just didn't get around to it.

Bullshit.

A more likely reason, the detectives believed, was that Hoyt didn't feel comfortable walking into a police station the day after he'd blown a guy's head off and set his body on fire. The problem Stewart and Blades had, though, was that they didn't have any evidence to support charging Hoyt with murder. They knew it and Hoyt knew it.

What about the sawed-off shotguns?

Hoyt said he'd gotten all three shotguns that month from his brother-in-law, Phillip Skipper. Skipper, he said, lived in a trailer on a gravel road outside Clinton.

"Does he have any more guns?" Stewart asked.

"I don't know," Hoyt said. "Maybe."

TWENTY-EIGHT

A couple of days later, Dennis Stewart, Cade Blades, and two ATF agents visited Skipper's trailer. Skipper claimed he knew about his brother-in-law's sawed-off shotguns but denied giving them to him. The two ATF agents asked Skipper if they could take a look around his home.

Skipper signed a consent-to-search form.

The ATF agents found a pair of shotguns, both legal, although one of the agents later noted in his report that one of shotguns was wrapped in black electrical tape just like one of the guns taken from Hoyt's trailer.

The illegal firearms case against Hoyt was turned over to the U.S. Attorney's Office in Baton Rouge for federal prosecution.

In August 2000, Cade Blades left the St. Helena Parish Sheriff's Office to take a job as chief of police in the town of Greensburg. Not much happened in Greensburg. The town was essentially a few businesses and a handful of resi-

dences thrown up around the intersection of Louisiana Highways 10 and 43. The town didn't even have a traffic light. For
that matter, neither did the parish. For a cop used to working
undercover for weeks at a time with no backup and chasing
million-dollar dope deals, there wasn't much in Greensburg
for Cade Blades to do. Except stay out of trouble.

He'd left the Sheriff's Office for a reason. He'd
guessed—correctly as it turned out—that the sheriff was
going to be indicted and arrested. While working as a sheriff's detective, Blades uncovered information that led him
to suspect that his boss, first-term Sheriff Ronald "Gun"
Ficklin, was involved with a chop shop operation run by a
convicted dope dealer named Barry Dawsey. Blades confronted his boss with what he'd found out.

"After talking to him, I knew he was involved," Blades
says.

A crooked sheriff was not big news in Louisiana, and
particularly not in St. Helena Parish, where it had become
the norm, at least in recent years. In 1997, the FBI arrested
four-term incumbent sheriff Eugene Holland for theft. He
spent sixteen months in federal prison. A year later, Holland's replacement, Sheriff Chaney Phillips, was indicted
for nineteen counts of theft and payroll fraud and was sentenced to eight years in federal prison.

Sheriff Ficklin was later hit with a twenty-two-count
federal indictment charging him with conspiracy, trafficking in stolen vehicles, mail fraud, aiding and abetting the
possession of a firearm by a convicted felon, misprision of
a felony, and defrauding the state Department of Public
Safety and Corrections out of $140,000 by using state pris-
oners to work at the chop shop.

In an strange twist in the Ficklin corruption case, after
Sheriff Ficklin's indictment, the twenty-one-year-old son
of Ficklin's girlfriend and the sheriff's twenty-four-year-
old son-in-law attacked State Police Detective Dennis
Stewart at a bar in Greensburg.

Stewart, who had been promoted to sergeant by then, had helped put together the federal case against Ficklin and was trying to track down a witness. Stewart was standing at the bar talking when the two men sneaked up behind him. One of them hit Stewart in the back of the head. More blows followed. When the stunned detective dropped to the floor, the two punks pummeled him with kicks.

According to federal court documents unsealed when Stewart's two attackers later pleaded guilty: "Witnesses observed that, as a result of the beating, Sgt. Stewart was bleeding from his ears, nose, and mouth and his eyes and cheeks were swollen. [The] defendants . . . knew that Sgt. Stewart was involved in the Ficklin investigation, and they attacked him in retaliation for such involvement and in an attempt to dissuade Sgt. Steward from assisting in Ficklin's prosecution."

In September 2000, after the departure of Cade Blades, and with the Sheriff Ficklin investigation and indictment, and his own subsequent beating at the hands of a couple of the sheriff's thugs still in the future, Dennis Stewart teamed up with another St. Helena detective named Michael Martin and continued to dig into the Edward Roberts murder case.

On September 27, the two detectives went back to the Hoyts' trailer on Highway 43. They had received third-hand information that in a trash can or trash pile behind their rented trailer Johnny and Lisa had burned the .45 pistol they'd used to kill Roberts. The Hoyts had moved after Johnny bonded out of jail on the state gun charges, but Stewart and Martin tracked down the property owner and obtained her permission to conduct a search. The detectives found two burn piles but no gun. A search of the trailer also came up empty.

On September 28, 2000, a federal grand jury in Baton Rouge indicted Johnny Hoyt for violating the National Firearms Act of 1934. Under federal law, the crime carried a maximum penalty of ten years in prison.

Less than a month later, on October 23, officers from the Denham Springs Police Department picked Hoyt up on a federal arrest warrant charging him with two counts of illegal possession of sawed-off shotguns. Hoyt later pleaded guilty in exchange for a three-year sentence. The U.S. Bureau of Prisons shipped him to the federal prison in Oakdale, Louisiana.

The fledgling Brotherhood had lost one of its founding members.

On October 25, Dennis Stewart interviewed Lisa Hoyt. Since shortly after Johnny's first arrest on the gun charges in July, Lisa had been staying with her father-in-law in Holden. Just as she had when Stewart spoke to her before, Lisa denied knowing anything about Eddie Roberts's murder.

Stewart found her condescending and arrogant.

Johnny did not own a .45 pistol, she said. He had never owned a gun of any kind. She had never even seen him with a gun. Lisa claimed that she and Johnny were home in bed when Roberts was killed. She volunteered to take a polygraph to prove that she was telling the truth.

Dennis Stewart scheduled a polygraph examination at State Police headquarters for November 3. Lisa didn't show up. Stewart called around looking for her. He got in touch with her brother. Phillip said Lisa had gone to stay with their mother, Isabella. Isabella didn't have a telephone, he said.

A few days later, Lisa called Stewart and told him she had hired an attorney to represent her.

Two days after that, on November 8, 2000, Lisa's attorney called Stewart. The attorney's name was Elbert Guillory, Genore Guillory's brother-in-law. At the time Lisa hired Guillory to represent her, the telephone call Joel Odom took from Tangipahoa Detective Mark Apperson that broke the Guillory case open and shifted the focus from Police Officer Steve Williams to Johnny Hoyt, Phillip Skipper, John Baillio, and Lisa Hoyt was still nine months in the future.

From Elbert Guillory's perspective at the time, Lisa Hoyt was simply the sister of Genore's friend and neighbor. She was a wife and the mother of three children and she was in trouble, suspected of a brutal murder in St. Helena Parish.

Stewart still wanted Lisa to take a polygraph. Elbert Guillory said he would get a written statement from Lisa and fax it to Stewart. If the detective still had questions after that, then they could talk about rescheduling the polygraph exam.

The written statement Lisa sent through her attorney to Stewart was useless. In it, she denied killing Roberts, whom she referred to as "Robertson." She denied knowing anything about his death. She also reiterated her claim that Johnny didn't own a .45-caliber semiautomatic pistol or any other firearms. In her statement, Lisa made no effort to try to explain the presence of the three sawed-off shotguns Cade Blades and Nat Williams had found behind her washing machine.

Following Johnny Hoyt's arrest in October for federal firearms violations, a U.S. magistrate judge ordered him held without bond. He was housed in the Livingston Parish jail under a contract with the federal government.

Around the middle of November 2000, Hoyt got a new cell mate, thirty-nine-year-old James H. Sanford. Life in a cage is a lot of things, but one thing it's not is entertaining. Hoyt had to find something to do to occupy his time, so he started talking. He told Sanford that he'd killed a guy named Eddie Roberts. He said Roberts was supposed to bring some weed to Hoyt's apartment, but the two of them had gotten into an argument on the phone and Hoyt told him not to come over. Roberts ignored Hoyt and showed up at his trailer on the night of July 6.

Hoyt said he was sitting on the sofa in the living room holding a .45 pistol under a cushion when Roberts walked in. As Roberts turned around to look at something, Hoyt jammed the gun against the back of his head and pulled the trigger. Hoyt then drove the body over to the Big Gravel and set it and Roberts's pickup truck on fire. Then he came home and cleaned up the blood and picked up the empty shell casing. He said he'd learned from some crime show on television that the police could match a shell casing to the gun it had been fired from.

At the first opportunity, Sanford repeated to deputies from the Livingston Parish Sheriff's Office what Hoyt had told him. The Sheriff's Office contacted Dennis Stewart, and on December 14, Stewart pulled Sanford out of jail for an interview.

On December 18, Stewart used Sanford's statement as the basis for an affidavit he wrote for a warrant to search Hoyt's old trailer on Highway 43. Stewart also went to a judge in East Feliciana Parish and got a warrant to search Phillip and Amy Skipper's trailer.

The next day, Stewart took a State Police forensics team to help him search the Hoyts' former residence. In addition to the murder weapon, they were looking for traces of blood. They didn't find anything.

Because Hoyt had admitted that Skipper had given him the sawed-off shotguns, and because a shotgun in Skipper's trailer had the same type of electrical tape wrapped around the butt that had been found wrapped around one of Hoyt's sawed-offs, Stewart figured there was at least an outside chance that Hoyt had stashed the .45 at his brother-in-law's trailer.

When Stewart hit the Skippers' trailer, the first thing he found were cockroaches. Lots of them. They were everywhere. He even found them crawling inside the refrigerator. "That was the filthiest place I've ever been in my life," Stewart says. The outside was no better. "It was a junkyard." Busted cars, auto parts, kids' toys, piles of garbage—there was even a dogfighting arena out back with an extension cord running to it to power a set of lights Phillip had rigged up.

The pistol wasn't there, but Stewart did find a couple of marijuana joints. It wasn't much, but it was enough to put Phillip and Amy in jail.

Genore's family couldn't take all of her belongings back to Eunice with them. One of the things they left behind was Cleo, Genore's overprotective, sometimes vicious guardian. As the family had seen time and time again while taking care of things at Genore's house, very few people could control Cleo. No one in the family could handle the chow, and neither could Genore's friends from work, several of whom had come by to help with the cleanup and the packing. Just about the only two people Cleo didn't try to rip apart were Phillip Skipper and John Baillio. Since Skipper had more than a dozen dogs penned up at his trailer, the Guillorys asked if he would keep Cleo.

Phillip agreed. He and John-John, one of his pet names for his "stepson," would take good care of Cleo.

Sometime after the Guillorys pulled out of Clinton for the last time, Skipper told Baillio to take Genore's dog out behind the trailer and kill it. Baillio says he never argued with Phillip or questioned Phillip's instructions. He did what Phillip told him to do, every time. It was the only way the teenager knew to avoid a beating, or at least minimize the number of beatings he got.

So Baillio dragged Cleo out back and hunted around until he found a suitable club. Skipper's friend Donny Fisher later described what happened: "John-John takes a rod . . . a steel rod . . . a crowbar-like object . . . ties the dog to a tree and flattens out the dog's head."

Genore was dead and now so was her dog.

Not long after John Baillio killed Cleo, Phillip Skipper accused him of having sex with Amy. Baillio denied it, but Phillip was so mad that he sent the teenager home to live with his mother.

Baillio was a severely screwed up kid, desperately trying to find a surrogate father or mother. Phillip was terrible in that role, but Amy was better. She wasn't abusive and she actually cared about him. Baillio thought of her as his mother, much more so than he did his biological mother, Shawn Smith, whose lack of discipline and concern had sentenced him to an adolescent hell of drugs, beatings, and sexual abuse.

Although Baillio denies he had sex with Phillip's wife, he admits he had sex with Phillip's sister. Baillio says he started screwing Lisa sometime after he got out of juvenile detention in 1999. He was about fifteen at the time. She was nineteen, maybe twenty.

Johnny Hoyt knew about it but didn't care, Baillio says, boasting that he once had sex with Lisa in the Hoyts' trailer while Johnny was in the next room rolling a joint. According to Baillio, Lisa's third child, Angel, who was born February 3, 2000, was his daughter, not Hoyt's.

Baillio later described his sexual relationship with Lisa this way: "I mean I'm sixteen years old. When my dick gets hard, what do you expect? What would you do if a woman bent over in front of you? She got doggie style and I just started humping her."

It was dating, Bubba-style.

After Johnny Hoyt was sentenced to three years in federal prison in late 2000, Baillio and Lisa continued their relationship in earnest. Looking back on it, having unprotected sex with Lisa worries Baillio. He says he doesn't know of Lisa having any sexually transmitted diseases, but he's concerned. "I don't know if I got AIDS from that nasty girl or what," he says.

TWENTY-NINE

On September 29, 2000, three months after Genore's murder, the Skippers got two checks in the mail for $12,500 each. One was made out to Phillip, the other to Amy. They were from Genore's JCPenny life insurance policy.

As part of his investigation, lead detective Don McKey pried into every aspect of Genore's life. He was used to finding dirt. In a lot of cases, it was the dirt that had led to the victim's death. Drugs, booze, jealousy, gambling, shady financial deals—they caused people to get angry, and angry people sometimes killed those who'd made them angry. But Genore Guillory was different. "I couldn't find one thing bad about this woman," McKey says. "She was a great lady."

Pauline Pitre worked with Genore at BlueCross for eleven years. "She was kind, gentle, compassionate, and generous," Pitre says. "She was a wonderful person."

Linda Cueno also worked side-by-side with Genore for many years. "Genore was the most generous person I've ever known," she says.

Carl Chenevert worked with Genore for more than a decade. He says they developed a relationship more like brother and sister than coworkers. He remembers her generosity. "She would give you the last dime in her purse."

Even one of Genore's killers agrees. "That woman would give you the shirt off her back," John Baillio says.

And it was that generosity that ultimately led to her death.

When McKey found out about the insurance policy, his instincts told him he had found the motive for the killing. All he had to do was prove it. Until then he had been confounded by the *why* of it.

Who, what, when, where, why, and how? Six questions well known to every cub reporter, and to every rookie cop, and McKey was a long way from his rookie days. Like every veteran detective, McKey was well aware that motive—the *why* of it—was not one of the elements of a crime that needed to be proved in court.

All that was needed for a conviction in a criminal case, from a legal standpoint, was proof that a crime had taken place within the jurisdiction of the court in which it had been charged, and that the person or persons accused of the crime had committed it knowingly, willingly, or negligently. The need to prove why the accused committed the crime was wisely kept outside the scope of the prosecutor's responsibilities. The nation's earliest jurists knew that to ascertain motive required the ability to peer into men's souls, something beyond the power of mere mortals. Motive was better left to God.

Make that God and homicide detectives. Motive is one of the first things a good murder cop looks for, because it is frequently the key to uncovering the identity of the killer. People kill for a reason. Regardless of how sick or twisted it is, there's always a reason. Murder victims are usually killed by someone they know, most often by someone close to them: a spouse, a lover, a relative, a friend, a neighbor. In a homicide investigation, the *why* often leads to the *who*.

If the *who* is obvious right from the start of an investigation, if physical evidence or witness statements point directly at the perpetrator, even though not legally bound to establish motive, a good detective will still dig for the *why* because a good detective knows that jurors are curious people. They want to know, regardless of legal requirements, why someone did what he or she did. The more horrific the crime, the more intense the curiosity.

Criminal cases can, and often do, reach the point where juries apply their own standard of proof, above and beyond what the law requires. Any police investigator who's been through a few trials knows that juries are unpredictable and often stubborn. They want to understand the crime, and they want to understand the person they have been asked to judge. If they can't understand the crime, they can't understand the person.

Some motives are obvious. Robbery, burglary, fraud, and embezzlement don't usually require much of an explanation. Someone needed money so they stole it. Some motives are not so obvious. Beatings, shootings, stabbings, and murder often require more of an explanation. Was it anger, jealousy, revenge?

What McKey had in the Genore Guillory murder was a horrific, seemingly senseless act of utter brutality. At least three weapons had been used. A dog everyone described as vicious and terrifying had been subdued. The crime scene itself suggested more than one perpetrator, and multiple attackers almost completely ruled out the idea that the murder had been a crime of passion. The remoteness of the location—a dead-end gravel road in the middle of nowhere—limited the number of potential suspects. How many people even knew the house was there? The only people nearby were neighbors and friends. People with no obvious animosity toward the victim. People who did not seem to benefit in any way from Genore's death.

At least that's what it looked like until McKey found out about the insurance policy. Twenty-five thousand dollars was a lot of money to someone living in a secondhand trailer way out in the woods. Twenty-five thousand dollars would buy a lot of booze and a lot of dope and would back more than a few bets at the Saturday night pit bull fights. Twenty-five thousand dollars was a whole lot of motive.

Phillip Skipper wasn't happy about the money. It wasn't enough.

Although Genore's insurance policy represented a good-sized chunk of cash, certainly more than Skipper had ever had at one time, he thought there was going to be more, a lot more.

In the weeks after Genore's murder, when Donny Fisher and his girlfriend were staying with him, Phillip had bragged to Fisher that he was expecting at least a hundred thousand dollars from Genore's insurance policy. Later, after the insurance company notified Skipper that the total amount of the death benefit was going to be $25,000, split between him and his wife, he was visibly angry. Fisher later said Skipper stomped around his trailer all day with a "disgusted look" on his face.

Years later, after the case finally went down, East Feliciana Parish Sheriff Talmadge Bunch dismissed the idea that race had been a factor in Genore's death. "The motive for the murder was one thing—money," the sheriff said.

It's an understandable and convenient explanation that money was the sole reason Genore Guillory was killed, especially coming from a man charged with keeping the peace in the deep South, a place where racial tensions frequently boil over. But that explanation ignores the bigger picture, specifically the attitude about race shared by those involved in the crime. Money was part of it to be sure, but there was something else.

According to John Baillio, if Genore had been white, they wouldn't have killed her. "I helped kill a woman for no reason other than the color of her skin," Baillio says.

In the early summer of 2001, while Lisa Hoyt was staying at her father-in-law's house in Holden and her husband was doing his federal time on the ATF gun charge, she asked a neighbor, Bill Thurman, to drive her to Georgia.

Like most of the rest of the Skipper clan, Lisa and Phillip's father, Gilbert Skipper Jr., had run afoul of the law. He was busy serving a life sentence at a maximum security state prison in Georgia for murder, aggravated sodomy, and rape when Lisa decided to pay him a visit.

"She comes from an evil family," Sheriff Bunch says.

In 1985, Gilbert Skipper lived with his wife and kids—Phillip was eight, Lisa six—in rural Appling County, Georgia. In late April, while visiting his neighbors, William and Gretchen Morris, Skipper and William Morris got into an argument because Skipper—probably in a drunken stupor—had dropped the Morris's baby. The argument got heated, and eventually William Morris threw Skipper out of his house and told him not to come back. As he was leaving, Skipper said, "Good luck living out here. You're going to need it."

Almost immediately, Skipper launched a harassment campaign against his neighbors. Williams Morris got tired of the dirty tricks and left a note in Skipper's mailbox. The note read, "Skipper, this . . . better stop. I have already talked to the landlord about you. If I catch you doing anything else, I'm going to the law."

The next day, Skipper told a friend, "I might have to kill the whole bunch—William, his wife, and baby." Skipper borrowed a pickup truck from his friend and went back to the Morris's house, this time carrying a shotgun and a pistol.

Skipper burst through the door of the Morris's home and aimed the shotgun at William Morris. Morris tried to run, but Skipper dropped him with a blast to the head. Then he dragged Gretchen Morris and her baby out of the house and through a cornfield. He threw Gretchen to the ground under a pecan tree and forced her to perform oral sex on him. Then he raped her. When he finished, Skipper took the wife and baby back to the house. On his way through the front door, he smashed the porch light with the barrel of his shotgun. After knocking back a quick drink, Skipper dragged Mrs. Morris into the bedroom, where he threatened her, beat her, choked her with the belt from her own bathrobe, and raped her again.

Skipper worked out what he thought was a deal with Gretchen Morris. He told her that he'd let her and her baby live if she would give him time to get home and then come to his house to call the sheriff (the Morris house did not have a telephone). She was to tell the sheriff that an unknown assailant had broken into her house and killed her husband. Gretchen Morris agreed and a half hour later, she used Skipper's telephone to call the sheriff.

When sheriff's deputies and GBI (Georgia Bureau of Investigation) agents arrived, Gretchen Morris reported the crime exactly according to Skipper's instructions. The entire time Gretchen Morris spoke to the police, Skipper and his wife remained glued to her side. The whole thing seemed weird to at least one of the GBI agents, who later said, "We couldn't separate the company of Mr. Skipper and Mrs. Morris . . . Everywhere Gretchen Morris went, the Skippers were around her."

After a deputy sheriff asked Gretchen Morris to get into his squad car so he could take her to the sheriff's station to give a formal statement, the deputy had to stop Gilbert Skipper from climbing into the backseat beside her.

As soon as Gretchen Morris got away from Skipper, she told the cops what had really happened. When sheriff's deputies and GBI agents returned to the scene, they found drag marks leading from the Morris house through the cornfield to the pecan tree. They noted flattened grass under the tree where it looked like someone had been lying down. At the house, they noticed the front porch light busted out and found grass on the bed, including a pecan leaf on the pillow.

A year later, a Georgia judge sentenced Gilbert Skipper to death for the murder of William Morris. The judge also sentenced Skipper to life in prison for rape and gave him ten years for aggravated sodomy. Ironically, two years later, Skipper, a former Klansman, appealed his death sentence claiming that the prosecutor had unfairly excluded blacks from the jury. A Georgia appeals court didn't buy the race argument but did overturn Skipper's death sentence for a procedural error. Skipper was later resentenced, to two life terms plus ten years.

On the long ride to Georgia, Lisa passed the time by talking about killing Genore Guillory. As the thirty-three-year-old Bill Thurman drove, he listened as Lisa bragged about how she and Phillip stabbed and shot Genore to death in her own home. Lisa claimed a lawyer had paid them to kill Genore. Phillip used the money to buy a pickup truck and a Harley-Davidson motorcycle. Lisa didn't say what she'd gotten out of the deal, nor did she say if her husband had participated in the killing. She only said that Johnny Hoyt had come over to Genore's house while they were murdering her.

Lisa also bragged about an old-fashioned wristwatch she wore, saying she'd taken it from one of the corpses at Gatlin Cemetery.

Not long after Thurman got back from his Georgia trip, an anonymous male caller started phoning his house and threatening him. The caller said he would kill Thurman if he ever talked to anyone about what Lisa had told him.

THIRTY

Bill Thurman was just one of a growing number of friends Lisa bragged to about killing people. While her husband was in federal prison, Lisa was seeing a guy from Denham Springs named Michael Poole. Lisa told Poole about how she and Johnny had killed Eddie Roberts up in St. Helena Parish.

On July 23, 2001, Lisa's fifteen-month-old daughter, Angel Skipper-Hoyt, the child Baillio is sure he fathered, drowned in a plastic baby pool in Johnny Hoyt Sr.'s backyard. Despite rumors to the contrary, Baillio is sure that Lisa didn't kill the baby. It was an accident, Baillio says. "Lisa was too busy doing crank and didn't watch her."

Guilty or not, a couple of days after Angel's death, when an investigator from the state's Office of Social Services started poking around into the circumstances of the baby's drowning, Lisa made herself scarce. When the investigator contacted Lisa and Phillip's mother, Isabella Skipper, and asked where to find Lisa, Isabella said her daughter had been staying with Michael Poole in Denham Springs.

On Saturday morning, July 28, five days after her daughter drowned, Lisa gave her "friend" Michael Poole a ride to her brother's trailer. Poole needed a part for the steering column of his pickup truck, and Lisa said Phillip had a number of junked trucks on his property. Poole could probably find one there.

Almost immediately upon arriving at Phillip's trailer, Poole sensed something was wrong. Lisa and Phillip left him standing in the yard while they walked a short distance away and talked privately. Poole overheard part of what they said. They were talking about God and the devil. "He's the devil," Phillip said. "You need to get away from him and get right with God. He'll forgive you, Lisa."

After listening to a few minutes of their conversation, Poole figured out that Phillip and Lisa were using some kind of code. Johnny Hoyt was God. Poole was the devil. He started to get nervous.

As Poole strained to hear more, he heard Phillip tell his sister, "When I hit him in the head he'll know." A few minutes later, Phillip said, "You know he will be proud of us if we do this." From the context, Poole understood the person who would be proud was Hoyt. He also understood that the person Phillip planned to hit in the head was him.

Poole was scared.

Abruptly, Lisa announced that she was going inside to wash her hair. She didn't explain why she suddenly felt the need to wash her hair at her brother's trailer. A few minutes later, Poole went inside to talk to Lisa. He found her in the bathroom.

"Are you and Phillip planning on killing me?" he asked.

Lisa said he was being ridiculous, but Poole felt certain she was lying. He could feel the walls closing in around him. He guessed they were trying to get rid of him because Lisa had said too much about the Guillory murder, or because someone had gotten word to Johnny in prison that he was fooling around with Lisa.

A minute or so later, Phillip came into the trailer. As Poole stepped into the kitchen to get something to drink, Phillip ducked inside the bathroom with his sister and closed the door. Poole shuffled around for a few minutes then stopped in front of the bathroom door. He could hear Phillip and Lisa talking quietly. Poole knocked on the door. The conversation inside stopped.

"Come in," Phillip said.

Poole pushed the door open.

Phillip and Lisa stared at him.

"Lisa . . . uh, when can you take me back home?" Poole said.

"I'll bring you home," Phillip volunteered.

They're going to kill me, Poole thought.

Phillip left the tiny bathroom.

"Lisa, is something about to happen to me?" Poole asked.

Lisa copped an attitude. "Nothing is going to happen. You think I want to get charged with accessory to murder?"

Murder. There it was out in the open. A non-denial denial.

Poole stepped outside and started pacing the driveway. Phillip and Lisa stayed in the trailer. They came out thirty minutes later. Poole had to use the bathroom. As he walked past Lisa, she told him that if anyone from Social Services contacted him, she wanted him to say that he hadn't seen her recently and didn't know where she was staying.

Poole had serious doubts about whether he'd live long enough to speak to anyone from Social Services or from anywhere else. He figured Lisa was trying to placate him because she knew he was edgy.

As soon as Poole finished in the bathroom, he stepped outside the trailer again and saw Lisa pulling away in her car. Phillip just stood in the yard staring at him. Poole's stomach dropped into his shoes. There was nothing he could do except act cool, so he asked Phillip about the part for his steering column. Phillip led him to an old Ford F-100 pickup behind his trailer. As Phillip stood near the open driver-side window of the cab, he told Poole to come take a look inside the cab. When Poole peeked into cab, he saw a hatchet lying on the front seat. The handle was about a foot long. Although he was nearly scared out of his mind, Poole was still quick-witted enough to reach through the open window and grab the hatchet.

"This is neat," he said. He was trying to play it cool, hoping Phillip didn't suspect that he knew Phillip was about to try to kill him.

For the next few minutes, Poole clung to the hatchet, afraid that if he put it down Phillip would chop him to pieces with it. As casually as he could, Poole sauntered toward the driveway. He was trying to put some distance between him and Phillip, but Phillip followed him. It was a strange dance, with neither man willing to acknowledge what was really going on.

Phillip's new truck sat parked in the driveway. It was a four-by-four with oversized mud-grip tires. When Poole got close to the truck, he noticed a four- or five-foot-long tire tool lying in the bed. Phillip walked up to the truck and stood beside the truck bed. He was within an arm's length of the steel tire tool. Phillip motioned Poole to come closer. He said he had a Super Swamper mud-grip tire he'd melted down to the rim, sitting in the bed of the pickup, that he wanted Poole to see.

Poole said he didn't want to see it. Phillip reached over the side of the truck bed and wrapped his hand around the tire tool. He asked Poole again to come look at the tire in the back of the truck. Poole refused to budge. His feet stayed rooted to the ground. He knew if he took a step closer to the truck, Phillip was going to swing that tire tool at him.

Poole backed away toward the end of the driveway. "When are you going to give me a ride home, Phillip?"

Phillip let go of the tire tool. "In about an hour," he said. Then he asked Poole if he would like to see some junked cars down at the end of a trail that ran off into the woods.

Poole said no.

Phillip strolled to the end of the driveway and made a show of checking his mailbox.

"When are we leaving?" He asked again.

"Soon as I change clothes."

Poole watched from the end of the driveway as Phillip walked toward his trailer. He thought Skipper was probably going to get a gun. As soon as the trailer door closed, Poole bolted into the woods across the street, carrying the small ax with him. He ran just inside the wood line for a half mile or so, until he came to a house. He banged on the door until someone opened it, and he begged them to let him use their telephone.

He called 9-1-1.

A deputy from the East Feliciana Sheriff's Department came out and took a report, but there was nothing he could do. It wasn't a crime to ask a guy to look at a melted tire. Besides, Poole had been the only one with a weapon. The deputy took the hatchet as evidence anyway.

By August 2001, East Feliciana sheriff's detectives Don McKey and Joel Odom were convinced that Phillip Skipper, Johnny Hoyt, and John Baillio had murdered Genore Guillory.

Skipper clearly had the means and the opportunity to do it. Like everyone else who lived in the country, he had access to guns and knives, and he probably had a baseball bat or two lying around his trailer somewhere. He lived across the street from Genore. His wife at one time even had a key to their neighbor's house. And, as McKey and Odom had recently discovered, Skipper also had a motive—$25,000. A lot of people had been killed for a lot less.

But means, opportunity, and motive is just a theory. It's conjecture. And while theories are good, facts are better. In the real world of crime and punishment, only one thing can transform conjecture into reality, and only one thing can turn a suspect into a defendant—evidence.

McKey and Odom needed to find something that linked Phillip Skipper to the murder of Genore Guillory, something other than the fact that he was a racist skinhead who hated black people, that he lived across the street from her and had a key to her house, that he probably had access to the three known types of weapons used in the crime— guns, knives, and blunt objects—and that he was a dope fiend and had gotten a bunch of cash after her death.

On August 3, Donny Fisher gave them that link when he told them about the conversations he'd had with John Baillio and Phillip Skipper.

What would you think if I told you I killed . . . if we killed G? Skipper had said.

Fisher's statement was McKey and Odom's first real piece of evidence that tied Phillip Skipper to the murder. Secondhand confessions by two of the killers wasn't strong evidence, but it was a start. It was a step in the right direction, and it was certainly strong enough for a search warrant.

Statements made out of court and later testified to in court are usually considered hearsay. Generally, hearsay is inadmissible at a criminal trial. There are, however, several exceptions to the hearsay rule. Some of the exceptions are specific to particular courts; others are more universally accepted.

One of the universally accepted exceptions involves what is known as a *statement against interest*. If a person who later winds up seated at the defense table says something that incriminates him, the person who heard it can testify to what he heard. The legal theory behind that exception is that people rarely lie to make themselves look bad or to put themselves in prison. Therefore, the theory holds, if they say something that implicates them in a crime, what they've said is very likely to be true.

The bottom line for McKey and Odom was that Donny Fisher could testify before a jury as to what he'd heard John Baillio and Phillip Skipper say about killing Genore Guillory. However, as McKey knew all too well, one witness does not usually a conviction make. The detectives needed additional witnesses to back up Fisher's statement or, better yet, something physical to prove the link between Skipper, Hoyt, and Baillio and the murder.

THIRTY-ONE

On August 8, 2001, more than thirteen months after
Genore Gulliory's murder, Don McKey, Joel Odom, and
Dennis Stewart, who was still looking hard for a solid link
between Skipper and the Hoyts in the Edward Roberts
murder investigation, banged on Phillip and Amy Skipper's trailer door. The detectives had another search warrant, this one in connection with the Guillory investigation.

Two days before, East Feliciana State District Judge
George Ware had signed a warrant authorizing Sheriff's
Department and State Police investigators to search the
Skippers' property and comb through their belongings
looking for:

> any and all baseball bats, any .22-caliber firearms, any
> .22-caliber ammunition, any .22-caliber shell casings,
> any .22-caliber spent bullets, any and all knives that
> may have facilitated the death of Genore Guillory, any
> and all papers, books, documents, forms, notes, or elec-
> tronic storage or recording material regarding life

insurance policy beneficiary information on Genore
Guillory, a class ring from Eunice High School listed as
taken from the residence at the time of the homicide,
any articles of pearl jewelry listed as taken from the
residence at the time of the homicide, a pair of shoes
matching the impressions of the shoe imprint in blood
taken into evidence after the time of the homicide.

The detectives didn't hit the mother lode they'd hoped for,
but neither did they come away empty-handed. Out behind
Skipper's main trailer—the one Genore helped him buy—
they found a red MacGregor baseball bat shoved inside a
doghouse. Another bat, a silver MacGregor, McKey found
hidden behind an old Ford Bronco. In the front yard they
picked up a spent .22-caliber shell casing. Inside the trailer,
lying in a glass jar in the den, were four unfired .22-caliber
bullets. And despite the execution of the previous search
warrant and subsequent arrest of both Phillip and Amy for
possession of marijuana, the detectives found a small stash of
weed and four pipes caked with burned marijuana residue.
They also found four documents relating to Genore's life insurance policy, a notebook containing dogfighting records,
and another notebook filled with Nazi drawings.

When the detectives left, they also took Phillip Skipper
with them. In addition to the search warrant, McKey had
brought another warrant, an arrest warrant for Phillip Skipper charging him with "First-degree murder upon Genore
Guillory by shooting, stabbing, and beating Guillory in the
head, causing her death."

When McKey jerked Skipper's hands together behind
his back and snapped handcuffs on his wrists, Amy Skipper unleashed a barrage of curses at the detectives so foul
they would have made a sailor blush. Every other word out
of her mouth was "fuck." When Amy finished with the detectives, she started screaming at reporter James Minton,
who was there to cover the arrest for the Baton Rouge

newspaper *The Advocate*. "When God works this problem out, you'll look just as silly as they will," she told the newspaperman.

Amy followed the detectives to the jail and continued to berate them as they led her husband toward the booking desk. While she sat waiting on a hard plastic chair in the lobby, near the restrooms and the Coke machine, Amy told the newspaper reporter that State Police Detective Dennis Stewart wasn't really there to investigate the Guillory case.

"He's just trying to put Phillip in the middle of something else with Hoyt," she said. "Me and Phillip has been with the Guillory family ever since this happened. We've been by them for whatever they needed done. Phillip has passed a lie detector test and we've helped Don McKey every way we could."

As Stewart crossed the lobby on his way to the booking desk, Amy told the detective that she'd been praying for him and praying that Genore Guillory's killer would be caught.

"Maybe the prayer's been answered," Stewart shot back.

Once Skipper was fingerprinted and photographed, McKey read him his Miranda rights from a printed Sheriff's Department form.

"Do you understand the rights that I have just read to you?" McKey asked.

"Yes," Skipper said.

"Having had those rights explained to you, do you wish to waive those rights now and answer questions without a lawyer?"

"Yeah."

McKey handed the rights form to Skipper along with a pen and asked him to sign in two places, once to acknowledge that he'd been read and had understood his rights and once to waive his rights. The nearly illiterate Skipper scrawled his name on both signature lines with big printed letters.

After a few preliminary questions, McKey got right into what he wanted to talk about. "Where were you when Genore Guillory was killed?"

"I was at home asleep," Skipper said.

No one but the killer or killers knew exactly when Genore had been murdered. Dr. Emil Laga, the pathologist who'd performed the autopsy on Genore, had only been able to narrow down the time of death to sometime between noon Saturday, June 24, and noon Sunday, June 25. For Skipper to claim he had been home asleep when Genore was killed implied he had more information about exactly when she was killed than did those investigating her murder.

It was an implication not lost on McKey.

Skipper said Johnny Hoyt, Lisa, and their kids had stayed over that Saturday night. He didn't mention anything about his mother spending the night. Sunday morning, Skipper said, Hoyt woke him up early and demanded a ride home. It was unusual, Skipper claimed.

After being under arrest for less than an hour, Skipper seemed already to be toying with the idea of throwing his brother-in-law and Brotherhood brother under the bus.

McKey was tired of listening to the bullshit.

"Why did you and Hoyt and Baillio kill Genore Guillory?" he asked.

"I don't know," Skipper mumbled, not even denying the accusation.

"Did y'all kill her for the money?"

"I don't know."

"Why'd you rape her?"

"I don't know."

Skipper had nothing else to say. The interview was finished. McKey turned him over to the jailers, who locked Skipper in a cell.

After more than a year of frustrating work, justice had prevailed. McKey had one arrest and more on the way.

There was a lot of cleanup work left to do to prepare the case for trial, but the Genore Guillory murder had finally gone down, or so McKey thought.

On August 10, McKey went back to Judge Ware for another arrest warrant for Phillip Skipper. This time, McKey added aggravated burglary and aggravated rape to Skipper's booking sheet. The detective needed the additional felony counts to make the first-degree murder charge stick. As bloody and brutal as the killing of Genore Guillory had been, under Louisiana law it was only second-degree murder unless the state could prove certain other factors were involved.

The limited scope of the state's first-degree murder statute only applied to murders like the Guillory case if they were committed while the killer or killers were engaged in the perpetration or attempted perpetration of another serious felony. That list of felonies included aggravated burglary and aggravated rape. A conviction for second-degree murder carried a mandatory life sentence. A charge of first-degree murder brought with it the possibility of death by lethal injection, something McKey felt the Guillory case clearly warranted.

On the afternoon of August 14, John Baillio's mother, Shawn Smith, showed up at the East Feliciana Sheriff's Office. She had driven there from her trailer in Denham Springs and wanted to talk to a detective about what she'd learned about the murder of Genore Guillory.

Joel Odom set a tape recorder on his desk and turned it on.

Shawn Smith said her son had come to live with her the previous summer, after Skipper kicked him out. He'd stayed with her for a little while and then gone to live with his friend Donny Fisher in the town of Folsom, in St.

Tammany Parish. After spending some time at Fisher's, John came back. When he came back, he started telling her things about the murder that had happened across the street from Phillip's trailer, things maybe only someone who'd been involved would know.

According to Shawn Smith, her son never told her he was involved in the murder, but he said he knew that Phillip, Johnny, and Lisa had been. The reason her son had left Phillip Skipper's house, Smith said, was because Phillip threatened to kill him after he found out that John had told Donny Fisher about the murder. John was scared of Phillip, so he'd left. John had also told her about a note he'd found at the Skippers' trailer. Lisa had printed it in red crayon. The note read, "Phillip knew the dogs and we did it just for fun."

Smith told Odom that she had seen Phillip handle and feed Genore's dogs several times, including the vicious chow named Cleo. She also knew that Phillip had a key to Genore's house.

Smith said her son told her that Genore Guillory had been shot five times, stabbed five times, beaten, and raped. All of the clothes Skipper, Hoyt, and Lisa had worn when they committed the murder—including the Reeboks they'd stolen from Skipper's mom—had been burned, according to her son.

Skipper knew about the insurance policy Genore had taken out and had bragged to Shawn Smith that when Genore died he was going to come into some serious money. After Genore's death, Skipper spent the money on two trucks, a Harley-Davidson motorcycle, and more pit bulls.

Smith also told Odom about the cultlike gang Skipper and Hoyt had formed called The Brotherhood. John had shown her his G.F.B.D. tattoo and had explained what it meant. She told Odom the gang was "extremely racist."

John had admitted to his mother that he and Skipper had

loaded up on pills before they'd taken their polygraph examinations and that's how they'd passed them.

The next day, August 15, Don McKey, Joel Odom, and Dennis Stewart made the three-hour drive to the federal prison in Oakdale, Louisiana, to try to talk to Johnny Hoyt. With a little more than eight thousand residents, the city of Oakdale is essentially the expanded intersection of two highways in rural Allen Parish—U.S. Highway 165 and Louisiana Highway 10. The town's main industry is housing federal prisoners and immigration detainees.

On a cold night in November 1987, Oakdale's industry exploded. The day after the U.S. government announced a deal with Cuban dictator Fidel Castro that would allow the Justice Department to send back to Cuba 2,500 of the most undesirable of the more than 125,000 Cubans who had washed up on the shores of south Florida during the 1980 Mariel boatlift, 1,000 Cuban detainees rioted at the Oakdale federal prison. Armed with a variety of makeshift weapons, including machetes, spears, knives, and clubs, the prisoners captured twenty-eight guards and set fire to most of the buildings on the forty-seven-acre prison complex.

The next day, 1,400 Cubans took over the maximum security federal penitentiary in Atlanta, capturing dozens of guards and setting fire to everything that would burn.

Of the 2,400 Cuban detainees rioting in both Oakdale and Atlanta, eight had been convicted of arson, fourteen of kidnapping, eighty-eight of murder, more than four hundred of burglary, and nearly seven hundred of drug charges.

An article in the *Los Angeles Times* described the prisoners this way, "They ran the gamut from homicidal maniacs to penny-ante con men."

In Oakdale, the takeover and hostage crisis dragged on for eight days. Inmates waved a misspelled message spray painted on a sheet of plywood at television news cameras and the hundreds of heavily armed law enforcement officers who had surrounded the prison. The sign read, "Liberly our die" (Liberty or die).

In the end, the Cubans got neither. They surrendered without a fight. None of the hostages were killed, but ten of the prison's fourteen buildings had been gutted by fire. The damage totaled $15 million.

A week later the Cuban prisoners in Atlanta surrendered.

There's no good way to get to Oakdale from Clinton, which is why the 130-mile trip takes three hours, give or take. From Clinton you either have to cross the Mississippi River on the ferry at St. Francisville or drive all the way down to Baton Rouge and cross the old U.S. 190 bridge. Then there's the tedious and often jarring journey on south Louisiana's pockmarked highways, with frequent stops in tiny, one-light towns whose traffic signals seem stuck on red.

McKey, Odom, and Stewart weren't in the best of moods by the time they reached Oakdale. Soon their mood would get worse.

To enter the prison itself was a complicated procedure involving signing in, searches, and the issuance of visitor badges. The three detectives left their guns in the car. Finally, after all the security procedures were exhausted, they were escorted to an interview room where they were told to wait. Inmate Johnny Hoyt, less than a year into the three-year sentence he drew for pleading guilty to federal weapons charges, would be along any minute.

When Hoyt arrived just before noon, sporting a bright prison jumpsuit, he looked slightly less demonic than he had in his June 2000 booking photo, taken when he got picked up for weed in Livingston Parish. Perhaps prison had sapped some of his cockiness. Hoyt took a seat across from the three detectives at a small table.

Although unnecessary, McKey, Odom, and Stewart reintroduced themselves to Hoyt. It was unnecessary because Hoyt was unlikely to have forgotten the three men who'd been hounding him for more than a year over two murders in two different parishes and who were responsible for landing him in federal prison on gun charges.

McKey slid a Louisiana State Police rights form across the table to McKey and asked him to read it. A paragraph near the top of the form described a suspect's rights against self-incrimination and explained that an attorney would be provided free of charge if requested. Hoyt took his time reading the form and then drew a check mark in a little box below the top paragraph. The mark indicated that he had read the statement of his rights and that he understood them. He printed his name just under the check box and signed to the right of his printed name.

McKey and Odom then signed and dated the form, using two signature lines and a date block down near the middle of the form.

So far so good.

McKey then read the next paragraph, titled "WAIVER OF RIGHTS." "I understand what my rights are and I elect to waive them. I am willing to answer questions and make a statement. I do not want a lawyer. I understand and know what I am doing. No promises or threats have been made to me and no pressure of any kind has been used against me."

McKey then signed another signature line below the waiver and slid it back across the table. Hoyt shook his head. "I'm not signing that," he said. "I'm not waiving my rights. I want to talk to my attorney."

Just like that, the interview was over. The three detectives filed out of the interview room and piled back into their car for the three-hour drive back to Clinton.

They were going to have to get someone else to cooperate, because Johnny Hoyt clearly wasn't going to.

THIRTY-TWO

On Friday, August 17, a grand jury in East Feliciana indicted sixteen-year-old John Baillio for first-degree murder, aggravated burglary, and aggravated rape. District Attorney Charles Shropshire sought the indictments against Baillio because he wanted to prosecute the teen as an adult, a move that would leave the death penalty on the table.

The grand jury also indicted Johnny Hoyt and Phillip Skipper for the same trio of charges.

As soon as the indictments were handed down, Don McKey and Joel Odom went to Judge Ware and obtained three arrest warrants for Baillio, one for each charge.

They found him back on Sallie Kinchen Road in Tangipahoa Parish. In three unmarked police cars, McKey, Odom, Stewart, Sheriff Bunch, and several local deputies pulled up in front of a tiny house near the graveled end of Sallie Kinchen. Baillio was outside in the yard, shirtless and wearing a pair of jeans.

When Baillio saw the cars coming, he knew immediately they were police cars. He also knew they were coming for him. He just wasn't sure why. His best guess was that it was over a dope deal. Since he had left the Skippers' trailer, he'd been selling plenty of dope: OxyContin, heroin, marijuana, and ecstasy. He was carrying a .38-caliber pistol, a bag of dope, and a bunch of knives. He was a knife freak and often had on him at least half a dozen fighting knives of varying sizes.

When Baillio saw Don McKey step out of the lead car, he knew it was about Genore Guillory.

Baillio turned and ran.

He got into the woods and got away—for a little while.

"He was a fast little ole boy," Sheriff Bunch says. "We had to get some dogs to track him down."

While the East Feliciana detectives and the local cops waited for a bloodhound team from the Tangipahoa Sheriff's Office to help track Baillio, Joel Odom took at look around at the place where Baillio had been hiding out. They'd spotted him outside a small, red shotgun-style house owned by a relative.

Shotgun houses are common in the South, especially in and around New Orleans. They're long and skinny, with a central passageway running down the middle. Because they take up less road frontage, they fit onto narrower lots than other styles of houses. They're shaped like a big shoe box with the front and back doors lined up with each other. Tradition holds that the name comes from the idea that a person could stand in the front doorway and fire a shotgun down the length of the house, and have the shot go out the back door.

The house where they'd spotted Baillio was a shithole. Four small children wearing nothing but dirty diapers padded around outside, unsupervised. One toddler wobbled up to Odom. The baby looked up at the detective with a vacant, cross-eyed stare. Its backside and legs were covered in feces. It was as clear a case of child neglect as Odom had ever seen. He asked one of the Tangipahoa deputies to call out their parish's child welfare agency.

Meanwhile, Baillio was trying to get rid of his dope and his gun. He stashed them under an old tree and then concealed himself beneath a bush at the edge of a pond. He knew from living on Sallie Kinchen that three alligators, one a seven-footer, lived in the pond. If the cops called for tracking dogs, which Baillio figured was very likely, he hoped the smell of the alligators would keep the dogs away.

In the end it didn't matter. Even before Baillio heard the first dog bark, he walked out of the woods with his hands in the air. He'd only lasted thirty minutes on the lamb. "I was tired of running," he says. Baillio claims he went back to the tree where he'd hidden his dope and recovered a dozen or more hits of ecstasy so he'd have something to take while he was in jail. He knew he wasn't going to get out anytime soon.

McKey and Odom waited until the Tangipahoa deputies had gone through the procedure of booking Baillio into their jail in Amite, as a fugitive from East Feliciana. After that, the sixteen-year-old was released into their custody and they drove him back to Clinton.

By the time they got back to the East Feliciana jail Friday evening, McKey, Odom, and Sheriff Bunch were hot and tired. Baillio wasn't going anywhere. Because the law requires that juvenile offenders, even those charged as adults, be kept separate from adult prisoners, the sheriff locked Baillio up in the jail's medical cell and left him there for the weekend.

The following Monday morning, Joel Odom threw open the medical cell door. He and McKey were ready to question Baillio, but the teenager had something else on his mind.

"Man, I'm hungry," Baillio said.

Odom looked at his watch. It was just past seven

o'clock. The jail served breakfast at six. "You just ate," he said.

"Man, I ain't ate since y'all put me in here."

The weekend jail shifts hadn't known anyone was in the medical cell. Odom looked at his partner. "Dude, that's bad."

The detectives called a jailer and told him to get the kid some food. Their much anticipated interview could wait for a few more minutes.

"They hadn't fed the son of a bitch all weekend," Odom recalls. "The sheriff left him with a tennis ball that he could throw against the wall . . . a couple of comic books and a Snickers bar."

After Baillio got something to eat, McKey and Odom sat him down in the tiny cinder-block detective office. They read him his rights at 7:52 a.m. Baillio signed that he understood them and signed again that he agreed to waive them.

It was only a recent change in state law that allowed McKey and Odom to even consider trying to interview Baillio by himself. The detectives were the beneficiaries of a Louisiana Supreme Court decision made three years earlier. For the twenty years prior to that decision, state law mandated that for a law enforcement officer to interview a juvenile suspect in a criminal case, it was not enough that the juvenile waive his or her rights and agree to give the police a statement. A kiddy suspect, regardless of whether he or she was being prosecuted as an adult, as Baillio was in the Guillory case, had to "engage in meaningful consultation with an attorney or an informed parent, guardian or other adult interested in his or her welfare before the juvenile waived the right to counsel and the privilege against self-incrimination."

The adult had to remain with the juvenile suspect during the interview, to ensure that the cops didn't turn around and trample on the kid's Fifth Amendment rights as soon as they were alone with him or her. Violating that court-sanctioned procedure would cost the state the use of any incriminating statements and any evidence obtained as a result of the interview.

A long-standing U.S. Supreme Court doctrine, imaginatively dubbed "fruit of the poisonous tree," which was developed as an extension of the Fourth Amendment's exclusionary rule, forbids prosecutors from introducing even *legally* obtained evidence that was discovered as a result of an *illegal* search or interrogation.

A classic example of the doctrine at work:

If a suspected murderer under police interrogation asks for a lawyer, the law dictates that the interrogation must stop immediately. However, if the police press on with the interrogation, disregarding the suspect's request for counsel, and the suspect eventually gives up the locations of the body and the murder weapon, and the police later obtain search warrants to seize that evidence, in nearly all circumstances a judge will not allow the body or weapon to be presented at trial because they are considered "fruit of the poisonous tree," the poisonous tree being the illegal interrogation, the borne fruit of which is the body and the weapon.

In Baillio's case, the recent change in the law was, for McKey and Odom, a stroke of luck. At least one of John Baillio's two so-called guardians, Phillip Skipper, was already under arrest for the same crime. Amy wasn't charged yet, but the case had already taken so many strange twists and turns that no one knew where it was going to lead or who was going to be implicated. Baillio's biological mother, Shawn Smith, could have certainly represented her son's interest, but she lived way over in Denham Springs, worked at a bar somewhere, and had no telephone.

And any attorney worthy of the title would have told his client to keep his mouth shut. There is no advantage in talking to the police unless you have a deal worked out, in writing, with the district attorney.

Had the old law been in effect, the Guillory case would

have likely ground to a screeching halt right then and there. There would have been no prosecution and no justice for Genore.

Yet even with the new law working in their favor, for the first fifteen or twenty minutes of their interview, it didn't look to McKey and Odom like the change in the law was going to matter one bit. Baillio wasn't talking. Then without warning he changed his mind.

"All of a sudden he went to telling us about it," McKey says.

The detectives wanted the statement on tape. They sat Baillio in a chair with his back to the inside wall of the office, in a small open space wedged between two desks, and set up a video camera in front of him. McKey and Odom sat on either side of the camera, out of sight of the shot. They were joined by State Police Detective Dennis Stewart and Sheriff Talmadge Bunch.

Baillio wore an orange prison uniform, baggy pants, and a short-sleeved V-neck T-shirt. His head was shaved like a brand-new boot camp recruit's, his hair cut down to within a sixteenth of an inch of his scalp. Under his chin grew an ungroomed tuft of hair. The inside of his right forearm was covered with a tattoo of a muscular pit bull surrounded by red flames. Baillio looked scared as he fidgeted in the chair, his elbows pressed against the armrests, his fingers laced tightly in front of him.

With the videotape rolling, Odom introduced everyone in the room. He read Baillio his rights again and asked the teen if he understood them, if he had agreed to waive them and give a statement, and if he was aware that the interview was being video recorded. Baillio answered yes to all of the detective's questions.

McKey had been with this case from the beginning. He'd spent fourteen frustrating months investigating it. Now he had his first real witness. John Baillio wasn't someone with second- or thirdhand information. He wasn't someone who'd been told about the crime. Baillio was there. He actually saw and helped commit the crime.

McKey was tired of pussyfooting around. He was ready to find out exactly what had happened.

"We're investigating the murder of Miss Genore Guillory, y'all knew her by Miss G," McKey said. "Let's start with what happened that weekend. Let's start with Friday. Do you remember what happened that Friday?"

Baillio started with the trip to Johnny and Lisa Hoyt's trailer and the discovery that a car had run over and killed the group's prized first pit bull. "We started drinking, eating Valiums, and smoking weed," Baillio said to the detectives. "On the way back to Phillip's house, Johnny started asking me if I thought it would be fun to go kill somebody."

Baillio told the detectives how Skipper and Hoyt had come up with a plan to kill Genore. Then he explained in graphic detail just how they'd done it.

McKey asked what Baillio's involvement had been.

Baillio twisted in his chair and wrung his fingers. "They wanted me to watch them kill Miss G."

"Did they say why they wanted you to watch?" McKey pressed.

"It would be my true test of Brotherhood."

"Tell me a little bit about The Brotherhood," McKey said.

"It was their idea of a close-knit gang."

Baillio described Genore's final moments. She fought hard, he said, but when she realized she couldn't get away, she pleaded for her life. "She begged them to quit," he said. "She kept hollering to stop and leave her alone . . . She begged Lisa to make them quit and they wouldn't."

"What did she actually say?" Dennis Stewart asked.

"She said, 'Lisa, please make them stop.' And they just wouldn't. They kept on doing it. After Miss G stopped breathing, they started raping her."

Baillio claimed he didn't participate in the rape, also that Phillip and Johnny wore condoms they had picked up from a local health clinic. As Phillip and Johnny took turns raping Genore, Baillio said, he and Lisa watched. "Lisa was standing there laughing the whole time. She was laughing and talking about how it was fun . . . fun to watch someone die."

Don McKey was shocked to hear about the extent of Lisa's involvement in the murder. Donny Fisher either hadn't known about Lisa's participation or had elected not to mention it when McKey and Odom interviewed him earlier that month. Baillio's mother, Shawn Smith, had told them that Lisa had been part of it, but Smith hadn't known how far Lisa's involvement went. Her statement was at best secondhand information anyway, probably aimed at helping minimize her son's participation.

Young John Baillio's story was different. If what he was telling them was the truth, Lisa, a young mother of three, whose infant daughter had recently drowned, had not only helped her husband and her brother murder a neighbor, but she had then stood by and laughed as she watched them rape the dead woman's body. It was nearly inconceivable to McKey. He was used to dealing with scumbags, with killers of almost every stripe, but this . . . this was almost too much.

But there was more. Baillio told the detectives about robbing graves, about pulling rings, watches, necklaces, cash, even gold teeth from rotting corpses in several cemeteries.

He also confirmed what Detective Dennis Stewart already suspected: that Johnny and Lisa Hoyt had killed Eddie Roberts and then set him on fire. Months after the St. Helena Parish murder, Baillio said, Hoyt had bragged to him about killing Roberts.

"He said he had shot that man and it was because he was getting ready to rat," Baillio told Stewart. "It was over drugs. Little Ricky Young said he was there and he touched a man's brains."

Hoyt had said he would kill Baillio if he ever told anyone about the murder.

Then Baillio told the detectives about the monstrous sexual abuse he had suffered at the hands of Phillip Skipper—the rapes, the beatings, the strangulations, the cigarette burns, the hot nail branding. "He used to make me suck his dick," Baillio said, his voice suddenly high-pitched and childlike. "He used to make me have sex with him. I told him I didn't like it, but he wouldn't stop."

THIRTY-THREE

After McKey and Odom finished their interview with John Baillio, they went to Judge Ware and got an arrest warrant for Lisa Skipper Hoyt, charging her with first-degree murder.

That evening, McKey and Odom, along with Dennis Stewart and Sheriff Talmadge Bunch, drove two unmarked police cars to Livingston Parish. They found Lisa at 7:30 that night, at her father-in-law's ramshackle house on Lake Brandy Drive in Holden. Johnny Hoyt Sr. answered the door and called for Lisa. While everyone waited, Hoyt Sr. lambasted the detectives. It was the usual diatribe. They didn't know what they were doing. They were charging the wrong people. They just had it in for his son and daughter-in-law.

A few minutes later, Lisa came out. She stared right through McKey. It reminded him of Linda Blair's character in *The Exorcist*. "She had the devil in her eyes," McKey says. He handcuffed her and shoved her into the backseat of Sheriff Bunch's car.

They booked her in Livingston Parish first as a fugitive. Then after the local cops released her, McKey and Odom transported Lisa to Clinton. The ride was anything but pleasant. "She cussed us from damn near Hammond all the way to East Feliciana," Odom recalls. "That's an evil bitch."

At one point during the ride, McKey tried to make a religious appeal to Lisa just to get her to do something besides cuss at them. "Do you go to church?" he asked.

"Yeah, I go to church," she said.

McKey was surprised. "Really, what church do you go to?"

"The church of fuck you!"

McKey had to laugh. "I never heard of that one," he said.

Two days later, on August 22, 2001, Don McKey was back in front of Judge George Ware with another affidavit, this one charging Phillip Skipper with an additional count of aggravated rape. This time the victim was John Baillio. McKey felt he had enough information, based on John Baillio's recorded statement, to charge Skipper with rape for his repetitive sexual assaults on his teenage "stepson."

McKey's affidavit read, in part:

The victim (John Baillio), age 16, did advise that while in the care of Phillip Skipper for the past three years he was forced to perform sexual intercourse and perform oral sex with Phillip Skipper. With Phillip Skipper threatening the victim with bodily harm if the victim did not comply or if the victim ever reported the crime. Affiant [McKey] further states that the victim informed him that the sexual acts occurred once a week up until three months ago until the victim left the residence of Phillip Skipper . . . to get away from the mental and sexual abuse.

Later that afternoon, McKey pulled Skipper out of his cell at the East Feliciana jail and rebooked him, on the new rape charge.

It had been exactly two weeks since Skipper's arrest for murder, burglary, and rape in the Guillory case. Two weeks locked up in jail had evidently exacted a toll on the five foot, six inch, 130-pound tattooed skinhead. His first booking photo, taken on August 8, shows a tight-lipped, defiant, perhaps cocky Skipper, with a bushy goatee sprouting from his chin, staring straight into the camera. The photo taken two weeks later as McKey booked him for repeatedly raping a teenage boy shows a young man who appears dazed and confused, his intense stare replaced by a cock-eyed, openmouthed gape. All that remains of the bushy goatee is a patch of stubble on his sagging chin.

A couple of weeks later, federal prison officials transported Johnny Hoyt to Clinton, where he was booked for first-degree murder, aggravated burglary, and aggravated rape. During his brief return, Hoyt remained defiant. When the East Feliciana detectives tried to talk to him, he made it clear that he had nothing to say. "He lawyered up real quick," McKey says.

On October 12, 2001, an East Feliciana grand jury returned a two-count indictment against Lisa Hoyt, formally charging her with first-degree murder and aggravated burglary. The first count of the indictment left Lisa staring straight into the unflinching face of the death penalty.

While John Baillio sat in the East Feliciana jail with a first-degree murder charge hanging over his head and the possibility of a death sentence looming in his future, he did some soul searching and decided that maybe cooperating with the cops wasn't such a good idea.

Since Baillio's arrest, East Feliciana deputies had locked up Little Ricky on charges from another parish. Whether

Ricky was Johnny Hoyt's stepbrother, half brother, or cousin didn't really matter. He belonged to the Hoyt clan and he was locked up in the cell right next to Baillio. Phillip and Lisa were there, too. They were all being housed together, just one big happy family, except that everyone knew Baillio had snitched.

A few weeks after his arrest, an inmate passed Baillio a message from Phillip: "Keep your mouth shut."

On November 1, Baillio wrote a letter to Amy. In it he tried to reassure her that, despite appearances, everything was okay and that he was hanging tough. Baillio addressed the letter "Dear Mom," which was what he called Amy. He claimed that when he was taken to jail he had stuffed a handful of acid strips in his mouth. "I was tripping on acid and I was drunk out of my fucking mind," he wrote as a way of explaining why he had agreed to talk to the cops. He went on to tell "Mom" that the cops didn't have any evidence against him. They had nothing on Little Ricky, Johnny Hoyt, or "Daddy," which was what he called Phillip Skipper. "The pigs are fucking with us because they want to make this look like a hate crime."

Baillio also wrote a letter to Johnny Hoyt in which he reiterated what he'd told Amy, that he was solid and wasn't cooperating with the detectives.

During the fall of 2001, as they were preparing the case for trial, Detectives Don McKey and Joel Odom were eagerly awaiting a report from the Louisiana State Police Crime Laboratory. When the report finally came in, it wasn't good.

The Genore Guillory investigation wasn't crime scene TV. The cops didn't crack the case in an hour (forty-four minutes after subtracting for commercials), and the lab techs didn't come up with the a last-minute indisputable piece of forensic proof that sealed the case.

The Guillory case was real life—very messy and very imperfect.

All of the advancements in forensic science and technology during recent years did McKey and Odom no good whatsoever. Ultraviolet lights; blood reactive chemicals; improvements in fingerprint-lifting capability; computerized databases and fingerprint identification systems; enhancements in ballistics comparison, matching, and identification; the discovery of DNA and its application to law enforcement—none of it meant anything in this case, because the State Police Crime Lab didn't find anything to link the suspects with the crime scene. No prints, no hair, no fibers, no blood, no DNA. Nothing.

The results of the examination of the evidence taken from Phillip Skipper's trailer were equally disappointing.

Without a gun to compare it to, the spent .22-caliber shell casing found in the yard meant nothing. Probably everyone in East Feliciana Parish had a .22 rifle or pistol. The unfired .22 cartridges found inside might have been significant if they had been the same brand as spent shells found at Genore's house, but since no shells had been found—probably because the perpetrators had either picked up the spent shells or used a revolver—they also meant nothing.

The two baseball bats, although arguably significant in a blunt trauma beating case, had been outside for more than a year, exposed to the frequent rains and steamy heat of south Louisiana's subtropical climate. They had no blood, hair, or tissue on them, and also likely meant very little.

The documents McKey collected—the insurance papers, the dogfighting records, the book of Nazi drawings—meant something but proved nothing. No one disputed, least of all Phillip Skipper, that Genore's death had resulted in a windfall profit for the Skippers. Dogfighting was illegal, but had nothing to do with murder. The Nazi drawings were meaningless. They had probably been drawn by the state's future star witness and only demonstrated that The Brotherhood was composed of racist idiots, and there was no law on the books against being a racist or an idiot.

When District Attorney Charles Shropshire received his copy of the lab report, he realized he had a dog on his hands. The case consisted of a tiny pile of circumstantial evidence and nothing more. A few months in jail had done nothing to loosen the tongues of Phillip or Lisa, who for once was keeping her mouth shut. Amy wasn't talking, other than to cuss out the investigators whenever she got the chance. Johnny Hoyt, locked up at Oakdale, had no reason to cooperate. Admitting he had sawed-off shotguns and marijuana in his trailer had landed him in federal prison for three years. Admitting he'd been involved in the brutal murder and rape of a sweet, middle-aged black lady wasn't going to help him any.

"The only thing we had was John Baillio's statement," Don McKey says.

Which everyone knew wasn't going to be enough.

Not surprisingly, District Attorney Charles Shropshire offered no objection when Phillip Skipper's attorney, DeVan Pardue, asked Judge Ware to set a bond for his client. On December 18, 2001, the date originally set for the opening day of the murder trail, Judge Ware set Phillip Skipper's bond at $150,000. If Skipper's family could raise 10 percent of that amount in cash for a bondsman or, through their attorney, convince the court to accept a property bond, they could get Skipper out of jail. The judge also set a bond hearing for Lisa Hoyt for the following day.

When reporter James Minton questioned First Assistant District Attorney Bill Carmichael about why the DA's office didn't object to the judge's decision to set such a relatively low bond in a first-degree murder case, particularly one so gruesome, Carmichael said, "Based on the evidence that's available to us, we're not prepared to go to trial."

Unlike Baillio's attorney, who was busy filing pretrial motions, and who had a serious evidentiary hurdle to overcome, in that his client had confessed, the lawyers representing Johnny Hoyt, Lisa Hoyt, and Phillip Skipper were ready to go to war and had been pressing Judge Ware to enforce their clients' right to a speedy trial.

At Phillip Skipper's December 18 bond hearing, Judge Ware granted a motion by the district attorney to delay the trial, but he gave prosecutors just six weeks to get their act together. The judge set a new trial date of February 4 and warned Shropshire that he had better be ready to present his case to a jury.

In addition to a lack of physical evidence, Shropshire had another problem with the case. Baillio, through his lawyer, had refused to testify against his codefendants. His lawyer was also challenging the admissibility of his videotaped statement and fighting to get it suppressed so that it couldn't be used against Baillio at trial.

Even if Shropshire could get Baillio to testify, he still faced yet another complication. The Guillory family was opposed to the DA's office making any kind of deal with John Baillio. The family wanted the death penalty for Johnny and Lisa Hoyt and Phillip Skipper, and life in prison for Baillio.

Without Baillio's cooperation, Shropshire found himself with nothing. No physical evidence, no witness testimony, and very little circumstantial evidence.

The case was dead and everyone knew it.

Shropshire threw in the towel.

On January 22, 2002, he dismissed the indictments against Phillip Skipper, Johnny Hoyt, and Lisa Skipper Hoyt. That afternoon, after five months in jail, Phillip and Lisa walked out of the East Feliciana Parish Prison. They were free.

The news that all of the charges against him in the Guillory case had been dismissed must have been a relief to Johnny Hoyt, but he was still in prison. For the short term, the news had little effect on him. He had about two more years to serve on his federal gun conviction. For the long term, however, Shropshire's decision meant Hoyt no longer faced the prospect of life in prison or the death penalty. He'd be a free man after the feds got through with him.

John Baillio was another matter, though. A grand jury had indicted him for aggravated burglary, aggravated rape, and first-degree murder; and he'd confessed to detectives that he'd committed two out of the three (to this day, Baillio denies raping Genore Guillory). Shropshire couldn't let a confessed murderer go free, so he left him in jail, the indictments still in place, hanging over his head like a noose.

"The main evidence at that time was the statement of John Baillio," says former First Assistant District Attorney Bill Carmichael, now a state district judge in East and West Feliciana Parishes. "Without that statement it would have been almost impossible to get a conviction because that's all there was. There wasn't any physical evidence."

At the time they dismissed the case against Skipper and the Hoyts, prosecutors Shropshire and Carmichael tried to put the best spin on the situation that they could. "The investigation is continuing," Carmichael said, "and if additional evidence is discovered, we can seek another indictment, and we certainly will do so."

Sheriff Talmadge Bunch was livid. Through hard work, perseverance, and luck, his detectives had solved a case that had once seemed unsolvable. Now the sheriff wanted the killers brought to justice. He was disgusted that the DA's office was dropping the case without a fight. "Why not bring it to a jury and let the people decide," he told reporter James Minton.

On the other side, the defense lawyers were cocky.

Flushed with what seemed to them an easy victory, they were eager to strut in front of the press.

Skipper's attorney, DeVan Pardue, a bolo tie–wearing, ex-jock, trashed the detectives and their investigation. "They just jumped the gun here," he said. "I think that's what happened. They arrested and indicted him before they gathered the evidence. To date, they haven't produced a single piece of evidence against him. They assumed he would talk if he sat in jail for two years. It just didn't pan out."

Pardue apparently didn't know that his client had only been in jail for five months.

Attorney Michael Thiel, representing Johnny and Lisa Hoyt, was more magnanimous in his comments about what seemed to be the end of the case. "Obviously, I wasn't in the grand jury when the evidence was presented, but from the discovery responses I've received, I just didn't see that the state had a sufficient amount of evidence to meet its burden of proof."

Thiel praised the decision of Shropshire and Carmichael to dismiss the case against his client. "I have to give them credit. There are some prosecutors who might have proceeded regardless of whether they had enough evidence."

Both Pardue's and Thiel's words would eventually come back to bite them on the ass. The wheels of justice may turn slowly, but they do turn.

THIRTY-FOUR

Two months after being released from jail in East Feliciana Parish, Phillip Skipper was back in jail in Livingston Parish. This time he was charged with three counts of aggravated assault. On March 8, 2002, Skipper got into a beef with three members of the Madison family, Edward, Samuel, and Ward, while visiting their house in the town of Livingston, the parish seat. During the argument, Skipper pulled a knife and threatened to slash the three of them. Then he ran off.

The Madisons called the sheriff's office and reported the assault. That same day a judge issued a warrant for Skipper's arrest. Two weeks later, with sheriff's deputies sniffing around trying to find him, Skipper turned himself in.

In 2002, the Florida Parishes of southeast Louisiana experienced an explosion of methamphetamine. Manufacture, use, and arrests were climbing with no ceiling in sight. Unlike cocaine, every gram of which has to be smuggled into the country, methamphetamine is synthetic and can be manufactured in the United States. It can be made in a bathtub. On the street it's known as crank, crystal meth, or ice. It can be snorted, smoked, swallowed, or injected. German soldiers used it during World War II to keep alert and keep fighting.

A meth high is more intense and lasts longer than a cocaine high. Users feel euphoric. They stay awake for hours or days and eat very little. They lose weight. They fuck like rabbits—at first. With prolonged use they break out in rashes. They get paranoid. Their teeth fall out. Men go limp, something called "crystal cock." They have psychotic breakdowns. They die.

The principle ingredient of methamphetamine is ephedrine or pseudoephedrine, both now carefully monitored by the Drug Enforcement Administration but still readily available. It's the same stuff used in diet pills and energy boosters.

The problem was not new, but it was quickly getting worse. According DEA statistics there were only fifteen methamphetamine laboratory "incidents"—seizures, arrests, accidents, injuries, explosions, deaths—in Louisiana in 2000. In 2001, there were sixteen. Suddenly, in 2002, that number jumped to 133.

A new plague—the white death—had come to Louisiana.

A DEA report also noted that along with meth came ancillary problems. "State agencies note a direct relationship between methamphetamine distribution and abuse and violent crime, particularly domestic violence, child abuse, aggravated assault and murder," the report said.

Johnny Hoyt, Phillip Skipper, John Baillio, and Lisa Skipper Hoyt were all meth freaks. Before he got locked up on the weapons charges, Hoyt was the group's meth cook. According to Baillio, he was pretty good. It's the recipe that makes a good meth cook, Baillio says. Too much of any one ingredient can ruin it. He compares mixing meth to cooking spaghetti. "If you put salt in it and it tastes good, then the next time you put more salt in and it tastes like shit," he says.

Most of what cash the Hoyts, Skipper, and Baillio got, they plowed back into meth. John Baillio says he once won $6,000 on a dogfight. "Not that it did me a lot of good," he says. "I just went and bought a lot of dope. I used some and sold the rest."

As the plague of methamphetamine swept across southeast Louisiana's Florida Parishes, there was one unexpected benefit. It led to a break in the Genore Guillory case and eventually to justice for her killers.

*In the summer of 2002, Steven Johnson was a twenty-*six-year-old meth freak, meth cook, marijuana dealer, and dogfighter from Holden. He had a prison-yard weight lifter's body and a shaved head. He'd known Johnny Hoyt and Phillip Skipper for several years. They sold dope together and fought pit bulls. He also knew a lot of Hoyt's other friends and relatives and had heard of the gang Hoyt was starting called The Brotherhood. The way he heard it, there were as many as thirty people in the gang.

That summer, Livingston Parish sheriff's deputies arrested Johnson for the manufacture and possession of methamphetamine with the intent to distribute and for possession of a firearm during a drug trafficking crime. Johnson was looking at hard time. He was also looking for a way to help himself out. So he called Detective Joel Odom.

On July 18, McKey and Odom put Johnson in an interview room at the Livingston Parish jail. Johnson told the detectives that sometime during the late summer or early fall of 2000, he'd ridden with Hoyt to Phillip Skipper's house to pick up some marijuana. On the way there, while the two of them were popping Valium and washing it down with shots of vodka, Hoyt started talking about how he'd killed a guy up in St. Helena Parish. Hoyt said he did it because the guy had an affair with Lisa and was trying to take her and the kids away from him.

Hoyt also bragged that he, his wife, Phillip Skipper, and John Baillio had killed a black neighbor of Skipper's for her insurance money. Skipper had promised Hoyt part of the proceeds, but Hoyt was still waiting on the money. He claimed they were going to get somewhere around $80,000. Hoyt told Johnson that he had beaten the woman with a bat, Phillip had shot and stabbed her, Lisa had stabbed her, and Baillio had raped her.

Johnson said he wasn't sure where the woman lived but he remembered that Hoyt said they'd walked there, so it had to be close.

Johnson also said that he was frequently at Phillip Skipper's trailer and had often seen him with a long-barreled, nine-shot, .22-caliber revolver strapped to his side. He'd seen Skipper fire the pistol several times around his trailer and watched as he dumped the empty shells in the grass. It was the same gun Skipper used to kill pit bulls that lost a fight.

When Hoyt and Johnson reached Skipper's trailer, Skipper gave a package of marijuana to Hoyt and told him to deduct the cost from what Skipper owed him. Johnson said he guessed Skipper was talking about the money he owed Hoyt from the dead woman's insurance policy.

Sometime after their trip to Clinton to score weed from Phillip Skipper, Hoyt brought up the murders again. This time they were at Johnson's house in Holden, not far from Hoyt's father's house. While they were sitting on the back porch, Hoyt told not only Steven Johnson, but several other people, including Johnson's two younger brothers, Dustin and Brandon Smith, and Stacey Stringer, about the murders in Clinton and St. Helena Parish.

*The next day, July 19, 2002, McKey, Odom, and Stew-*art interviewed Steven Johnson's younger brother, twenty-year-old Dustin Smith. Smith, who had a string of drug arrests and at least one conviction, for which he drew a five-year suspended prison sentence, acknowledged to the detectives that he had been at his brother Steven's house when Johnny Hoyt was talking about killing Phillip Skipper's neighbor. They did it, Hoyt said, so they could collect $25,000. Smith said it sounded to him like the money was going to come from a will.

Smith also said he heard Hoyt talking about how he and his cousin (probably a reference to Ricky Young, who had been telling everyone who would listen that he had been involved in the Roberts murder) had shot a dude, taken his weed, and burned him in his truck.

Next, the three detectives interviewed Stacy Dale Stringer, who was locked up in the Livingston Parish jail on a dope charge. Stringer said he'd sold dope for Hoyt for about six years and had seen Hoyt with as much as thirty pounds of marijuana at one time. Hoyt kept some of his stash in his dad's attic in Holden, Stringer said. Hoyt also sometimes packed a .45-caliber semiautomatic pistol.

Stringer said Phillip Skipper, who he knew had a long-barreled .22-caliber revolver, admitted to him that he, Johnny Hoyt, and Lisa Hoyt had killed Genore Guillory. Skipper called Genore a "tough old broad" and said they had to use a bat, a knife, and a gun to put her down. They did it for the money, Stringer said.

THIRTY-FIVE

It is a given that in Louisiana, as well as across the South, politics and race are intertwined. There is rarely, if ever, one without the other. It is a legacy of the Civil War, of the Ku Klux Klan, of Jim Crow, of the civil rights movement.

East Feliciana, like its neighbor to the west, is proud of its Confederate heritage; yet however proud of it they are, it is certain that the vast majority of East and West Felicianians would be quick to point out that no one is proud of the hate that heritage has spawned in the hearts of some.

Together, the two Felicianas form Louisiana's 20th Judicial District. They share a judiciary, a clerk of court, and a district attorney. One courthouse is in Clinton, the other in St. Francisville. Standing at attention in front of each is a statue of a Confederate soldier. West Feliciana has several beautifully preserved antebellum plantations. East Feliciana is home to the Confederate Cemetery and Museum. Confederate battle flags are a common sight.

Standing behind the statue of its Confederate defender, the Clinton courthouse predates the Civil War by a generation.

Built in 1840 to replace the original wooden courthouse, gutted by fire in 1839, the colonnaded, two-story Greek Revival building stands in the center of the town square and is the oldest courthouse still in use in Louisiana, perhaps the country.

On the ground floor are a couple of offices. The courtroom and judge's chambers are upstairs. On either side of the main entrance two sets of ancient wooden stairs rise to the second story. There is no elevator. Anyone with business in the courtroom who has a disability that prevents him or her from climbing stairs has to be carried. A women's restroom is tucked into an alcove under the stairs near the front entrance. The men's restroom is an outhouse.

In 1996, voters in the two Felicianas had chosen by a razor-thin margin the state's first black elected district attorney. Former Assistant DA Charles Shropshire edged out his white opponent by less than four hundred votes to fill the post vacated by his boss, George H. Ware Jr., who successfully ran for state district judge.

With Shropshire's historic victory in a majority-white voting district, it seemed that at long last some of the ghosts of the past had finally been laid to rest. The racial wall had been breached.

Less than a week after the election, in an editorial that turned out to be surprisingly prophetic in its irony, *The Advocate* newspaper wrote: "Realistically, a lot of people on either side of the racial barrier are likely to test Shropshire's mettle. From all indications so far, that will be a mistake. During his tenure as an assistant, Shropshire never shrank from prosecuting black defendants, and he isn't likely to shrink from prosecuting white suspects now that he's the boss."

If during his first term in office Shropshire was interested in demonstrating to black voters that he had not sold out to the white power structure, and that as district attorney he could be trusted to prosecute white criminals just as he had prosecuted black criminals as an assistant, the Genore Guillory case was tailor-made for him.

In the unwritten, ice-cold handbook of prosecutorial politics, Genore Guillory was an ideal black victim: attractive, hardworking, and clean living. Conversely, her alleged killers were ideal white defendants: tattooed, violent skinhead dope dealers. No one could say anything bad about Genore, nor could anyone say anything good about her suspected killers.

Shropshire had a rare opportunity to make black voters and white voters happy. In a legal system commonly perceived—especially among minorities—to grant leniency to white defendants while cracking a whip across the backs of black defendants, Shropshire had the chance to use the Guillory case to prove to suspicious blacks that he was not afraid of being tough on white criminals, while at the same time demonstrating to skittish whites that he was a color-blind, law-and-order district attorney who did not play favorites.

He failed on both counts.

By dismissing the charges against Skipper and the Hoyts, Shropshire fed the fears of everyone. Black residents were angry that four whites were going to get away with murdering a black woman. White residents were scared that four psychos were going to be turned loose to kill again. (Technically, John Baillio was still under indictment, but the DA's Office had no plans to prosecute him.)

By the fall of 2002, Feliciana voters—black and white—were ready for a change.

Thirty-seven-year-old Sam D'Aquilla had grown up in St. Francisville. He'd struggled in school until he found the Marine Corps. As it has with countless other young men during its 225-plus-year history, the Marine Corps instilled in Sam D'Aquilla a sense of honor, discipline, and uncompromising integrity. Compared to marine boot camp, law school was a piece of cake.

After graduating, D'Aquilla served as a special assistant district attorney alongside Charles Shropshire during the mid-1990s, and then when Shropshire was elected DA in 1996, D'Aquilla went to see him in his office. Seated across the desk from Shropshire, D'Aquilla told his former colleague that he would like to keep his position as a special assistant. Although it was a part-time position and paid only $800 a month—D'Aquilla also had a private law practice—he wanted to keep the job as a special assistant because he liked the sense of satisfaction he got from putting criminals in jail.

Shropshire looked at him for a minute. Then he leaned back in his chair and shook his head. "We don't have a place for you."

D'Aquilla went to work for the Public Defender's Office and learned the other side of criminal law.

In 2000 he found out about the Genore Guillory murder just like everyone else: He read about it in the newspaper and saw it on TV.

D'Aquilla's work naturally brought him in close contact with a lot of cops. Police officers and public defenders usually mix like oil and water, but the five foot, eight inch D'Aquilla had such an easygoing, affable manner that the cops liked him despite the fact that he was a defense attorney. A lot of them also remembered the former marine as a tough prosecutor. D'Aquilla could keep a smile on his face the whole time he was choking the life out of his opposing counsel's best argument.

As D'Aquilla watched Shropshire bungle the Guillory case and another high-profile case involving the murder of a correctional officer at the state penitentiary at Angola in West Feliciana, his friends in law enforcement were quietly encouraging him to run for district attorney.

Halfway through his first term, Shropshire had managed to alienate just about everyone. The two sheriffs didn't care for him, and a lot of the deputies couldn't stand him. "He wasn't doing his job," D'Aquilla says. "He wouldn't talk to people. He almost wouldn't give you the time of day."

D'Aquilla announced he was a candidate for district attorney.

As the November 2002 election drew near, Sheriff Talmadge Bunch asked D'Aquilla what he intended to do about the Genore Guillory case if he won. The sheriff wasn't the only one asking. As D'Aquilla campaigned, a lot of people asked him the same thing: *What about the people who killed Genore Guillory?*

D'Aquilla told voters what he'd told Sheriff Bunch. If he were elected district attorney, he would take the Guillory case to trial.

Don McKey was one of the ones lobbying D'Aquilla to prosecute the case. "He [D'Aquilla] was on board from the get-go," McKey says.

On November 5, D'Aquilla beat Shropshire by a whopping 20 percent margin. By a vote of 6,700 to 4,700, Feliciana residents, especially black residents, had delivered a mandate. In electing a white Southern Democrat, they let it be known that race wasn't the only issue. What they wanted was someone who would work with law enforcement to clean up their district and someone who would prosecute the killers of Genore Guillory.

THIRTY-SIX

On December 19, 2002, two years to the day since he searched Phillip Skipper's trailer looking for the .45-caliber pistol Johnny Hoyt used to shoot Eddie Roberts, State Police Detective Dennis Stewart obtained arrest warrants for Johnny and Lisa Hoyt for second-degree murder and for Mark Hoyt for accessory after the fact to second-degree murder.

Stewart was after Johnny and Lisa. They were the ones who had killed Eddie Roberts. The charge against Mark Hoyt was a throwaway, a bargaining chip. The charge carried a maximum sentence of five years. Under state law, an accessory after the fact is "anyone who, after the commission of a felony, shall harbor, conceal, or aid the offender, knowing or having reasonable ground to believe that he has committed the felony, and with the intent that he may avoid or escape from arrest, trial, conviction, or punishment."

Stewart had heard enough second- and thirdhand information to convince him that Mark Hoyt had helped his brother dispose of Eddie Roberts's body after Johnny Hoyt had shot him in the head, and that made Mark an accessory after the fact. The detective hoped to use the charge as leverage against Mark to get him to flip on his brother.

Ten days later, on December 29, at one-forty-five in the afternoon, Dennis Stewart, Sheriff Talmadge Bunch, Detective Joel Odom, and two state troopers arrested Lisa Hoyt at a house where her mother was staying on Glascock Lane in Walker. They booked her into the Livingston Parish jail as a fugitive and then drove her to the jail in St. Helena Parish, where Stewart booked her for second-degree murder. Because Lisa was nearly nine months pregnant, she was released on bond.

As with her daughter Angel, who'd drowned in a wading pool the year before, the paternity of the child Lisa was carrying when she was arrested was the subject of some speculation.

Since Lisa's husband had been in federal custody for more than two years and John Baillio—the alleged father of Angel—had been in the East Feliciana Parish jail since August 2001, the identity of the father of the new baby was a mystery.

Lisa's "sister-in-law" Carrie Keen provided some clues. In a statement to Dennis Stewart, Keen told the detective that Lisa had admitted to having an affair with Mark Hoyt while Johnny was in prison. Lisa also told Carrie that she had had an affair with her best friend Tonya Nienstedt's husband, George. Tonya later left George and moved in with Mark Hoyt. It was a game of musical beds, Bubba-style.

Guessing who caused Lisa's latest pregnancy, one person who knew her said: "It was probably Mark's or Ricky's baby. She was fucking everybody."

At five-thirty that same evening, Dennis Stewart and company scooped up Mark Hoyt at his trailer on Black Mud Road in Walker. As the troopers had with Lisa, they booked Mark locally as a fugitive and then hauled him

back to St. Helena Parish and booked him as an accessory
to murder.

During the twenty-five-minute drive north to the jail in
St. Helena Parish, Dennis Stewart, who had been a police-
man for more than a decade, kept an eye on Mark Hoyt.
Mark, who didn't have much of a rap sheet, looked rattled.
It was the first sign Stewart had seen that someone in-
volved in the Roberts murder might be willing to talk.

Because Johnny Hoyt was still doing time at Oakdale
and not going anywhere, Stewart sent a copy of the murder warrant to the U.S. Bureau of Prisons. Hoyt's earliest
projected release date was July 3, 2003. Stewart could pick
him up then.

After Stewart finished processing Mark Hoyt at the St.
Helena Parish jail, he led him to an interview room and
asked him if he wanted to talk. Mark said yes. Stewart took
out an advice-and-waiver-of-rights form and a pen. After
acknowledging that he understood his rights, Mark Hoyt
agreed to waive them. He wanted to tell the detective what
happened.

"The night Eddie Roberts was killed, Johnny called me
about eight o'clock or eight-thirty . . ."

Johnny wanted to borrow Mark's girlfriend's car. Mark
said no. He knew she would get pissed if he lent her car
out. Then Johnny asked if Mark could pick up his kids for
a while. He had something he needed to do. Mark picked
the kids up and took them to his grandmother's house in
Holden. Later, he brought them back to Johnny's trailer,
along with a five-gallon jug of gas. Mark claimed he never
saw the body and didn't know anyone had been killed.
When Johnny burned the truck on the Big Gravel, Mark
thought his brother was just pulling some kind of insurance scam. He didn't figure it out, he said, until a few days
later when he read in the newspaper that a body had been
found in the backseat of a pickup truck on the Big Gravel
just across the parish line.

When Johnny asked him to get rid of the .45, Mark said, he didn't think it had anything to do with burning the truck. Johnny was into so many things, there was no telling why he wanted Mark to get rid of the gun.

"Where's the gun now?" Stewart asked.

"I guess it's still in the mud hole where I threw it," Mark Hoyt said.

"Did you tell anyone where you put it?"

"No. No one."

"Can you show me where you threw it?"

Mark shrugged. "Sure."

*Later that night, Dennis Stewart drove back to Liv*ingston Parish. He and Trooper Richard Newman hiked down a logging trial just north of Interstate 12 with a hand-cuffed Mark Hoyt in tow. Four hundred yards off of James Chapel Road near Holden, Mark pointed to a water-filled hole. It was just one of dozens of similar holes scattered along both sides of the trail.

"That's the one right there," Mark said. "That's where I threw the gun."

Stewart shined his flashlight at the hole. It was about twelve feet across. In the darkness the water looked black.

"How can you be sure that's the right one?" Stewart asked.

"I grew up in these woods. I've been rabbit hunting here my whole life."

Dennis Stewart took a deep breath and stepped into the cold December water. He was so eager to find the murder weapon that he forgot to take his ankle holster off, and he got his own weapon soaking wet. In the middle of the hole the water was waist deep. Stewart waded around for as long as he could stand it, bending over and digging his hands into the soft mud under his feet whenever he felt something hard, but he couldn't find the gun.

The next morning Stewart called the White metal detector company. He owned a White Classic III metal detector and wanted to know if it would work under water. The surprised White company employee said it should work fine as long as the control head stayed dry.

Then Stewart called Jim Churchman, head of the Louisiana State Police Crime Lab. If Stewart found a gun that had been under water and mud for a couple of years, how should he preserve it?

Churchman told him to put it in a bucket filled with water dipped from the same source.

Stewart got Mark Hoyt out of jail in St. Helena and took him back to the logging trail. It was pouring rain when they got there. Mark swore that he was sure they were at the right mud hole. Dressed in camouflage military pants and a dark blue State Police T-shirt, and wearing boots still waterlogged from the night before, Stewart stepped back into the muddy hole carrying his metal detector.

As he sloshed around in the frigid water, the metal detector gave off a couple of screechy beeps and each time the dogged State Police detective bent down and probed the muddy bottom with his bare hand. Nothing.

Stewart kept at it, determined to cover the entire hole. A little while later, his White metal detector let out a strong beep. Stewart reached down and shoved his hand into the muck. He felt nothing, so he pushed deeper. With his arm buried halfway to his elbow, Stewart's fingers brushed something hard. He closed his hand around it. To a man who'd spent his entire adult life training with and carrying firearms, the object buried in the thick gunk had a familiar feel to it. It was a gun.

Against all probability, he had found Johnny Hoyt's pistol. Stewart had brought along a white five-gallon bucket just in case he got lucky. He filled it with water from the hole and set the gun down inside it.

Within minutes the rain stopped and the sun came out.

Back at the State Police Crime Lab, forensic firearms examiner Patrick Lane carefully cleaned and examined the gun. It was a badly corroded and damaged, blue steel Smith & Wesson model 745 .45-caliber semiautomatic pistol. It was not functional in its present condition. Lane repaired and test-fired it. Three weeks later, he issued his report. The barrel had six lands and groves and a right-hand twist, characteristics it shared with the gun used to kill Edward Roberts. Beyond that, though, Lane could not say conclusively that it was the same gun that fired the bullet found inside Roberts's skull. The barrel was just too damaged by two and a half years buried in mud and water to be positive.

What science couldn't prove, a determined detective's shoe leather could. Stewart tracked the gun from its manufacture by Smith & Wesson in Springfield, Massachusetts, to its shipment to a federal firearms dealer in Anchorage, Alaska, through several private transactions to an owner in Mississippi, through another personal sale to a man who lived in a trailer on Pinemont Drive in Livingston, Louisiana, its theft from the trailer, to its sale at Phillip Skipper's uncle's house in Baton Rouge to Johnny Hoyt for $100, to the hands of Mark Hoyt, and finally to its eventual internment in a mud hole beside a logging trail outside Holden, Louisiana.

There was no doubt in Stewart's mind, the .45-caliber pistol he had found at the bottom of that Livingston Parish mud hole was the same one Johnny Hoyt used to kill Edward Roberts.

In January 2003, Sam D'Aquilla was sworn in as the district attorney for East and West Feliciana parishes, replacing the man who six years earlier had told him he didn't have a place for him at the District Attorney's Office.

Even before D'Aquilla took office, he went to the parish Police Jury (the equivalent of a County Commission in many states) and got their approval to move the District Attorney's Office from the commercial space Shropshire had been leasing back to the courthouse. Space in the 162-year-old courthouse was free and saved the parish money, but even more important, the courthouse was where D'Aquilla felt the District Attorney's Office should be. D'Aquilla was a trial lawyer. He liked being near the courtroom.

As soon as he reported for work, D'Aquilla found his desk piled with police and Sheriff's Office case files.

"Where did these come from?" he asked his secretary.

For months, police officers, sheriff's deputies, and detectives had been saving files, waiting for D'Aquilla to take office before they turned in cases they considered important. They didn't feel Shropshire was going to prosecute the cases. Dangerous criminals would go free. The cops knew Sam and they trusted him.

Don McKey had a case he wanted prosecuted, too.

At 1:30 in the afternoon on May 13, 2003, Livingston Parish Sheriff's Deputy Ryan Coon was dispatched to a disturbance at the cemetery behind the Lighthouse Pentecostal Church near Walker. The Lighthouse Church is a small redbrick building on Arnold Road, a patched-up, two-lane piece of blacktop that winds through a rural landscape dotted with mobile homes and junked cars.

Behind the church is a cemetery with fifteen to twenty graves. Several are without headstones and are marked only with index-sized cards covered in plastic and mounted in small metal frames. Beside the cemetery is a basketball court and a broken-down church bus.

Deputy Coon pulled his cruiser around the left side of the church and stopped in the parking lot next to the chain-link fence surrounding the cemetery. A pickup truck sat just outside the fence. One man and two women were inside the cab, while another man stood beside the truck. They were all arguing. Coon knew one of the men, a local tough everyone called Buffalo. Coon had dealt with Buffalo before.

Not far from the truck was a partially dug grave. A couple of shovels stood upright beside it in a mound of fresh earth.

Coon ordered everyone out of the pickup. The man inside the truck stepped out. He wore a dirty T-shirt and a pair of shorts. He raised his hands and rushed at Coon. The deputy ordered the man to stop. When he didn't, Coon pushed him against the truck. The two women climbed out. The shorter one started crowding Coon. Buffalo stayed where he was. He knew Coon and knew the wrong move could land him in jail, or worse.

Coon told the woman to back off and asked the man he had jammed against the truck what his name was.

"Phillip Skipper," he said.

When Coon patted him down, he felt something soft in Skipper's left front pocket. The deputy reached into the pocket and pulled out a clear plastic Baggie. Inside was a quarter ounce of marijuana and three pills that later turned out to be Xanax.

Coon tossed the Baggie on the hood of the truck and reached for his handcuffs. The shorter woman, who turned out to be Skipper's wife, launched herself at Coon, cursing and flailing away at him with her arms. The deputy shouldered her aside long enough to get handcuffs on Skipper and to key his portable radio and call for backup. As the scuffle was going on, Buffalo and the other woman stood frozen in place.

Coon pulled a second set of handcuffs from his belt and snapped them on the shorter woman's wrists. Then he turned to double-lock Skipper's handcuffs. As soon as he touched Skipper's arm, Skipper fell to the ground shaking and choking. Between gasps, he claimed to be having a seizure.

Coon radioed for an ambulance.

While he waited, Coon pieced together enough of the story from everyone—except Skipper, who was still flopping around on the ground—to figure out what happened. Skipper's thirty-four-year-old brother, James Skipper, had died in a hospital in Baton Rouge two days before. To save money, Phillip decided to recruit a couple of relatives to help him dig his brother's grave.

While they were digging, tempers flared.

"I think they were drinking or something and the family got into a fight," says Lighthouse pastor Jerry Arnold.

The ambulance arrived and the crew checked Skipper out. He'd stopped flopping by then, and the medics decided he had faked the whole thing. They cleared Deputy Coon to take him to jail.

Coon booked Phillip with two counts of possession of a controlled dangerous substance and charged Amy with battery on a police officer and interfering with a police officer.

That evening, Lisa Hoyt bailed them both out of jail.

THIRTY-SEVEN

On July 1, 2003, Detective Joel Odom resigned from the Sheriff's Office and announced that he was going to challenge Sheriff Talmadge Bunch in the October election.

Earlier in the year, Odom had been caught up in the hunt for the Baton Rouge serial killer, an investigation that led to the arrest of a local pervert named Derrick Todd Lee. Lee, who split his time between the house he shared with his wife in West Feliciana Parish and his girlfriend's apartment in East Feliciana, was later linked through DNA evidence to the disappearance and murder of seven women in and around Baton Rouge and is suspected in half a dozen more.

During the serial killer investigation, Odom was introduced to the dark side of police politics. He says he saw high-ranking police officials scrambling to cover up fatal missteps in the investigation that would have led to Lee's capture much sooner, and then he saw the same officials trampling over one another to claim credit for breaking the case after Lee was identified as the serial killer.

Odom and a couple of detectives from the city of Zachary, in East Baton Rouge Parish just south of the East Feliciana Parish line, suspected Lee of killing and raping two women in Zachary in the 1990s.

In July 2002, after police in Baton Rouge realized a serial killer was stalking the streets of their city, raping and murdering at will, they formed a multiagency task force to capture him. Joel Odom and the Zachary cops told members of the task force of their suspicions about Derrick Todd Lee but were told their input wasn't needed. Based on information contained in an FBI profile, the task force, they were told, was looking for a white male. Lee was black. He wasn't the serial killer.

"It bothered us," one of the Zachary detectives admits.

In April 2003, Odom had lunch with an investigator from the Louisiana Attorney General's Office and mentioned his suspicions about Lee and the similarity between the two Zachary cases and the five murders then known to be linked to the man dubbed the Baton Rouge serial killer.

The serial killer task force was still denying the Baton Rouge and Zachary cases were related.

On May 5, Odom, along with the two Zachary detectives and a couple of the attorney general's investigators, tracked Lee down in West Feliciana Parish and took a DNA swab from his mouth.

Three weeks later, the State Police Crime Lab matched Lee's swab to the then five known serial killer victims. At eleven-thirty Sunday night, May 25, 2003, Joel Odom got a call at home. He was asked to report immediately to the serial killer task force office in north Baton Rouge. The match proved that he and a handful of other investigators, who had ignored the profile and had been forced to work outside of the task force, had been right, but the delay in identifying Lee as the serial killer had cost lives. "It was the sickest feeling," Odom says.

At the task force office, everyone was congratulating everyone else. There were smiles and high fives all around.

On May 27, Odom had his picture taken with the Zachary detectives and AG investigators he'd worked with. Sheriff Bunch told him what a great job he'd done.

The next day everything changed, Odom says. State Attorney General Richard Ieyoub, who was running for governor, was reluctant to acknowledge anyone's contributions to breaking the case other than those of his own investigators. Odom says he was told to keep his mouth shut about his part in the case.

Everyone craves recognition of some sort for doing a good job, and cops are certainly no exception. "I did want credit," Odom says. "I'm not going to lie. I worked my ass off on that case."

At work, the atmosphere grew frosty, Odom says, almost as if he'd done something wrong. As far as he knew, all he'd done was spend a lot of his own time working on the serial killer investigation and then accepted a couple of pats on the back for being part of a small team that had bucked the conventional wisdom and helped break the case. For that, he was being treated like a pariah. "It kind of left a bad taste in my mouth, especially for the politics," he says.

A few weeks later, Odom threw his hat in the ring to run for sheriff. In announcing his candidacy, Odom had no harsh words for his former boss, Sheriff Bunch. "The current sheriff is a good man, but he has no training in the cutting-edge law enforcement techniques and strategies that our parish needs," Odom said. "We are in an era of new threats to public safety, and these new threats need a new breed of lawman to deal effectively with them. Just being a well-liked person is no longer enough."

A few months later, despite mounting an aggressive campaign that highlighted his training and experience in law enforcement's newest technologies and techniques,

Odom got an old-fashioned drubbing at the polls. He finished a distant second in a three-way primary, with 29 percent of the vote to Bunch's 54 percent. A third, no-name candidate pulled in 16 percent.

After his election loss, Odom went into his family's grocery business. He works part-time for the Jackson, Louisiana, Police Department and hasn't ruled out another run for sheriff.

On July 3, 2003, the U.S. Bureau of Prisons released Johnny Hoyt from the federal prison at Oakdale after he'd completed a little more than two and a half years of his three-year sentence for possession of two sawed-off shotguns. State Police Detective Dennis Stewart was there waiting for Hoyt as he out-processed. Stewart formally arrested Hoyt for the second-degree murder of Edward Roberts and for an unrelated second-degree battery charge in Tangipahoa Parish.

Stewart drove his prisoner to the Tangipahoa Parish jail in Amite. During the ride, Hoyt chose to exercise his Fifth Amendment right against self-incrimination. "It was a quiet ride back," Stewart says.

Later that same month, Sam D'Aquilla made good on his promise. He took the Guillory case to an East Feliciana Parish grand jury and came out with fresh indictments. Johnny and Lisa Hoyt, Phillip Skipper, and John Baillio were all indicted for first-degree murder, aggravated burglary, and aggravated rape. Under Louisiana law, Lisa could be prosecuted for rape just like the men because, although she didn't commit the act herself, she was alleged to have helped the others commit it.

D'Aquilla was determined to take the case to trial. In the year and a half since Shropshire had dismissed all the charges in the Guillory case, except those against Baillio, nothing significant had come to light except perhaps for a few more second- and thirdhand admissions by the defendants, admissions that might be ruled hearsay and thus excluded from presentation at trial.

"We didn't have any physical evidence that directly linked them to the case," D'Aquilla says, but he was determined to present what he had to a jury. "Sometimes . . . you just have to roll the dice."

Sheriff Talmadge Bunch saw the new indictments as a vindication for his detectives and as a validation for his support for Sam D'Aquilla during his campaign to unseat the previous district attorney. "I'm very comfortable with the indictments today," Bunch said just hours after the grand jury handed them down.

On July 22, at four-thirty in the afternoon, Livingston Parish sheriff's deputies arrested Phillip Skipper during a traffic stop on Milton Road near Walker. They booked him in jail as a fugitive from East Feliciana Parish. On the booking sheet, Skipper used big block letters to print his name on the signature line and listed his occupation as "disabled."

A short time later, Livingston Parish deputies picked Lisa up at a house on Glascock Lane in Walker, the same house where Dennis Stewart had arrested her seven months earlier for the murder of Edward Roberts.

Later that same day, the new charges were added to the list of charges pending against Johnny Hoyt as he sat in a cell in the Tangipahoa Parish jail.

On August 5, D'Aquilla filed a motion with the court notifying the judge that he was seeking the death penalty against all four defendants. The motion also served as notice that there was a new DA in town and he was playing hardball. He was also playing for keeps.

Faced with the possibility of dying with a needle stuck in his arm while lying on a gurney in the death house at

Angola in front of a dozen witnesses, John Baillio caved. D'Aquilla made him an offer. Testify against the others in exchange for being prosecuted as a juvenile. The maximum sentence Baillio could get was "juvenile life," which meant he'd be released the day he turned twenty-one. Not a bad deal for slaughtering a woman in the middle of the night in her own home.

But before D'Aquilla inked the deal with Baillio, he talked to Genore's family. They wanted everyone who had a hand in Genore's death punished, but her brother-in-law, Elbert Guillory, with decades of experience as an attorney behind him, realized certain practicalities inherent in the criminal justice system. Sometimes you have to make a deal with a demon in order to catch the devil.

Speaking for the Guillory family, Elbert gave his blessing to D'Aquilla to do whatever it took to bring Genore's killers to justice.

Sam D'Aquilla was determined to go to trial with what evidence he had. The new agreement with John Baillio certainly helped. However, when it comes to evidence, as with many things, more is usually better.

Back in 2001, Detective Joel Odom had persuaded Sheriff Bunch to spend $1,500 so Odom could send the fingernail clippings collected from Genore Guillory during her autopsy to ReliaGene Technologies laboratory in New Orleans. During their analysis, ReliaGene had found trace amounts of male DNA under the nail clippings. A DNA match with any of the male defendants would transform the case overnight from a crapshoot into a slam dunk.

D'Aquilla decided to test the DNA against his three male defendants.

On November 5, he brought Hoyt, Skipper, and Baillio into court for a hearing before Judge Ware. D'Aquilla planned to ask the judge to compel the three men to provide DNA samples for comparison to the male DNA found under Genore's fingernails. To the district attorney's surprise, all three men waived their right to a hearing and agreed to submit to a saliva swab.

Hoyt's attorney, Michael Thiel, told the judge that he believed the state had enough information to meet the burden of proof necessary for the court to force his client to submit a DNA sample.

Later that afternoon, an investigator from the state Attorney General's Office took oral swabs from Hoyt, Skipper, and Baillio at the jail. The investigator videotaped the samples being taken in order to forestall any questions that might pop up later about the origins of the samples. The saliva swabs were sent to the State Police Crime Lab for comparison.

In the spring of 2004, D'Aquilla's case suffered a major setback. The male DNA under Genore's fingernails didn't match any of the defendants.

D'Aquilla had gambled and lost. A DNA match would have made the case a lead pipe cinch. No match was a monkey wrench in a gearbox.

"It put us further back than when we started," D'Aquilla says.

The test had also given the defense their biggest weapon.

The number one television program in the country at the time was *CSI: Crime Scene Investigation*. Everyone on the jury was going to expect a DNA match, and when the state didn't produce one, and when the defense attorneys hammered the point home again and again that the state had failed to produce one, the jurors were going to wonder why. Enter a defense attorney stage left to tell them why: There was no DNA match because the defendants were innocent. Someone else had killed Genore Guillory and left his DNA under her fingernails. In the back of their minds, the jurors were going to hear echoes of Johnnie Cochran, *If it doesn't fit, you must acquit.*

The best defense is a good offense. It's true in sports, it's true in war, and it's true in a courtroom. D'Aquilla knew he couldn't wait for the defense attorneys to raise the issue of the failed DNA comparison. He had to bring it up first. To do that, he planned to turn to Natasha Poe.

Poe was a DNA analyst with the Louisiana State Police Crime Laboratory in Baton Rouge, and D'Aquilla was going to use her to explain to the jurors that DNA material found under fingernails is common, especially under women's nails, which are traditionally longer than men's.

"I can shake your hand and get it under my fingernails," Poe says. "You don't have to draw blood." And it can remain there for days, depending on how often a person washes her hands.

Still, many jurors demand scientific proof, something that often puts an unreasonable burden on the state. Not every case yields scientific evidence. People committed crimes before the advent of DNA. The discovery of DNA and the development of the technology to use it in criminal cases didn't invalidate every other type of evidence, nor did it absolve a jury from the responsibility of using common sense in evaluating a case.

Veteran Louisiana prosecutor Hugo Holland, who has tried nine capital cases and sent eight defendants to death row, calls jurors' unrealistic expectations about forensic evidence the "*CSI* Effect."

"The presence of forensic evidence means everything," Holland says. "The absence of forensic evidence means nothing. You have to look at the totality of the circumstances."

D'Aquilla's argument was going to be simple: Just because Johnny Hoyt, Lisa Hoyt, Phillip Skipper, and John Baillio didn't leave DNA evidence behind when they murdered Genore Guillory doesn't mean they didn't do it.

• • •

On May 4, D'Aquilla made a strategic decision, one he hoped would help him overcome the fact that he had very little physical evidence, and none of what he had directly linked the defendants to the crime. His witness list also read like a *Who's Who* of local scumbags, replete with stalkers, wife-beaters, dogfighters, dope dealers, and at least one confessed murderer.

D'Aquilla reduced the charges against all four defendants. He dismissed the aggravated burglary and aggravated rape charges and dropped the first-degree murder count to second-degree murder. The death penalty was off the table.

In the courtroom, the move would give D'Aquilla an advantage, one he hoped would make up for the inherent disadvantages in his case. Louisiana is one of but a handful of states that allow nonunanimous jury decisions in criminal cases. Under state law, any serious felony case, *other than a death penalty case*, can be decided by a ten-to-two vote of the jury. Most states require a unanimous verdict. D'Aquilla could have two die-hard votes for acquittal on the jury and still get a conviction.

Outside the courtroom, the move would save the parish a ton of money. State law requires that juries in death penalty cases be sequestered for the duration of the trial. With twelve jurors and at least two, sometimes four, alternates, that meant up to sixteen hotel rooms, three meals a day, around-the-clock security. Capital cases also require the defense to put together a mitigation team, usually composed of a psychiatrist, a psychologist, and a social worker. If the defendant can't pay for it, and few can, the state has to pick up the tab.

The costs for a capital case could be enormous and could bankrupt a poor parish like East Feliciana. In the Guillory case, D'Aquilla was looking at the possibility of three separate capital murder trials.

"I don't think this parish could afford to try a death penalty case," D'Aquilla said the day he announced his decision to reduce the charges.

THIRTY-EIGHT

"Trust, friendship, and betrayal—that's what brings us here today," Assistant District Attorney Kathryn "Betsy" Jones told a jury of eight women and four men in her opening remarks at the start of Phillip Skipper's murder trial on July 8, 2004.

Genore had been in the ground for four years. Several members of her family traveled back to Clinton to witness the trial. Some of Skipper's family were also in the gallery.

Seven of the jurors were white, five were black.

Jones, serving as co-counsel with D'Aquilla, who was prosecuting the case himself, described Genore as "a kind and compassionate person," a good neighbor who cared for Skipper and his family. She showered them with gifts. She gave them access to her home. She gave them money. She helped them purchase a newer mobile home, one in better condition than the one they'd been living in. She went so far as to name Phillip and Amy as beneficiaries of the life insurance policy she once had in her boyfriend's name. She trusted them.

"Her mistake was trusting the wrong person and she paid for that with her life," Jones said.

Jones told the jury about the last minutes of Genore's life, about how she had answered the late night knock on her door, then the brutal attack that started right there in the doorway, her flight into the kitchen to try to get a knife with which to defend herself, her attempts to use the telephone to call for help, the stabbing, the shooting, the beating she suffered, the rape, and how it had all finally ended with Genore lying crumpled on the floor in a pool of blood, her nightshirt pushed up around her chest.

"It happened at the hands of someone she trusted," Jones said. "It happened at the hands of Phillip Skipper."

Jones called Skipper's actions the ultimate betrayal. "He murdered her for money. He murdered her for that life insurance policy."

During Jones's opening statement, Skipper sat motionless at the defense table beside his attorney. He stared at the back of the prosecutor's head and never once looked at the jury. His hair was short but not shaved, and he had a goatee. He wore a long-sleeve shirt and khaki pants.

After Jones finished her remarks, Skipper's attorney, DeVan Pardue, stood to address the jury. Pardue was tall and broad-shouldered and looked like a former football player. He wore a dark suit and a bolo string tie. Pardue's father, an attorney whose license to practice law had been suspended, sat nearby and served as a legal advisor.

Pardue jumped on the state's Achilles' heel right away. "There is not one piece of evidence that directly links Phillip Skipper to this crime," he told the jury. Not surprisingly, Pardue didn't mention the incriminating circumstantial evidence or damning witness statements.

Like the vast majority of defense lawyers, Pardue's argument was based on selling the notion that the state had the wrong person in custody. Generally, defense attorneys don't believe the police have *ever* arrested the right person for any crime. In the helter-skelter world of criminal defense, for some inexplicable reason the police *always* arrest the wrong person. But Pardue was willing to take things a step further. In a bit of high drama, he suggested that the real killer was well known to the detectives and to the prosecutor. Pardue even promised that as the trial moved forward the jurors would discover his identity. "There is a person out there who needs to be tried for this case, but its not Phillip Skipper," Pardue said.

The first four witnesses were Genore's coworkers and friends. They described how kind, gentle, and compassionate she had been. They also talked about Steve Williams, the former Baton Rouge police officer who'd been harassing Genore at work with constant telephone calls, and his sudden, unexpected appearances in the parking lot at her office and at the stable where she kept some of her horses.

Deputy Ronald Johnson told the jury about how he'd discovered Genore's body. Detective Don McKey and former Detective Joel Odom took the stand and described their investigation and why they eventually focused on Phillip Skipper. (The rules of criminal procedure did not allow anyone to mention Johnny or Lisa Hoyt.)

Don McKey identified copies of two checks Sam D'Aquilla showed him, one each to Phillip and Amy Skipper in the amount of $12,500. McKey told the jury that the checks represented the death benefit for the $25,000 life insurance policy Genore had taken out on her life. The detective also described how he'd found four .22-caliber bullets in Skipper's trailer and one spent .22 shell casing in his yard.

On the second day of the trial, Adam Becnel, a foren-sic scientist with the Louisiana State Police Crime Lab, took the stand. Becnel was an expert on crime scene investigation and had worked more than a hundred such scenes during his career. The job of introducing the crime scene videotape shot at Genore's house the day her body was discovered fell to Becnel.

Sam D'Aquilla set up a television in front of the jury and pushed the VHS tape into a video recorder. A bailiff dimmed the lights in the courtroom. Everything fell silent. The tape had no audio track. The jury stared at the screen as the opening scene showed Genore's neatly furnished, immaculate den. Then the camera moved to the front door and the blood-smeared deadbolt. A few jurors shifted uncomfortably in their hard-backed wooden chairs in anticipation of the gruesome scene they knew was coming.

When the camera operator, whom Becnel identified as former East Feliciana Detective Drew Thompson, got to Genore's bedroom, the jurors leaned forward, their faces tight. The television showed a room upended by violence. Blood smeared the walls. Most of the furniture had been knocked over. Genore Guillory lay dead and nearly naked in the corner, her face covered by her bloody nightshirt.

As the camera zoomed in on Genore's wounds, a female juror moaned in horror.

As the horrific images rolled across the television, Sam D'Aquilla stared at the screen from his seat at the prosecutor's table, his face pinched, his eyes blinking rapidly. At least once he wiped a finger across the corner of one eye.

When the video ended, Judge George Ware gave the jury a few minutes to compose themselves.

When testimony resumed, D'Aquilla, who wore a dark suit, a starched white shirt, and a yellow and black tie, stood and asked Becnel to identify a series of crime scene photos.

As Becnel progressed through dozens of photographs, he came to one with an indistinguishable black mass in the center. D'Aquilla asked him to identify it for the jury. Becnel held the photo up so the jurors could see it, then touched the middle of the picture with his finger. "That dark object in the center is the victim's head. Her head's been bashed in."

On the afternoon of the trial's second day, pathologist Dr. Emil Laga testified about the cause of death.

Dr. Laga told the jury in a calm, measured voice, one traced with an eastern European accent, that he asks himself three questions at the start of each autopsy. Who was the person? Why did they die? When did they die?

He described for the jury in clinical terms the injuries Genore had suffered. There were five nonfatal abdominal punctures that were consistent with stab wounds, the doctor said. Each one was from five to seven inches deep. One had penetrated her left lung. He described bruises and abrasions on Genore's hands, knees, and legs, all consistent with defensive wounds commonly suffered during an attack. Then he described the gunshot wounds: one each in her left arm, wrist, and hand; one in her left buttock; and one in her right shoulder. All nonfatal. All from a small-caliber weapon.

Finally, the doctor came to the wounds to Genore's head. She had been struck five times with a blunt object. "There was a massive loss of blood," Dr. Laga said. "The one behind her left ear killed her. It was blunt, massive, high-velocity type of damage that caused a major fracture of the skull. There was a big crack of the skull." The head injuries were consistent with Genore having been beaten with a baseball bat. She had bled from her ears, nose, and mouth. Her jaw had been dislocated and fractured. "Her teeth were all loose," he said. "Some of them had come out."

As Dr. Laga spoke, some of the female jurors became visibly upset. At one point in the doctor's testimony, Genore's mother gasped out loud and had to be helped from the courtroom by relatives.

On cross-examination, DeVan Pardue tried to argue that Genore had been hit in the face with the shattered lamp that had been found lying next to her and that she'd fallen backward onto an overturned houseplant and cracked the back of her skull. Pardue seemed to be trying to create a scenario in which Genore had been attacked, but not fatally so, and then had died from an accidental fall.

Dr. Laga shot Pardue's argument down by explaining to the jury that a fall could not have generated enough force to fracture the base of Genore's skull the way hers had been fractured. That part of the skull, Dr. Laga said, was one of the hardest parts of the human body. Additionally, no blood had been seen on the houseplant Pardue was trying to finger as the culprit, nor had the plant been found under or near Genore's head.

Patrick Lane, a State Police firearms and ballistics expert, testified that eight gunshots had been fired at the crime scene. Four bullets had been recovered from Genore's body during the autopsy. Using a comparison microscope, he had positively identified three of the four as having been fired by the same gun. The fourth recovered bullet was too heavily damaged for him to be certain it had come from the same gun, but it shared many of the same characteristics as the other three. All were .22-caliber.

No spent shells had been recovered, which suggested to him that a revolver had been used. Lane said he knew of several companies that manufactured seven-, eight-, and nine-shot .22-caliber revolvers.

Convicted dope dealer Steven Johnson testified he'd seen Phillip Skipper firing a nine-shot .22-caliber revolver in his yard. When the gun was empty, Skipper dumped the empty shells on the ground.

Donny Fisher told the jury that Phillip Skipper had admitted to him that he'd killed Genore. At first, Fisher said he thought Skipper was going to kill him because he'd found out about it from John Baillio, but then Skipper started bragging about it, even calling it the "perfect murder." Fisher told the jurors that Skipper had boasted to him that he'd injected someone else's semen inside Genore to throw the cops off. "He said he had bought it from a—excuse my language—a nigger that he had gotten it from and planted it."

Natasha Poe tried to explain to the jury why no DNA material had been found on the two bats Don McKey recovered from Phillip Skipper's house in August 2001. The bats had been sitting outside for more than a year, she said, which was more than enough time for nature to remove any trace of blood, tissue, or hair.

Genore's own DNA had been found under her fingernails along with that of an unidentified male. There had been no blood, no hunks of tissue, which suggested to Poe that the male DNA had come from "casual contact," not murder.

THIRTY-NINE

On the morning of the trial's third day, Sam D'Aquilla called Steve Williams. D'Aquilla asked the former Baton Rouge police officer to explain his relationship with Genore Guillory.

"I used to visit her, but not as, per say, dating," a nervous Williams said. "I talked with Genore more as a family member than as someone trying to have a relationship with her."

During his testimony, Williams surprised everyone when he pulled out a set of family photographs and tried to explain to the jury that Genore had been light skinned like his sisters, and that his two wives had been dark skinned. He seemed to think he was proving the point that he couldn't have been romantically attracted to Genore because she looked too much like a family member.

Williams admitted calling Genore at work as often as two or three times a day, but he denied stalking her. He said he had approached her one night at her horse pasture, but he claimed not to remember if he had been wearing military-style pants. He certainly hadn't snuck up on her, he said, although he did remember tossing a rock into some nearby bushes.

His involvement with Genore had cost him his second marriage, Williams told the jury. His wife left him after local television news broadcasts showed his picture and identified him as a suspect in the case. "We separated because of this mess," he said. "My wife couldn't handle it. She didn't understand friendships."

She hadn't known about his interest in Genore.

Williams said he stopped cooperating with the investigation after his failed polygraph examination. "When they took the polygraph, they did it improperly," he tried to explain. "I felt a frame was in the making. I felt they were trying to frame me."

While on the stand, Williams produced a book filled with notes and names of people he said could verify his whereabouts on the weekend Genore was murdered. His confused testimony seemed to suggest he still thought he was being blamed for Genore's death despite the fact that he was at that moment testifying on behalf of the state at the murder trial of someone else who'd been charged with the crime.

Defense attorney DeVan Pardue asked Williams why he hadn't given the list of names of people who could provide an alibi for him to the police early in the investigation.

"They didn't ask for them," he said.

John Baillio took the stand on the afternoon of the third day of the trial. Nearly three years in jail had added nearly sixty pounds of bulk to the once scrawny teenager.

D'Aquilla asked Baillio how'd he'd ended up in the custody of Phillip Skipper.

"I was placed in his care upon my release from LTI [a juvenile prison] because my mother couldn't control me," Baillio said. He explained his connection with Skipper as a submissive "love-hate" relationship. "I loved him in some ways," Baillio said. "I hated him in some ways. My grandmother was in prison. Phillip Skipper was the only person I had."

He also described for the jury his participation in the fledgling skinhead group known as The Brotherhood, calling it "a gang-type organization." At D'Aquilla's request, Baillio took his shirt off and showed the jury the letters G.F.B.D. tattooed across his back.

"What do those letters stand for?" D'Aquilla asked.

"God forgives, The Brotherhood doesn't," Baillio said.

In often monotone, mostly unemotional tones, John Baillio took the jury through the events surrounding Genore's murder. He told them about riding in Skipper's truck to Johnny Hoyt's trailer in St. Helena Parish and the discovery that their first pit bull had been killed. "We started drinking and eating some Valiums," he said.

He told them about Hoyt firing a nine-shot, .22-caliber revolver from the back of the truck on the ride back to Skipper's trailer. About Hoyt waking him up in the middle of the night telling him it was time to earn the tattoo on his back. The murder was his initiation into The Brotherhood. About walking over to Genore's house carrying a rope for the dog, everyone else carrying a weapon. About Genore answering the door and her initial confusion. And about the sudden, violent attack they launched on their neighbor and friend.

In the bedroom, Genore grabbed the telephone to call for help. "Lisa had the gun at the time," Baillio said. "She shot her. It hit her hand."

A lot happened to Genore in that bedroom, Baillio said. "That's where she was beaten up, stabbed, and shot, and raped."

A couple of months after the murder, Baillio got away from Phillip. He went back to live with his mother. Whenever Skipper came around looking for him, Baillio avoided him. "I was running," he said.

"Running from what?" D'Aquilla asked.

"I was scared Johnny and Phillip was going to do me in."

In jail, Baillio was even more scared. Skipper was locked up in the East Feliciana jail with him. So was Hoyt's "stepbrother," Little Ricky, who was there as part of a work release program from another parish. Skipper passed threatening messages to Baillio through other inmates. "I didn't see him, but he could have gotten to me," Baillio said.

To ease the tension, Baillio wrote letters to Amy Skipper and Johnny Hoyt telling them that he was solid, that he hadn't talked, and that he wasn't going to talk.

"Why didn't you write a letter to Phillip Skipper?" DeVan Pardue asked on cross-examination.

"Because he can't read," Baillio said.

During his opening statement, defense attorney DeVan Pardue had promised to unmask the real killer, but in the end he didn't deliver. Instead he engaged in long, rambling cross-examinations that went nowhere. Instead of attacking the prosecution's assertions, much of Pardue's questioning seemed aimed at countering points the prosecutors hadn't even made. He asked Adam Becnel, the State Police forensic scientist, if he'd tested the tan chow to find out if the dog had been shot with pepper spray.

Pardue based his defense on two conflicting propositions. He alternated between arguing that Steve Williams killed Genore Guillory *and* that John Baillio had committed the crime alone.

To Sam D'Aquilla, the mutually exclusive defensive arguments were a sign of desperation. "It seemed like he was shooting bird shot out there hoping it would hit something," D'Aquilla says.

In her closing argument, Kathryn Jones reiterated what she'd told the jury the case was really about. "Trust, friendship, and betrayal," she said. "That's what we had here. Genore trusted Phillip Skipper, she befriended him, and he murdered her."

She reminded the jury that the state had little forensic evidence linking Skipper to the murder. "This is not television. This is not the *CSI* TV show. This is real life and real death."

But she also reminded the jurors of what they did have: a mountain of circumstantial evidence, statements from some of Skipper's friends that he had admitted to the murder and that he owned the type of gun used in the crime, and the admission of one of the killers that he had helped Phillip Skipper kill Genore Guillory.

In his closing, Pardue mentioned a third possible perpetrator, Tommy Alexander of Zachary, a friend and perhaps one-time boyfriend of Genore's with whom she shared a love of horses. Pardue was trying his hardest to give the jury an alternative to the state's case. He was asking them to take their pick of potential killers: Baillio, Alexander, or Williams. Anyone but Skipper.

Pardue wrapped up his remarks to the jury with a bizarre comment. To buttress his argument that Steve Williams was the real killer, Pardue suggested a connection between Genore's injuries—five gunshot wounds, five stab wounds, and five blows to the head—with the month and year of Williams's birth, May 1955. According to Pardue, five-five-five was the answer to the riddle of who really killed Genore Guillory.

On Monday, July 12, 2004, Judge George Ware gave the jury its instructions, dismissed the two alternates, and sent the twelve remaining jurors into the jury room to deliberate.

According to the judge's instructions, the jury had three options. They could find the defendant guilty of second-degree murder, which carried a mandatory life sentence without parole. They could find the defendant guilty of manslaughter, which had a maximum sentence of forty years. Or they could find the defendant not guilty.

Elbert Guillory, an experienced trial lawyer himself, was optimistic about the state's chances to get a conviction. "I think they put on a strong case," Guillory said on the last day of the trial. "They were dealing with some hardened, experienced criminals who knew how to get rid of evidence."

After deliberating for less than an hour, the jury returned with a verdict. Judge Ware received the written verdict from the jury foreman and read it out loud. "We the jury find the defendant, Phillip Skipper, guilty of second-degree murder."

A poll of the jury showed the verdict had been unanimous. Skipper's mother, Isabella Skipper, burst into tears.

"Don't cry," Skipper told her as a pair of sheriff's deputies led him from the courtroom.

"One down, two to go," Elbert Guillory said.

Two months after being convicted of murdering Genore Guillory, Phillip Skipper was back in court for sentencing. Judge Ware didn't mince his words. He peered down from the bench at Skipper.

"I would like to say this to you, Mr. Skipper. I've been a member of the bar for almost thirty years. During that time I've been in the private practice of law; I've served as a public defender for six years, district attorney for twelve years, and district judge for eight years.

"In all that time I have never come in contact with a case in this district that involved a murder or killing or death so gruesome and so senseless as what happened in this case. The victim in this case took you under her wing. She helped you in numerous ways and considered you to be a friend. Her caring and generous conduct was rewarded with a most brutal and unimaginable death.

"The legislature in this case has decreed that for your crime there is but one penalty—life imprisonment. I wish I could do more.

"It is the sentence of this court that you are sent to the Department of Public Safety and Corrections for the rest of your natural life, without benefit of parole, probation, or suspension of sentence."

FORTY

The murder trial of Johnny Hoyt got under way on Monday, January 31, 2005. Hoyt had a few advantages over fellow skinhead and Brotherhood member Phillip Skipper. Hoyt had a better attorney, he didn't know Genore that well and lived in the next parish over, and he had not gotten a big fat life insurance check after she died.

After six hours of selection, Judge Ware impaneled a jury of four men and eight women. Three of the jurors were black, nine were white.

Before the trial began, Hoyt's attorney, Michael Thiel, asked Judge Ware for a change of venue. Thiel said too many of the jurors had heard about the case or read about it in the newspaper. The judge denied the motion and ordered the trial to begin.

Hoyt had dropped the skinhead look in time for the trial. He was clean shaven and had let his hair grow out some. He wore it medium length and slicked back. He sat at the defense table wearing a black shirt, a dark striped tie, and tan pants, staring stone-faced at Assistant DA

Kathryn Jones as she made her opening statement to the jury.

Jones began her remarks on what to her was familiar territory. "What brings us here today is greed. Johnny Hoyt murdered Genore Guillory out of greed." She told the jury about a gang of small-time racist hoodlums called The Brotherhood and their sick motto, "God forgives, The Brotherhood doesn't." She told them about Genore's life insurance policy. "They murdered her to get the proceeds of the life insurance policy."

She told the jury they were going to hear from one of the murderers, John Baillio, who was just fifteen at the time. He had thought the murder was supposed to be his initiation into the gang. No one told him about the insurance policy.

Jones called the murder "extreme, senseless brutality." She warned the jurors, "Be prepared for blood."

Defense attorney Michael Thiel, thickset, with a lot of hair, didn't have former Baton Rouge cop Steve Williams as a boogeyman. Phillip Skipper's conviction had closed that door. But he had John Baillio, a rage-filled, white racist skinhead who lived across the street from the black victim. The problem was, Baillio didn't have a reason to kill Genore, not unless he was helping Phillip Skipper collect on that insurance money, and Skipper, conveniently, had already been convicted of murder. In defending Johnny Hoyt, Thiel was going to throw Skipper—Hoyt's brother-in-law and fellow Brotherhood member—under the bus.

"In every trial the evidence tells a story," Thiel told the jury. "Every story needs a title and the title of this story is 'How to Get Away with Murder.' "

Thiel told the jury that Baillio was a troubled kid straight out of LTI when his mother placed him in the custody of Phillip Skipper. He told the jury that three years of mental, physical, and sexual abuse at the hands of Phillip

Skipper had transformed Baillio from simply an angry kid into a homicidal maniac.

He cautioned them not to leave their common sense at the door when they listened to Baillio tell them that all he did was hold onto the dog while Genore Guillory was being murdered. "John Baillio did more than watch," Thiel said. "He killed Miss Guillory."

Testimony began on February 1.

Sam D'Aquilla, believing in the adage "If it ain't broke, don't fix it," made few modifications to his original playbook. Unlike defense attorneys, prosecutors can't create whatever scenario they think will work best. They're stuck with the facts. D'Aquilla again called up several of Genore's coworkers to testify about what kind of person she had been.

He also gave jurors an early peek at the horrors of the crime scene through the early testimony. Pauline Pitre, who worked with Genore for more than ten years at BlueCross, said she and her husband had helped clean up Genore's house after the murder. Pitre's husband, a painting contractor, had repainted the walls in Genore's bedroom.

"Why did your husband paint the walls?" D'Aquilla asked.

"The walls were covered with blood and there were holes from the gunshots," Pitre said.

D'Aquilla next called a series of law enforcement officers and forensic examiners to the stand. The second day ended with Adam Becnel introducing the gruesome crime scene video. As in the Skipper trial, several of the jurors were shaken by the horrible images on the tape and its eerie silence. While the tape ran, Hoyt stared at the television, his face blank, apparently unaffected by the carnage he was watching.

On the morning of the third day of the trial, Sam D'Aquilla called Amy Skipper. Amy had not testified at her husband's trial because she had refused to comply with the subpoena and appear. On the stand, Amy testified that Johnny and Lisa Hoyt had slept at her and Phillip's trailer the Saturday night Genore was killed. Amy said she slept soundly and had no idea if they had gone out during the night. Phillip took the Hoyts home around noon on Sunday, she said. Amy Skipper's testimony was the first piece of evidence that put Hoyt in the area at the time of the murder.

To accept Thiel's theory, that Phillip Skipper and John Baillio committed the murder, the jury was now going to have to believe that Skipper had intentionally left Johnny Hoyt out of it and that Hoyt had slept through the whole thing. And if that were the case, why would Skipper pick that night—when he had Johnny, Lisa, and their three kids sleeping over—to commit the murder? Why not wait until the next night or the one after that or any other night except when he had overnight company?

Donny Fisher and Steven Johnson testified about the gang Hoyt and Skipper started. "They have a tattoo—God forgives, The Brotherhood don't—G.F.B.D.," Fisher said.

"What does that tattoo mean?" D'Aquilla asked.

"It means they're a brotherhood, they stick together through thick and thin. You know, they have each other's back. They stick together like glue, like superglue, so that nothing can peel them away from each other."

Meth cook Steven Johnson told the jury that Hoyt told him he had helped Phillip Skipper kill Genore Guillory so Skipper could collect on an insurance policy. Hoyt later bragged to Johnson and his brother about killing Guillory. Johnson said he remembered Hoyt talking about beating her with a baseball bat.

"Why do you remember that comment specifically?" Assistant DA Kathryn Jones asked.

"Because something like that sticks with you," Johnson said.

D'Aquilla called his star witness on the afternoon of the third day of the trial. John Baillio took the stand and explained to the jury how he and Phillip Skipper and Johnny Hoyt and Lisa Hoyt had murdered Genore Guillory.

He testified that Johnny Hoyt came up with the idea for The Brotherhood after watching the movie *Stone Cold*. Hoyt had been impressed with the line that The Brotherhood doesn't forgive. "He thought it was pretty cool," Baillio said.

Not long after Hoyt saw the movie, Baillio, Hoyt, and Skipper got the G.F.B.D. tattoos at the House of Pain tattoo shop in Ponchatoula.

At D'Aquilla's request, Baillio stripped off his shirt and showed the jury his Brotherhood tattoo. Judge Ware then ordered Johnny Hoyt to stand up and remove his shirt so the jury could see the tattoo on his back. A sullen Hoyt did as he was ordered, but he told the judge, "If you're looking for Nazi tattoos, I ain't got none."

On cross-examination, Michael Thiel tried to poke holes in Baillio's story and point out inconsistencies with some of his earlier statements and testimony, but Baillio was close to unshakable on the stand. Thiel was clearly frustrated that Baillio steadfastly maintained that he had only held on to the dog Cleo and had not participated in the actual murder.

If the murder was supposed to be Baillio's initiation into The Brotherhood, why hadn't Hoyt or Skipper demanded that he take an active part?

It was a decent argument, but Baillio's level of participation—he was a scrawny fifteen-year-old at the time, who weighed less than Genore—didn't do anything to lessen Hoyt's culpability, which was what the jury was there to determine.

Thiel called on just one witness to testify for the defense. On the morning of day four, he put Isabella Skipper on the stand. Skipper's attorney, DeVan Pardue, had tried to call Isabella to testify at her son's trial, but Judge Ware had barred her testimony because she had ignored his sequestration order, had sat in the courtroom during the prosecution's case, and had listened to the testimony of the state's witnesses.

Isabella Skipper looked frail and confused on the stand as she answered Michael Thiel's questions. Despite the cold February weather, she had worn sandals to court. She said she had worked the Thursday night shift at a nursing home and gotten off at 6:00 a.m. the Friday before Genore was killed. She spent the weekend at Phillip's. She said she went with Phillip and John Baillio to Hoyt's trailer to move a refrigerator, and she confirmed that Johnny and Lisa and their kids came back with them and spent Saturday night at her son's trailer. Sometime during the night she was awakened by the sound of Genore's dogs barking. She slept late Sunday. "We was all tired." She said she lost her shoes that weekend and never found them.

During his cross-examination of Isabella Skipper, D'Aquilla infuriated Thiel with a line of questioning.

"Do you live with your husband?" D'Aquilla asked.

"No, sir," Isabella Skipper said. "I haven't lived with my husband in a long time."

"Why not?"

"Because he's incarcerated."

"For what?" D'Aquilla asked, knowing perfectly well what the answer was.

"For killing someone."

Michael Thiel shouted his objection, and the judge told the jury to ignore what Mrs. Skipper had just said.

The defense rested its case.

"Greed destroys," Kathryn Jones said as she began her closing argument. "It destroys friendships. It destroys lives. Greed is why Johnny Hoyt murdered Genore Guillory. The Brotherhood is why Johnny Hoyt participated in killing Genore Guillory."

Phillip Skipper wanted to collect on that life insurance policy and he knew he could count on Johnny Hoyt to help him get it, Jones said. "Johnny Hoyt was greedy. He wanted some of that insurance money."

The goat incident had ruined the relationship between Genore and the Skippers, Jones told the jury. Phillip Skipper knew that if he wanted that money he had to act fast, before Genore dropped him and Amy as beneficiaries.

John Baillio was a seventh-grade dropout, Jones said. He wasn't smart enough to make up a story that so precisely matched the evidence at the crime scene. The only reason Baillio knew what he knew was because he had been there, Jones argued, but he had not been there alone.

At the time of her murder, Genore Guillory outweighed John Baillio by nearly forty pounds. She very likely could have kicked his ass. Three weapons had been used to kill her, a fact that clearly suggested multiple attackers. The murder had been committed on the night that Johnny Hoyt was spending the night at Phillip Skipper's.

"You don't bring witnesses when you're fixing to commit a crime," Jones said. "You bring accomplices when you're fixing to commit a crime."

It was a strong argument.

Jones turned away from the jury box and pointed her finger directly at Johnny Hoyt. "Ladies and gentlemen of the jury, this man is a murderer, and it's time for him to face the consequences of his actions for the brutal and vicious murder of Genore Guillory."

In closing the defense case, Michael Thiel spent more than an hour attacking the credibility of the witnesses, particularly John Baillio and Steven Johnson. He called Johnson a "drugged-up dopehead." He hammered away at minor inconsistencies in their testimony. "If you want to believe Steven Johnson, then you can't believe John Baillio," Thiel said. "The fact is, you can't believe either one of them."

Thiel compared believing Baillio's testimony to eating a rotten, worm-infested apple. "You don't eat around the rotten part," he said. "You throw the whole thing away."

To believe that John Baillio had wandered around the house holding a vicious dog by a rope looped around its neck while everyone else participated in a bloodbath was ridiculous, Thiel said. "Why would he tell you he was holding the dog? Because if he's holding the dog he's not holding a knife or a gun or a bat and he's not taking a lamp and smashing her on the face."

Thiel suggested that Baillio had committed the murder alone while the others were sleeping in Phillip Skipper's trailer, but he didn't explain how Baillio could have taken control of Cleo and overpowered Genore, or how he'd manage to use a gun, a knife, and a bat during the attack.

Thiel also attacked the investigators, calling their work sloppy and accusing them of incompetence.

During the more than three hours of closing arguments, Johnny Hoyt yawned frequently. He looked bored.

FORTY-ONE

The case went to the jury at four-twenty on the afternoon of February 3, the fourth day of the trial. Judge Ware had instructed the jury on the same possible verdicts as he had the jury in the Skipper trial: guilty of second-degree murder, guilty of manslaughter, not guilty.

At 6:00 p.m. the jury sent out a question to the judge. They wanted clarification on the punishments for second-degree murder and manslaughter. Judge Ware answered the jurors' question and gave them a twenty-five-minute bathroom break.

The jury returned to its deliberation at six-twenty-five.

Nineteen minutes later, at 6:44 p.m., the jury foreman sent a message to Judge Ware. They had reached a verdict. The judge read the verdict in open court. On a vote of ten to two, the jury convicted Johnny Hoyt of second-degree murder. A poll of the jury revealed that two white male jurors had voted not guilty.

In the courtroom gallery, Hoyt's mother and sister broke

down sobbing. Two female jurors started crying. At the defense table, Hoyt sat stone-faced.

Outside the courtroom, Elbert Guillory told a reporter: "The family is satisfied with the verdict. Life in prison, death, nothing could compensate us for the love of that beautiful, loving, caring person."

On April 5, 2005, Judge George Ware sentenced Johnny Hoyt to life in prison without the possibility of parole.

In May, Lisa Skipper Hoyt pleaded "no contest" to manslaughter in the death of Genore Guillory and received a twenty-five-year sentence.

On July 22, 2005, Lisa also pleaded "no contest" to manslaughter in St. Helena Parish for her role in the death of Edward Roberts. The judge handed her an eighteen-year sentence but ruled that it could be served concurrently with her sentence in the Guillory case. She'll be out on parole by her early forties.

Johnny Hoyt is awaiting the results of his appeal in the Guillory case before deciding what to do about the charges pending against him for killing Edward Roberts. According to his attorney Michael Thiel, if Hoyt loses his appeal in the Guillory case, he'll plead guilty to manslaughter in the Roberts case in exchange for a twenty-five-year sentence. If his conviction for the murder of Genore Guillory is overturned, he wants to go to trial in the Roberts case.

In exchange for his testimony, John Baillio was sentenced to "juvenile life" for his part in the murder of Genore Guillory. On December 10, 2005, on his twenty-first birthday, he was released from the East Feliciana Parish jail, where he'd spent the last four and a half years. He has no real job skills and little formal education. He knows how to sell dope and fight pit bulls. He says he plans to make a living as a tattoo artist and intends to study graphic art.

Baillio says he is sorry for what happened. "I can still hear that woman scream."

He faults Skipper and Hoyt for turning him into what he became. "They created a monster," he says. Among his many tattoos, Baillio has "Psycho" on one arm, "White Devil" on the other, and "UNBROKEN" across the knuckles of both hands.

After Genore's murder, Baillio says he tried to commit suicide. "I loved that woman. My grandmother was in prison and she was the closest thing I had to a grandmother. If I had my choice, Miss Guillory would be alive and they would be dead. She had more balls than both of those faggot motherfuckers put together."

In August 2006, a white school-bus driver in a rural parish in Louisiana was suspended after she made nine black elementary schoolchildren cram into two seats in the very back of the bus. Just to fit into the seats, the smaller children had to sit in the laps of the bigger ones. The bus driver said the rest of the seats were assigned to white children.

A representative of the Louisiana NAACP said, "We fought that battle fifty years ago, and we won. Why is this happening again?"

The Bubba culture lives on.

Chuck Hustmyre spent twenty-two years in law enforcement and retired as a special agent with the Bureau of Alcohol, Tobacco and Firearms (ATF). He now works as a freelance journalist for several national, regional, and local publications, and is the author of the Berkley true crime book *Killer with a Badge* and the novel *House of the Rising Sun*. He lives in Baton Rouge, Louisiana, and can be reached at chuck@chuckhustmyre.com.

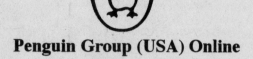